Knowledge, Culture
and Power

Pittsburgh Series in Composition, Literacy, and Culture
David Bartholomae and Jean Ferguson Carr, Editors

Knowledge, Culture and Power:
International Perspectives on Literacy as Policy and Practice

Edited by
Peter Freebody and Anthony R. Welch

University of Pittsburgh Press

UK   The Falmer Press, 4 John St., London WC1N 2ET
USA   University of Pittsburgh Press, 127 North Bellefield Avenue, Pittsburgh,
        Pa. 15260

The authors would like to acknowledge the financial support of the
Australian International Literacy Year (ILY) Secretariat.

First published 1993 by The Falmer Press

Published in the United States by the University of Pittsburgh Press,
Pittsburgh, Pa. 15260

A catalogue record for this book is available from the British Library

Library of Congress Cataloging in Publication Data are available on
request

ISBN 0-8229-1177-9
ISBN 0-8229-6102-4 (pbk)

Jacket design by Benedict Evans
Typeset in 9.5/11pt Bembo
by Graphicraft Typesetters Ltd., Hong Kong

Printed in Great Britain by Burgess Science Press, Basingstoke on
paper which has a specified pH value on final paper manufacture of
not less than 7.5 and is therefore 'acid free'.

Contents

Contents

Introduction

Sign of the times: a Canadian rock band, signed to a multinational recording contract, declared itself 'post-everything', specifically, 'post-punk', 'post-new wave', 'post-rap' and, of course, 'post-postmodern'. This is new, improved, first world marketing discourse *par excellence*. To declare difference in the context of a culture which thrives on traditions of the new is to sell. To be at the aesthetic margins has become a commodity, a means to enter profitably into the very discourses and practices which promote differences of economic centres and margins in the first place.

For the significant majority of the world's populace, to stand at the economic, political and aesthetic margins is not a matter of choice, of guise, or of marketing. Like Third World debt and First World under-employment, it is non-negotiable, whether scripted in terms of gender or colour, poverty or disease. However represented and mass mediated, *this* marginality is not a figment of discourse. Nor can it readily be critiqued and reconstructed by the individuals and groups in question. This is particularly the case for those without rudimentary access to economic, social and human services — and, not coincidentally, as this volume points out, for those without access to literacies.

If we take 'rewriting', 'writing and reading against the grain' and deconstruction as current metaphors for political action, it is important to recall that one cannot rewrite when one cannot write. If we take 'high tech', on-line literacies as the new nexus of power — the job skills upon which an updated human capital model of social and economic development turns — it is important to recall that one cannot get on-line without rudimentary hardware, affordable access to a reliable telecommunications network *and* a base mastery of the alphabetic system. The privilege of textual criticism and analysis, information and interpretation is, feminists of colour remind us, an occupational brief dominated by First World, male intelligentsia (Hooks, 1990; Mohanty, Russo and Torres, 1991).

What has come to count as post-modern culture is driven by what has been variously described as 'late', 'advanced' and post-industrial capitalism. But running beneath the narrative of post-modernism is a transnational division of labour and resources (Lash and Urry, 1987). Although the names of the key players, social movements and 'isms' have changed, many communities' socio-economic possibilities and opportunities have remained the same, or deteriorated. The outsiders remain underemployed and disenfranchised women, ethnic and cultural minorities, Aboriginal peoples, and an emergent white underclass in late capitalist countries. In what have been deemed 'developed' and 'developing' countries, many of these communities labour silently in the shadows and margins of the cultural 'post-everything'. As the case studies in *Knowledge, Culture and Power* show, a significant aspect of these communities' and groups' disenfranchisement is still tied up with illiteracy, undereducation and miseducation.

These concerns are shunted to the sidelines in educational discourse, to the subfields of language planning, comparative education and minority education: 'electives' at best in most educators' study and training, add-on topics in discussions of pedagogy and curriculum, and exceptional cases in mainstream accounts of psychological development. Hence it is important, as Welch and Freebody remind us in their initial chapter, to return to material factors of class and power, however elusive such phenomena might be, and however inseparable from gender and colour. Particularly in light of recent reorganizations of European nation-states, the persistence of regional and ethnic identity — it is also crucial for educators to return to recognition of those 'outsiders' from cultures of literacy described by the likes of Freire and Fanon, Garcia Marquez and bell hooks, but with renewed focus on the dynamics of post-colonialism, multinational economies, and policies of economic rationalism.

It has been over a decade since Graff (1979) coined the term 'literacy myth' to refer to those longstanding ideological claims which have dominated nineteenth and twentieth century political and academic debate over literacy. As Collins, O'Connor, Freebody and Welch point out, the uncritical affiliation of literacy with a range of social and economic effects — and of its 'other', illiteracy, with diametrically opposing effects — has retained a great deal of currency among policy-makers, educators and the public. Belief in literacy as a singular cause of technological, social and economic development continues to rhetorically mask economic and social problems of marginal groups — whether the Indian underclass described by Kumar, Northern Territory Aborigines described by Walton, the adult unemployed in Australia discussed by O'Connor, or the 'underprepared' American university entrants studied by Collins. In such instances the literacy/human capital rationale acts as a discourse technology for blaming victims, for shifting responsibility from systemically constituted inequality to already marginal individuals and groups.

Knowledge, Culture and Power presents case studies of literacy policies and campaigns, pedagogies and methods. These cover a broad range of contemporary national and regional contexts, tracing the social and political contingency of literacy and education in neo-colonial and post-colonial, industrial and post-industrial, North and South countries. As Limage's overview chapter suggests, international patterns can be drawn from these and other cases, especially those of consistent declines in public sector spending and the emergence of powerful discourses of 'economic rationalism'. Basic educational services of children and adults have been hard hit in 'developed' and 'developing' countries alike and, in spite of the progress in world literacy campaigns documented by UNESCO, it is increasingly difficult to sustain international, regional and local efforts at literacy education.

Yet Limage's overview of post-war literacy campaigns and Welch and Freebody's hypotheses about current 'literacy crises' caution against over-generalizations about the causes and consequences of the social and economic 'problem' of illiteracy. As importantly, they enable us to put into historical and comparative perspective claims about the universal relevance and efficacy of particular pedagogical schemes. Literacy pedagogies and curricula are by definition the textual representations and products of particular cultural contexts, institutional conditions and political interests. The educational formation and framing of a literate 'tradition' — an official language of instruction, a corpus of texts, reading and writing practices and events — is not an arbitrary or 'natural' decision, but is an extension of extant ideological, discursive and material relations. How pedagogies are done, and what they enable and disenable for students and teachers in programmes and classrooms, is further constrained by local and regional contexts. Hence, we can identify particular international trends in educational and social policy. But to judge literacy pedagogies in terms of their putative 'universality' and 'truth' is to deny in the first instance their basis in the local and regional politics of curriculum. Such a perspective risks perpetuating the century-long Anglo-American assumption — introduced into post-war international education by William S. Gray and other educational psychologists — that the real work of literacy education is about articulating and deploying the scientifically 'correct' and most 'efficient' pedagogy.

An alternative is to reconsider pedagogies in terms of the kinds of literacies they are capable of constructing for particular populaces, and of the applicability of these literacies to the economic and political possibilities and aspirations of the populaces in question (Baker and Luke, 1991). If indeed pedagogic discourse and power are realized differently in local institutional sites (Foucault, 1972) — the same pedagogy, the same curricula, even the same textbooks or materials, can generate varying, if not outright contradictory effects. What might appear an emancipatory agenda for a specific clientele can have very different effects and consequences in other educational systems and contexts. We can contrast, for instance, Walton's critique of progressive education for Northern Territory Aborigines, with Kumar's view of student-centred pedagogy as a seminal means for enfranchising students from Indian underclasses. Kumar, and Ahai and Faraclas argue that 'rote', skills-based approaches to literacy effectively construct 'failure' and 'deficit' for lower socio-economic class students in the post-colonial educational systems of, respectively, India and Papua New Guinea. Traditional and 'technocratic' approaches, they argue, should be supplanted by some of the very methods and approaches to literacy education which Walton and colleagues criticize as having reproductive, stratifying consequences in Australian systems. These and other analyses point to the site specificity and relevance of pedagogical constructs and effects, an insight at the heart of Freire's early project but often lost in the will towards grand designs, radical and conservative alike, for literacy education.

What seems key is the hypothesis developed by Heath (1986) at the micro-ethnographic level: without significant, institutional supports and functions in everyday life, literate practices are at best difficult to teach, and, at worst, practically unsustainable. Like language maintenance, the propagation of literacy in a given community is contingent on: first, enabling 'institutional supports', strategies and policies; and, second, the necessity for texts and textuality in daily economic and cultural practices. These would appear to be necessary and sufficient conditions for sustainable cultures and subcultures of literacy. Particular strategies discussed here — among them Papua New Guinea's English language education policy, Northern Territory Aboriginal education policy — founder not because they are 'wrong' in any absolute scientific and ethical sense (though they well could be), but precisely because they fail to consider the local, the tactical, the quotidian. At the same time, the case studies by Hassanpour, Ahai and Faraclas and Lankshear show that it would be equally erroneous to view language and literacy education as 'stand alone', local matters. The futures of diverse strategies like Kurdish revolutionary literacy, Singaporean 'Speak Mandarin' language reforms and the Nicaraguan literacy campaign hinge on their continued centrality in the cultural and political lives of these communities.

These cultural and political lives are increasingly implicated in geopolitical and multinational corporate agenda far beyond the immediate control of any particular domestic policy and jurisdiction, revolutionary or otherwise (Mintz and Schwartz, 1990). First world economic and legitimation crises have global effects, including the tendency to 'export' economic rationalist, technocratic approaches to social and cultural problems. In this regard, the 'literacy crises' to which Freebody and Welch return in their final chapter have a dual effect: first, to shift the focus away from the localized and regional character of literacy and language education problems; and second, to obscure larger socio-economic and increasingly transnational forces which shape the structure and character of work, culture, and ultimately such sectors as schooling. A focus on the universal 'prom ise' of literacy as a protagonist in the narratives of skill expansion and economic growth is an ideological move *par excellence*. As Collins here eloquently comments, it at once silences and naturalizes a powerful 'dark secret': that literacy has been and continues to be a crucial means not for social integration and enfranchisement into a public domain of democratic discourse, but a means for institutionally constructing and imposing difference and marginality.

We can change and rename the rules of the game: from industrial to post-industrial, from monopoly to multinational, from modern to post-modern. But for the communities described here, the next century appears to hold in store more of the same: an educational politics of exclusion and marginality. For these same communities, the advent of microchip technologies has superimposed another grid — that of information 'wealth' versus information 'poverty' — on top of longstanding economic and cultural exclusion. *Knowledge, Culture and Power* focuses us on the need for tactical analyses of the politics of literacy in local institutions — whether regional schooling jurisdictions, rural communities, or urban universities. At the same time, it insists throughout on the futility of literacy reform without larger socio-economic analysis and strategy.

Allan Luke
Townsville
Queensland, Australia
31 November 1991

References

BAKER, C.D. and LUKE, A. (Eds) (1991) *Towards a Critical Sociology of Reading Pedagogy*, Amsterdam, John Benjamins.

FOUCAULT, M. (1972) 'The Eye of Power', in GORDON, C. (Ed.) *Power/Knowledge: Selected Interviews and Other Writings by Michel Foucault*, New York, Pantheon, pp. 145–65.

GRAFF, H.J. (1979) *The Literacy Myth*, New York, Academic Press.

HEATH, S.B. (1986) 'Critical factors in literacy development', in DECASTELL, S., LUKE, A. and EGAN, K. (Eds) *Literacy, Society and Schooling*, Cambridge, Cambridge University Press, pp. 209–32.

HOOKS, B. (1990) *Yearning: race, gender, and cultural politics*, Boston, South End Press.

LASH, S. and URRY, J. (1987) *The End of Organized Capitalism*, Cambridge, Polity Press.

MINTZ, B. and SCHWARTZ, M. (1990) 'Capital flows and the process of financial hegemony', in ZUKIN, S. and DIMAGGIO, P. (Eds) *Structures of Capital*, Cambridge, Cambridge University Press, pp. 203–26.

MOHANTY, C., RUSSO, A. and TORRES, L. (1991) *Third World Women and the Politics of Feminism*, Bloomington, Indiana University Press.

Chapter 1

Introduction: Explanations of the Current International 'Literacy Crises'

Anthony R. Welch and Peter Freebody

Introduction

The almost archetypal innocence of a scene in which one person helps another learn to read or write is matched by the ideological innocence claimed by the disciplines that once exclusively informed that scene — Psychology, Human Development, and Educational Measurement. But the study of reading and writing has become a political pursuit. The most significant events in recent theorizing about reading and writing have been the applications of critical perspectives from sociology, anthropology, history, politics, linguistics, and economics to the study of literacy and literacy education. These perspectives, exemplified in anthologies edited by Baker and Luke (1991), Street (in press/1992), and Wagner (1987), have not only contextualized but have often countered the three traditionally dominant accounts of literacy: the growth-through-heritage account, the cognitive-psychological account, and the skills-and-measurement account (Gilbert, 1989, see especially Chapter 1).

The perspectives on literacy arising from this comparatively new cross-disciplinary attention in turn provide the grounds for critiques of both technicist and progressivist accounts of literacy education. The 'great debate' between so-called skills and meaning approaches to literacy teaching (presented by Chall, 1967) has been put into its historical and ideological context (Christie, 1990), and the ways in which it has blinkered the exploration of literacy practices are beginning to be documented (Gee, 1990).

The increasingly prevalent use of the term 'literacy practices' instead of the massifying term 'literacy' reflects the variety of social activities to which literacy is crucial, and the interconnections of literacy activities with other cultural practices in specific settings such as schools, factories, and churches (Grillo, 1989). The term 'literacy practices' also signifies that it is daily material activities that are the topics of literacy study, rather than abstractions drawn from psychological or institutional theorizing.

It is fast becoming commonplace, therefore, to assert that literacy practices are not ideologically innocent. They do not merely meet cultural and individual needs: rather they shape both the ways in which cultures develop socio-economic arrangements and the ways in which literate individuals develop 'adaptive'

6

psychological dispositions and cognitive strategies (Ong, 1982, presents the strongest case for the influence of literacy on consciousness). In a literate culture, neither inter- nor intra-personal conditions are unaffected by the technologies of literacy. This idea — which may be expressed by the slogan that literacy practices are culturally and psychologically emergent — is a central scaffold that is taken for granted by a growing number of scholars, educators, and policy-makers. The aim of this book is simply to give body to that scaffold — to provide practical and visible illustrations from around the world of the point that literacy practices reflect and themselves build dominant political and socio-cultural experience.

Understanding the process by which literacy practices come to be the matter of ideology, as much as they are its vehicle, depends partly on understanding the idea of 'selective tradition' (Williams, 1977). Of the many possible forms in which literacy activities could develop and be put to work (in schools, offices, factories, churches, government departments, homes, and so on), some are re-cruited by a culture and others are ignored or marginalized. The successful forms themselves, by the psychological attributes and interpersonal relations they encour-age, highlight and value some ways of behaving, using language, and knowing, and marginalize others. It is this understanding, shown in its many expressions in this volume, that most directly challenges the assumption that literacy is exhaustively defined as a set of psychological skills, and is thus measurable, trans-portable, and packagable.

In this book the political edge of literacy practices is given a wide variety of manifestations: in the chapters that follow, the idea that literacy both builds and reflects socio-economic and political contexts is acted out, in some circumstances, by soldiers who forcibly enter houses to search for and destroy printing presses, in other circumstances, by a government's withdrawal of funding from multi- or bilingual programmes in schools, and, in yet other circumstances, by the writers of university policy documents that subtly interweave propositions about eco-nomic and cultural capital with advice about literacy 'help'. This book is about why events such as these have more in common than first appears. As such it is a distinctive documentation of inflections — differences that together point directly toward the need to embed descriptions of literacy practices in the broader socio-economic narratives in which they play crucial parts. It is a book in which the contributors collectively lay to rest, through concrete illustration rather than through assertion, the innocence of literacy.

The contributors' task was to show, in material social and political practices and in the documents that support them, the heavy ideological duties to which nations and sub-national cultures have put selective notions of 'literacy'. As such it is a collection written for and about its time. Perhaps many of the examples described in the following chapters will not obtain within just a few years or even months of writing. But the goals of the contributors are partly heuristic: to stimulate and focus impatience with the preoccupation with 'white-room/black-box' descriptions of literacy practices, and equally with intellectualized generalizations about the liberating or oppressing effects of some unitary version of literacy; and to show the variety of sites in which to view the versatile and generally unobtrusive ways that literacy practices connect knowledge, culture, and power in the process of enhancing or challenging privileged discourses.

These are the themes that give coherence to the diverse instances presented in this book. Many of the chapters demonstrate how literacy and language policies are cut across by discourses based on racist, classist, sexist, or adultist ideologies. By linking literacy to economic development, certain malformations of power (Luke, McHoul and Mey, 1990) may deny authority and even involvement to the very people in whose interests the literacy and language policies were said to have been formulated. Thus, important questions about literacy hinge on relativities of power: what political, social and economic agenda are pursued under the guise of literacy policies? Whose interests are being served by particular literacy and plans?

Many of the contributors to this book explicitly consider literacy practices in the context of class, ethnicity, and gender; but all to some extent relate their analyses of literacy to marginalized groups in society. A few examples: Limage's chapter discusses principally large-scale policy issues, but also draws attention to some features of the micro-processes at work in the allocation of human and capital resources for literacy education from nation to nation and within each nation. Her argument points out some of the international dilemmas arising from differentiations based on racial and economic distinctions. The chapters by Walton and Hassanpour examine the problems and prospects of Fourth World, dispossessed minorities in a situation of diminished cultural and thus educational power. Collins examines the ways in which certain discursive formations constituting race, class and gender relations are evidenced in writing programs in American colleges.

Thus, in this collection, forms of literacy education and policy are interrogated for the ways in which they value and build certain kinds of competences and dispositions: ways of thinking and feeling, and ways of positioning oneself with respect to sub-cultural reference groups (based on gender, class, ethnicity, or generation) and to the society's powerful institutions. Literacy educators and policy-makers show the influence they have in shaping these competences and dispositions most dramatically when the question arises of what will be defined as acceptable levels and forms of competence with written text — that is, in debates on 'standards'. The ways in which contesting groups argue out the business of standards, and the assumptions they make about the need for and significance of literacy standards are a function of the historical, political, and economic conditions pertaining in a given culture. It is important, then, prior to a more formal introduction to the chapters that follow, to clarify some issues concerning literacy standards and the ways in which that notion is used in public debates.

Connecting Literacy and Power through 'Standards'

Literacy education is at the centre of debates about society and instruction, in and out of school. As such it is a site from which to view the shifting fortunes of contesting interests: public and private, working class and bourgeois, male and female, host communities and ethnic minorities, and, increasingly, school, workplace, and market-place. Further, these contests often target the issue of standards of literacy, rather than, say, the methods or materials of literacy education. Over many decades, perhaps most forcefully in Western nations, there have recurred assertions that school and community standards in literacy are falling and that this decline has direct consequences for economic performance and cultural levels. As a starting point, then, it seems important to explore and critique the major hypothetical explanations for these assertions about literacy standards, as a way of providing the broad context for the contributions that follow.

Many arguments about literacy standards can be seen as inflections of one or more of the following four hypotheses:

1. *The Slide Hypothesis*: That the rhetoric of concern about literacy standards is indeed a result of genuinely declining standards in the recent past in the literacy competence of school students or perhaps of nations or sub-national groups;
2. *The Demands Hypothesis*: That, while competences have not declined, the requisite literacy competences for effective civil, social, and cultural functioning have increased and diversified in our society;
3. *The Credentials Hypothesis*: That, while neither competences nor cultural demands may have changed significantly, the increased competitiveness of the labour market, and/or the decline in work-force numbers of low-literacy occupations in a society have led to an increase in the necessary formal credentials for any given job; and
4. *The Invention Hypothesis*: That the rhetoric of concern about literacy standards is, like the concept of 'standards' itself, a confection, designed or at least functioning to undermine certain progressive or socially powerful educational trends that have developed in the recent past.

We will now deal with each of these hypotheses briefly, pointing at times to the ways in which these considerations frame the contributions that follow.

The Slide Hypothesis

What empirical support is there for the hypothesis that there has been a recent and general decline in literacy competences in recent years? We need first to consider some methodological issues involved in possible answers to this question. It turns out that serious problems arise for researchers aiming to document generalizations about changes over time in literacy competence. Attempts to plot performance rates for groups of people over a period of time must deal with a shifting average. The establishment over time of stable levels of literacy performance with changing samples of people becomes possible only in the most abstract terms.

Comparing the performance levels, for example, of a certain group of same-aged students over a long period assumes that the composition of the samples on the multiple occasions has remained stable on variables other than age that may relate to literacy performance (such as socio-economic status or ethnicity), such that all samples in fact represent the same hypothetical population. Assessing over time the literacy activities of a group standardized by the fact that they have successively worked at the same job calls into play similar questions about the stability of the work-force (first language status or educational levels) in that position at differing points in the economic or cultural history of that society. It is clear that in periods of migration or economic change the critical assumptions cannot be made safely in either of these cases. In addition, statistical and analytic capabilities and fashions among the research community change over time.

Confidence in item reliability, scoring reliability, comparability in testing conditions, and the nature of the statistical analyses applied are all issues which bear directly on the ability to compare literacy performance across extensive periods of time. These issues assume particular importance when it is considered that the sample sizes used in such survey test programmes are usually sufficiently large to allow small absolute differences in performance levels to assume statistical significance.

These are some of the doubts arising just on the grounds of sampling and measurement that trouble the 'slide hypothesis'. There are further significant theoretical questions that could be pursued: about the relevance of test materials to the actual literacy practices that have developed in the school or the workplace, and about the attendant difficulties and biases introduced by the incursion of the school's form of 'read-remember-comment' literacy into contexts other than school (Heap, 1987).

All of these constraints upon reliability and validity of empirical studies about standards of literacy over time need to be kept in mind when considering the available research, in particular on the matter of the onus of proof. In a statistical sense, the null hypothesis is that standards of literacy performance among comparable groups of people have not changed. In the light of changing school clienteles, changing pedagogies, and changing methods of performance assessment, the difficult task of proving that standards have either increased or decreased lies squarely with those who wish to argue for an observable change in performance levels. That is, until proven wrong, we need to assume that general standards of literacy have remained precisely stable over time.

In addition, some account needs to be offered that would describe the network of factors functioning to cause a genuine decline in text-management competences among members of a society or groups within it. These accounts themselves can then be interrogated for evidence of recruitment in ideological agenda. The following are a sample of such accounts:

1. Certain class-reproductive or ethnocentric pedagogical methods may become prevalent which, in subsequent times of economic contraction or in times in which previously disenfranchised groups come to be offered more complete educational access, result in overall sample decline (see Bernstein, 1975);
2. Governments may allow salaries and conditions of teachers to decline in comparison with comparable occupations such that the literacy experiences and competences of beginning teachers change, and/or available literacy materials for school and workplace literacy programs diminish;
3. Political pressure may be placed upon teachers and school authorities to respond to certain apparent market forces by emphasizing areas of curriculum that are, again apparently, less demanding of literacy competence in their study and assessment;
4. A process of migration of traditional groups to urban, Westernized commercial centres may initially bring with it an increase in the proportion of the population engaged in white-collar occupations. Thus these migrants encounter increased textual demands, and subsequently more of their children attend school. Later, this migration may subside or in fact be reversed such that a rural reconstruction is attempted

and earlier increases in overall community literacy competences are halted or reversed.

All of these accounts implicate genuinely changing socio-economic conditions, or changing perceptions in the relationship between literacy education and cultural and economic development. However, the 'slide hypothesis' is generally presented in a functional vacuum, as if teachers or students were wilfully derelict either in their appreciation of the value of literacy or in their competence to teach and learn it. Such characterizations hail the ideologies of both class and generation, and 'literacy', as an unquestioned commodity, comes to be used as a legitimator of class and generational privilege.

Thus there are serious empirical problems in substantiating the 'slide hypothesis', and the explanations that are generally called upon to account for this slippery phenomenon are generally ideologically motivated. In the face of a lack of reliable empirical support, the methodologically appropriate move is to 'fail to reject the hypothesis of no change'. Nonetheless, the point is worth making that, as this 'no change' discourse finds its way into debates about literacy standards, it does itself have ideological significance and practical consequences, especially for groups traditionally marginalized by educational practices.

In the light of the difficulties of establishing a 'slide', a case can be reconstituted in terms of a 'gap': the apparently increasing gap between the literacy competences of many people and the genuine and proper demands that societies are coming to place on those competences. That line of argument can now be developed.

The Demands Hypothesis

The Demands Hypothesis states that, while literacy performance standards may or may not have decreased, it is the social and cultural expectations of literacy performance that have increased markedly in recent times. That is, society demands increasing levels of literacy performance and the school system is increasingly missing this moving target.

Useful summaries of the historical changes in literacy expectations over time have been attempted by, for example, Graff (1986, 1987) and Resnick and Resnick (1977). As an example, Resnick and Resnick identified three major models relating to literacy expectations evident in European history: the Protestant-religious model, in which literacy skills were developed primarily for the memorization of religious writing; the elite-technical model, which emphasized the use of literacy for the development of theoretical knowledge and technical problem-solving; and the civic-national model in which literacy was used primarily to instil civic goals and national identity and pride, and which demanded understanding of familiar and routine textual material. Drawing upon historical policy documents in the United States, Resnick and Resnick claimed that it is only within the context of a growing civic-national model following the First World War that the demand for understanding and the use of textual information in new contexts developed. With reference to the USA, they claimed (p. 379) that to the extent that people are disturbed about literacy levels it is because they are applying an inappropriately demanding criterion and construing the problem not in that light but as less capable student performance. Compared with previous generations, increasingly sophisticated pedagogical techniques are required before the goal of having all students and workers 'fully literate' in these comparatively new terms can be attained.

It is useful to identify two inflections of the Demands Hypothesis. First this hypothesis may be taken to mean that the functional demands on literacy performance have increased because individuals need to cope with increasingly complex bureaucracies and job specifications, both of which call upon increasingly complex and specialized forms of dealing with written texts. A second version of the hypothesis is that many societies are demanding or at least aspiring to a more culturally literate community than previously — a community that reads 'good literature', that perhaps writes in a greater diversity of written genres, and that can respond more sensitively to literary works.

With respect to first version of the Demands Hypothesis mentioned above, the civil-functioning aspect, the research of Mikulecky (1981) is pertinent. He examined the literacy demands placed upon industrial workers and high school students, concluding that technical workers faced more difficult job-related literacy demands than did students in technical schools; further that workers reported reading more for job-related tasks than did students for school-related tasks, with workers reading an average of 143 minutes per day compared to 98 minutes for high school students and 135 minutes for technical school students (pp. 408–409). Mikulecky also revealed that the workers read more difficult materials than did the students, with even blue collar manuals and directions averaging a Year 10 level of difficulty.

So the civil-functional Demands Hypothesis may not apply evenly across various levels of the work-force. That is, we would have expected in the past that white collar jobs as well as professional employment would necessarily entail Year 10 or better levels of literacy performance, but we might not have expected in the past that semi-skilled, unskilled or blue collar workers would necessarily face these demands. Similarly, the cultural version of the Demands Hypothesis has a social-class dimension: current notions concerning the benefits of literacy in terms of personal enrichment have led to pressure on teachers (of children and adults) to believe that all members of the community should appreciate literary works acceptable in the canon of the ruling culture, when the function of that canon is to set itself in contradistinction to mass culture. The ensuing community 'disappointment' becomes a public feature of class-reproductive discourse (Bourdieu, 1983).

The Demands Hypothesis is difficult to establish empirically over the short term. Resnick and Resnick and, in a less direct way, Eisenstein (1979) have documented literacy demands and expectations that have increased dramatically and changed in their nature over the centuries. But it has yet to be documented that the genuine demands on literacy practices, either in civil-functional or cultural terms, have shifted radically in the recent past. What may be more readily documented is the phenomenon that formal credentials for attaining jobs of various kinds in any given society have increased. A most common impression, at least in many Western nations, seems to be that many of the so-called unskilled jobs that lower school achievers formerly filled are disappearing or have come to require formally some enhanced literacy and numeracy competences, especially in urban centres. This is in part then a matter of credentialing, a different kind of explanation.

The Credentials Hypothesis

This third thesis draws attention to the influence of rising expectations in the job market. The point of this hypothesis is that some societies may allow or encourage their school systems to become closely articulated to literacy criteria driven by competitive industrial selection. That is, this hypothesis draws attention to the economic and cultural conditions (market forces and cultural aspirations) that lead to increases in the formal requirements of certain occupations, independently of the degree to which changing job demands genuinely call for more or different forms of literacy competence.

Dore (1976), for example, has cited cases in which students pursue increasingly higher credentials in order to keep one step ahead of competitors for job places. He argued that in Third World nations this can be catastrophic for certain groups; but that it continues to form a popular option to large numbers of people drawn by the notion of earning more in the 'modern', commercial sector of the economy than could otherwise be earned in the traditional sectors.

> In the late sixties, the Ugandan graduate just entering the civil service could expect his (sic) income to be fifty times the average income in Uganda. Even in India, after a much longer period of independence under governments with a much more explicitly egalitarian philosophy, the ratio was twelve to one. (Dore, 1976, p. 3)

Increases and change in literacy practices, among individuals and social groups, have featured prominently in movements into commercial sectors. In some nations a job in the civil service calls for competence in selective literacy practices; at a national level, research in the 1960s appeared to give added strength to the simple 'human capital' position — that increases in literacy performance were causally and directly involved in increases in general affluence. In Bowman (1968), for example, it is shown that, in a purely correlational sense, the richest countries showed the highest literacy levels, and the poorest the lowest.

The outcomes of a belief in the human-capital model of literacy (and education generally) in promoting Third World economic development have been in some cases damaging. It has been used to legitimate the substantial growth of educational systems, often well in excess of the capacity of economies to absorb 'school-educated' labour in these quantities. Further, it has been argued that the economic advantages that accrue to individuals or groups as a result of increased or broadened literacy competences can, depending on other socio-economic conditions, be discriminatory: that the most advantaged groups in society gain most from rising standards of literacy, and that this further widens the social and economic gap between, perhaps, rich and poor, or rural and urban, or male and female (Soltow and Stevens, 1981; Fuller, Edwards, and Gorman, 1987).

Especially, but not only in the Third World, employers were witness to a process whereby increased levels of education were called upon to secure particular jobs. Where previously a primary education certificate was adequate, now several years of secondary schooling became necessary. Even in nations that attempted to deal explicitly with this problem, such as Sri Lanka, India, and some parts of Africa and Latin America, the competition for credentials has increased.

Because Western-style schooling has in these nations grown faster than the 'modern' commercial sector, an educated and no doubt frustrated cohort of unemployed has developed (Oxenham, 1984, p. 11). The issue then compounds: in both Third World and developed nations a surplus of educated individuals has meant that, in an increasingly competitive labour market, employers can afford to be more and more selective. There has grown an increasing divergence between the level of competence that is appropriate for a particular job and that which could be commanded. Thus some people with adequate competences are pushed out of a given level of the job market, with the necessary justification that their literacy competences are inadequate. In this way the credential market, independently of any documentable increases in the demands attached to a job, creates a rhetoric of falling literacy standards.

Viewed from this perspective, the literacy crisis may be something of a confection. Certain groups in all societies have been ill-served by formal schooling since its development, partly because of the comparative cultural and economic position of teaching as a job, and the consequent ready recruitment of educational practices as displays of ruling culture. The literacy competences of these groups has always been different from and lower than more privileged groups, and these competences in turn become a pivotal concept in student-centred legitimations of class reproduction. In this view the most parsimonious and powerful explanation for current concerns in many societies about literacy competences is not to do with job demands genuinely requiring increased credentials, but rather with the shifting configuration of cultural, economic, and political factors that give rise to the occasional need to confect a literacy crisis.

The Invention Hypothesis

It has been suggested that the contemporary 'literacy crisis', particularly as it is enacted in advanced industrial states, is largely an invention, at least in its most common inflections. If so, what might be its origins? Why has talk of a crisis surfaced at this time in many societies, and what does it signify? Are there correlative arguments about the nature of schooling and society which are associated with particular interest groups? What sort of 'standards' and 'crises' are these?

Using Canada as an example, Willinsky (1988) has pointed to the ways in which the discourse of literacy crisis has been constructed in recent years. His example is worth some close consideration. In Canada an important stimulus for 'crisis' discourse was the Southam Literacy Survey, sponsored by a group of newspapers and given prominence in 1987. This survey, claiming much higher rates of illiteracy than had been found previously, was sensationalized in the press with front page headlines such 'Survey Rates Five Million Canadians Illiterate'. The outcomes of the survey included the establishment of a Secretariat of Illiteracy by the Canadian Government, a formal, institutional statement of the 'problem of illiteracy'. Commenting on the Southam survey, Willinsky (p. 9) claimed that, among the panel selected as representing the community, which was to devise a standard test for literacy, there was no consensus as to how literacy was to be defined or assessed. A supposedly liberal standard nonetheless resulted in one in four Canadians being labelled illiterate, although the vast majority of respondents reported spending time each day reading the newspaper. The survey did not feel shy in allocating blame for the allegedly large numbers of Canadian illiterates it discerned. Some journalists in reporting the results imputed the poor levels to both liberal immigration policies and a 'flawed education system' (p. 12). The schools were accused of adding 100,000 extra illiterates to the Canadian population each year.

What is remarkable here is the ready ascription of the causes of the 'crisis' to areas of societal policy and practice about which there was long-standing debate in Canadian society, notably about workers, immigrants, and the 'Back to Basics' school curriculum. In these ways research programmes can be recruited to further marginalize certain segments of society, and to legitimate reactionary educational agenda. In the Southam case, the survey's results functioned to reaffirm nostalgic and reactionary industrial and educational values, evoking a past age in which curricular knowledge was supposedly more certain and social structures were more stable.

The recruitment of such surveys in these agendas is facilitated by the fact that typically the survey developers, as in the Southam example, have tended to adopt a technicist definition of literacy as that minimum level of competence necessary for 'public efficiency and civic function' (Heap, 1987; Willinsky 1988). De Castell, Luke, and Egan (1986) have shown how technicist approaches have underpinned the principal models of literacy in North America this century. Such models allow only an analytic, reductive notion of universal literacy competences. Thus they afford not only standardized and contextually transportable tests but also close and apparently objective monitoring by teachers, government departments and employer bodies. In much of the discourse that is sampled in the chapters to follow, technical and economic progress are seen to demand rising standards of these particular forms of literacy for all.

As a further example, in the USA the discourse of 'literacy crisis' displays features of invention and recruitment in reactionary agenda. The publication of *A Nation at Risk* (National Commission on Excellence in Education, 1983) did more than assert that educational standards were falling: it also used the device of literacy standards to position the schools as scapegoats for perceived national failings in the international economic stakes. The focus is placed unproblematically but squarely on the schools at the outset of the book at which point they are described as the 'cause' that 'undergirds American prosperity, security and civility' (p. 5).

So part of the explanation for the appearance of this powerful rhetorical device of literacy standards is the changing economic and political contexts. The current American rhetoric is similar to that which arose there in the late 1950s. Then there was a widespread fear that the USA was about to lose its technological lead to the USSR, a fear symbolized by the successful launch of the first Soviet spacecraft in 1957. There was considerable media attention given to the superiority of the Soviet educational system, widely assumed to be the principal reason for the new-found technological superiority of that nation. Much of the criticism for the alleged failure of the American scientific and technological communities was levelled at the American schooling system, which was charged with producing a nation of illiterates and innumerates (Barzun, 1959).

In the 'Sputnik era' publications with titles such as *Why Johnny Can't Read* (Flesch, 1955), and *Teaching Johnny to Read*, (Flesch, 1956) *Educational Wastelands*, (Bestor, 1953) *Crisis in Education* (Bell, 1949) and *What Ivan Knows that Johnny*

Doesn't (Trace, 1961) enjoyed high public profile. In the early and mid 1980s Cold War rhetoric was once more prevalent in the USA, but on this occasion the focus of American economic anxiety was Japan. The effect of this apprehension however, was the same — an increase in the use of the icon of literacy and numeracy standards, in reductive terms, to attack American schools.

None of this is to deny the individual, social and economic costs of illiteracy. It is rather to assert that analysis of and discourse about 'standards' cannot be divorced from contemporary social and economic changes. As is argued more closely in several of the following chapters (especially those by Ahai and Faraclas, Lankshear, Collins, and Freebody and Welch), it is not uncommon for a crisis of the state to be exported onto schooling systems, such that they are, at all levels from elementary school to university, under pressure from governing ministries, industry, and the general public. (This phenomenon has been pointed out by others, such as Apple, 1986, and Welch, 1991, in different cultural contexts.) Ironically this pressure has often been accompanied by the withdrawal of funding support for public education, thus widening the gap in educational levels between bourgeois and working class, host and minority, and rural and urban sectors of society. As Limage (this volume) describes, there are parallels in the disparities between nations, in that the literacy gap between First and Third World countries is likely to widen.

Indeed the following collection as a whole demonstrates the different ways in which nations deal with internal and external pressures to enhance their 'literacy education effort' in the schools and work-places. Much discursive work is put, in some cases, into apportioning fault for inadequate performance levels, elsewhere into convincing communities of a simple version of the human-capital view of literacy practices, and yet elsewhere into offsetting claims about the destructive effects of imported literacy education campaigns on indigenous ways of social and intellectual life. The common element in these various efforts draws attention to the principal motif running through this volume: that is the motivation to develop a critical understanding of literacy practices through an analysis of their material and visible relations to knowledge, culture, and power.

Previewing the Volume

The contributors to this collection are drawn from many disciplines and many parts of the world. The chapters include studies of literacy in Fourth, Third, and First World contexts, by philosophers, sociologists, psychologists, linguists, policy advisers, ministry authorities and teachers. There is an initial need in a book such as this to provide a background for the subsequent chapters that traces some of the changes which have occurred over the post-war era — changes in international commitments to the development of literacy competences, accompanied by changes in the definition of literacy, and changing views of the teaching strategies that optimize particular literacy goals. Limage's chapter performs this backgrounding function by analyzing changes in literacy policies and practices from the vantage point of the UNESCO International Literacy Year Secretariat. The change from the mass literacy movements of the 1950s to a narrower and problematic concept of 'functional literacy' closely reflects these changing currents. Of concern at the time of writing is the international economic recession, involving withdrawal of public funds from basic provision, as part of a more general constriction of the public sector, in favour of economic restructuring, a tendency that is widening the gap between First and Third World nations.

So literacy, as a topic of debate and contestation, and as a resource in which other topics are contested, plays significant roles in highlighting and marginalizing differences between national or sub-national groups. This role is seen dramatically in the case of Fourth World nations. The chapters by Hassanpour and Walton pursue the roles played by various literacy practices and the concept of standards through the past and future developments of two Fourth World nations.

Hassanpour illustrates the intimate connection between literacy and political struggle shown throughout the history of the Kurdish people. For centuries writing in Kurdish has constituted an act of political defiance. During much of the early history of the Kurdish people, literacy competences were confined to their priests (the mullahs) who were educated in Arabic or Persian. Thus demand for literacy in the Kurdish language was limited. Only with the temporary rise of Kurdish power in the fifteenth and sixteenth centuries did an indigenous Kurdish literature begin to develop. The end of political autonomy in the nineteenth century signalled the end of Kurdish as a basis for religious instruction and schooling. Much of the modern era is characterized by Hassanpour as 'linguistic genocide' with perhaps the singular systematic exception being a brief period in the early history of the USSR, when native tongue literacy was fostered.

Walton examines the contexts in which policies and pedagogies directed at Australian Aboriginal literacy, principally the context of domination in which Aboriginal Australians have lived for centuries. Most Aboriginals living in the Northern Territory are multilingual, speaking at least their own indigenous language as well as English and perhaps Kriol. A number of bilingual programmes exist, but Walton argues that Aboriginal cultures and languages are still undervalued rather than used as genuine cultural or linguistic resources. The crucial question here is whether or not cultural differences are valued only to the extent to which they leave existing power arrangements undisturbed.

Walton points directly to the critical effects of pedagogical philosophies, especially those derived from the progressivist notion of 'natural language', which she describes as a particularly inappropriate basis for multicultural education. At the heart of Walton's argument is her documentation of the workings of discursive devices such the ascription to Aboriginals of 'free choice' in the matter of schooling as a means of distracting attention from the failure of provision, even when evidence suggests that Aboriginal communities are explicitly requesting access to schooling. Walton displays the discourses that build a web of racist structures and practices in which Aboriginal Australians find themselves, and which saps the larger community's will to implement multilingual literacy programs. Walton outlines what she takes to be appropriate instructional approaches, framing the future in terms of a socially critical pedagogy that is based upon literacy practices embedded in their multicultural context, and that is responsive to social and historical features including racial subjugation.

Developing this line further in a different cultural context, Ahai and Faraclas account for illiteracy problems in terms of the prevailing language policies and socio-economic factors operating in Papua New Guinea (PNG). In this nation a large proportion of young children never attend school at all, while the 'English only' policy, in a country with 869 languages, and competitive examinations and fees together serve to create a large class of what the locals call 'pushouts'.

Ahai and Faraclas construct an iconography of education in PNG, and sketch a profile for each: the school leaver, often rural dwellers, who are typically seen, and see themselves as useless; the rascal/expert icons, portrayed by Ahai and Faraclas as reverse sides of the same coin; and the elite, who are seen as losers in all but a material sense. From here the authors examine two forms of discourse, each associated with definitions of literacy: integral human development, and technicism. The former parallels the notion of 'empowerment' as it has been deployed in literacy campaigns in other Third World countries. In PNG, however, the deference to English vitiates its impact. The technicist model is characterized by the authors as a variant of 'back to basics'. PNG development is seen here as a process of encouraging indigenous peoples to submerge their own cultural and economic interests, in favour of those imported from the Western colonizers. Literacy education work stands in an ambiguous position in socio-cultural contests such as this, being an equally powerful ally in any side's agenda. The assumed passivity and ignorance of the learner are redefined by Ahai and Faraclas as opposition to cultural colonizing, while the slogan that literacy will, of itself, allow people to partake in development is revealed as illusory.

A conventional explanation for poor literacy rates in the Third World has been that children of poor parents leave school for economic reasons, including child labour. Kumar's chapter examines the thesis that it is rather the traditional forms of reading pedagogy combined with India's place in the international economic order that constitute the major barrier to fuller participation by India's poor. While Kumar documents that more than half of all primary/elementary-aged children in India are not attending any form of school, he argues that it is the pedagogy of endless rote learning of the sounds and shapes of letters, entrenched in the Indian primary school, that suppresses many young children's motivation to learn literacy, as well as restricting their range of literacy practices in which they can engage.

Kumar argues that while such an approach might work with students in more supportive circumstances, it is inappropriate in a modern mass educational setting, whether capitalist or socialist. Kumar's tentative solutions include the investment of more resources in making primary education a more interesting and stimulating environment, and the provision of more sophisticated literacy education in teacher training programmes and more attractive career structures for primary teachers.

Despite the visible success of some national literacy campaigns, literacy education has not always been an arena of unambiguous success, nor is it always possible, for complex and sometimes contradictory reasons, to build on significant early successes. Lankshear describes the substantial extent of illiteracy that confronted the Sandinista regime in Nicaragua, and the differences in access to literacy education that existed along ethnic and gender lines. For example, the situation of the Miskitu and other indigenous minorities is discussed, including some of the background to their struggle for cultural identity. The changing policies of the Sandinistas during the 1980s culminated in bicultural and bilingual programs. As well as pointing to some successes such as increased retentivity,

Lankshear notes the problems that consistently undercut these programmes, in particular the choice of standard English rather than Creole.

The political complexity of literacy education programs and classroom strategies in multilingual contexts arises in part from the role literacy practices play in inter-lingual contests sometimes going back centuries. In Kwan-Terry and Kwan-Terry's chapter, the politics of language planning and contest for instruction in the vernacular is seen to be decisive in explaining the development of literacy in Singapore. Even after a policy of bilingualism was announced, English continued to be the prestige language, carrying with it increased earning power, to the point where the government felt moved to make mandatory the former policy of encouraging bilingualism. Bilingualism is still compulsory, and although all four languages are promoted in the Singapore media, in practice English and Mandarin are the preferred choices.

What, then, have been the results of the policy of bilingualism for the various cultural and linguistic groups in Singapore? Kwan-Terry and Kwan-Terry conclude that it has been of some use in sustaining the use of Chinese, of less relevance to the Malay group of languages, and of no help in maintaining Tamil. So a national policy is necessarily read in different ways by language groups located in different political positions due to their socio-economic status or ethnicity, both of which have, in turn, been shaped in part by the language and literacy status of these groups.

It is these contesting readings of policies that politicize debates over standards of education and literacy even at the tertiary level. Collins analyzes the relation between the on-going debate over college curriculum and the development of basic writing programmes in the United States of America. As the content of college curricula has grown more problematic, there has been a 'turn to language' which has presented unexpected dilemmas for various institutional parties — writing teachers, students, administrators and faculty. Collins develops a comparative case study of writing programmes at an urban university over a twenty- year period, showing how shifts in the class, race, and gender composition of students and faculty, changes in who controls writing programs, and changes in theories of writing, have all shaped the practices found in basic writing courses. These changes have thus created distinctive literacy competences in subsequent professional cohorts.

O'Connor's chapter on workplace literacy and more broadly on workplace basic education (WBE) also raises questions of state policy and political interest. WBE has at times been too closely tied to business and other economic interests to fulfil its promise to workers, much less the sometimes inflated expectations of governments and industrial sectors still convinced by the simple form of the human- capital definition of literacy. Workplace literacy can be seen as another example of ways in which a wider and deeper crisis of the state is being masked, and presented as a failure of school education in general, and workers' competences and knowledge in particular. On the basis of comparative evidence, O'Connor warns against generally ineffectual short-term schemes, which often do little other than promote bickering among trainers. Equally, he argues, the largely uncritical adoption by funding bodies and educational institutions of the agenda set by business is dangerous, in that the goals of workplace basic education do not come to be widely debated or pluralistically defined. Consistent with conclusions from the array of contexts described in other chapters, O'Connor shows how controlling interest groups can determine what counts as literacy competence, and what counts as an explanation of literacy success and failure in the workplace.

The final chapter, by Freebody and Welch, is set in Australia, and elaborates on some of the themes raised earlier in this Introduction. The neglect of the effects of social class in research on literacy in recent national surveys is exemplified. This is accomplished at a theoretical level partly through the domestication of literacy competences and the causes of literacy failure. This domestication in turn diverts attention, among researchers and the broader community, away from other crises of the state — massive unemployment levels, most particularly among youth, unsustainable economic problems, and difficulties in international economic competitiveness. Certain key texts are closely analyzed to show how this process of domestication works.

It is clear that the different contributors vary substantially in focus and exhibit different disciplinary backgrounds. The theme that emerges is the relation between forms of literacy and forms of state power acted out partly through the schools and the workplace. At times, pedagogical conventions, or more or less naked political and even military judgments have impeded the development of literacy competences that might allow more autonomy to more individuals, and to marginal groups in society. It is in the hope that this book can make more visible these concrete, daily practices and how they may be redefined and systematically reconstituted that we have collected these pieces.

Acknowledgments

In addition to the Australian Literacy Year Secretariat, who provided some funding for this project, a number of individuals deserve the editors' thanks for the parts they played in the volume's development. Allan Luke, the series editor, gave substantial support to the project from its inception and valuable editorial advice in the latter stages. Cameron Barnes provided sound research help and kept a close eye on formatting consistency, well beyond the call of duty. And finally, our publisher at Falmer Press, Jacinta Evans, deserves our thanks for her continued encouragement. The editors shared the work on this project equally; the order of editorship is alphabetical.

References

APPLE, M. (1986) *Teachers and Texts: Political Economy and Class and Gender Relations in Education*, London, Routledge and Kegan Paul.

BAKER, C.D. and LUKE, A. (1991) *Toward a Critical Sociology of Reading Pedagogy*, Amsterdam/Philadelphia, John Benjamins.

BARZUN, J. (1959) *The House of Intellect*, New York, Harper and Brothers.

BELL, B. (1949) *Crisis in Education: A Challenge to American Complacency*, New York, Whittlesey House.

BERNSTEIN, B. (1975) *Class, Codes and Control*, Vol. 3, London, Routledge and Kegan Paul.

BESTOR, A. (1953) *Educational Wastelands*, Urbana, University of Illinois Press.

BOURDIEU, P. (1983) *Distinction: A Social Critique of the Judgement of Taste*, London, Routledge and Kegan Paul.

BOWMAN, M. (Ed.) (1968) *Readings in the Economics of Education*, Paris, UNESCO.

CHALL, J.S. (1967) *Learning to Read: The Great Debate*, New York, McGraw Hill.

CHRISTIE, F. (1990) 'The changing face of literacy', in CHRISTIE, F. (Ed.) *Literacy for a Changing World*, Hawthorn, Victoria, Australian Council for Educational Research, pp. 1–25.

DAVIS, A. (1981) *Women, Race and Class*, New York, Random House.

DE CASTELL, S., LUKE, A. and EGAN, K. (Eds) (1986) *Literacy, Society and Schooling*, Cambridge, Cambridge University Press.

DORE, R. (1976) *The Diploma Disease: Education, Qualification and Development*, London, Allen and Unwin.

EISENSTEIN, E. (1979) *The Printing Press as an Agent of Change*, 2 Vols., Cambridge, Cambridge University Press.

FLESCH, R. (1955) *Why Johnny Can't Read*, New York, Harper and Brothers.

FLESCH, R. (1956) *Teaching Johnny to Read*, New York, Grosset and Dunlap.

FULLER, B., EDWARDS, J. and GORMAN, K. (1987) 'Does rising literacy spark economic growth? Commercial expansion in Mexico', in WAGNER, D. (Ed.) *The Future of Literacy in a Changing World*, New York, Pergamon Press, pp. 319–40.

GEE, J.P. (1990) *Social Linguistics and Literacies: Ideology in Discourses*, London, Falmer Press.

GILBERT, P. (1989) *Writing, Schooling, and Deconstruction: From Voice to Text in the Classroom*, London, Routledge and Kegan Paul.

GRAFF, H. (1986) *The Legacies of Literacy*, Bloomington, Indiana University Press.

GRAFF, H. (1987) *The Labyrinths of Literacy*, London, Falmer Press.

GRILLO, R. (1989) *Social Anthropology and the Politics of Language*, Cambridge, Cambridge University Press.

HEAP, J. (1987) *Effective Functioning in Daily Life: A Critique of Concepts and Surveys of Functional Literacy*. Paper presented to the National Reading Conference, Arizona.

LUKE, A., McHOUL, A. and MEY, J. (1990) 'On the limits of language planning: Class, state and power'. In R. BALDAUF and A. LUKE (Eds) *Language Planning and Education in Australia and the South Pacific*, Clevedon, UK, Multilingual Matters, pp. 25–44.

MIKULECKY, L. (1981) 'The mismatch between school training and job literacy demands', *Reading Research Quarterly*, 16, pp. 400–417.

NATIONAL COMMISSION ON EXCELLENCE IN EDUCATION (1983) *A Nation at Risk: The Imperative for Educational Reform*, Washington, US Government Printing Office.

ONG, W. (1982) *Orality and Literacy: Technologizing the Word*, London, Methuen.

OXENHAM, J. (Ed.) (1984) *Education Versus Qualifications: A Study of the Relationship between Education, Election for Employment and Labour Productivity*, London, Allen and Unwin.

RESNICK, D. and RESNICK, L. (1977) 'The nature of literacy: An historical exploration', *Harvard Educational Review*, 47, pp. 370–85.

SOLTOW, L. and STEVENS, E. (1981) *The Rise of Literacy and the Common School in the United States*, Chicago, The University of Chicago Press.

STREET, B.V. (in press/1992) *Cross-cultural Approaches to Literacy*, Cambridge, Cambridge University Press.

TRACE, A. (1961) *What Ivan Knows that Johnny Doesn't*, New York, Random House.

WAGNER, D. (1987) *The Future of Literacy in A Changing World*, New York, Pergamon.

Anthony R. Welch and Peter Freebody

WELCH, A.R. (1991) 'Education and legitimation in comparative education', *Comparative Education Review*, 34, p. 3.
WILLIAMS, R. (1977) *Marxism and Literature*, Oxford, Oxford University Press.
WILLINSKY, J. (1988) *The Construction of a Crisis: Literacy in Canada*, unpublished manuscript, University of Calgary.

Chapter 2

Literacy Strategies: A View from the International Literacy Year Secretariat of UNESCO*

Leslie J. Limage

International Literacy Year 1990 provided the opportunity to look critically at forty years of efforts to promote literacy and education in general as basic human rights. This chapter looks at some of the challenges and dilemmas raised in the current context. It also examines the literacy situation in the world and the various approaches used to define and address literacy issues.

As an intergovernmental agency, UNESCO (United Nations Educational, Scientific and Cultural Organization) has prodded and pushed, but above all, has served as a mirror of the state of the world's conscience and commitment in the field of literacy. As we shall examine more closely later in this chapter, UNESCO's approaches have varied. After a period of initial optimism and confidence in governments' will to introduce education massively to all, the Organization found that most countries were simply unable or unwilling to introduce such massive change. While UNESCO had promoted what it called the 'mass literacy campaign' approach in its early years, it turned to a more targeted strategy, called 'functional literacy' programmes in the mid-1960s and early 1970s. When learners in these latter programmes discovered that the only 'functionality' involved was to make them better workers, the majority of these experiments failed. That UNESCO's approach since the period has been to provide technical expertise and advice according to specific needs in specific contexts, is an indication of the world community's pulse in recent years. No single solution can be applied across countries. Programmes and strategies must emanate from perceived needs within individuals and their communities.

But as we move away from simple recipes and slogans to, for example, 'eradicate illiteracy by the year 2000', we have to convey a more complex message. Some of the challenges of that message are outlined in the next paragraphs. First of all, the fundamental message of International Literacy Year has been that literacy matters and it matters greatly. Also, literacy is everyone's concern. The number one responsibility remains that of the public sector but there is a place for every actor in a larger alliance to promote a fully literate world: the state,

---

* The views expressed in this chapter are those of the author and do not commit the Organization in which she is engaged.

the private and voluntary sectors, non-formal education non-governmental organizations, business, the media, community groups and so forth. Unfortunately, it is not easy to find a clear language to communicate across countries and to all sectors of society. Too frequently, international organizations have developed a special language to talk about literacy which gets in the way of international understanding. The media, too, have frequently presented a fairly unrepresentative stereotype of the individual who has insufficient basic skills, for example, in order to heighten drama, newspapers and television dwell upon the individual testimonial, the individual shame, and convey an image which likens the illiterate adult to someone with an affliction such as alcoholism. In reality, an individual who lacks sufficient basic skills to meet his or her own needs is usually a fully functioning family member with responsibilities and/or a person who perceives need in terms of employment possibilities. That person is not ignorant. The individuals who come forward to develop their literacy and numeracy skills know precisely who they are and what they want to learn as a result of personal life and family goals. The media and even certain well-meaning charitable bodies frequently convey the image that it is really the fault of the individual.

We would like to get beyond this negative approach and work with adult learners to formulate their learning goals. In the case of some peoples, it is a matter of seeing how best oral cultures can be enhanced and complemented by literacy. It is certainly not a matter of one replacing the other. In other instances access to the written word involves a form of bilingualism: for example the deaf who master sign language live in and communicate within an authentic culture of the deaf. They must have access to the written word to participate in the world of the hearing. Numerous examples could be given of groups whose right to the written word has not been fully recognized.

Another challenge, in addition to that of communication, is to define clearly what we are really talking about. During International Literacy Year, the ILY Secretariat expanded the narrow notion of literacy/illiteracy as black and white conditions. It attempted to look at literacy acquisition as a lifelong constantly evolving process. Everyone, at different stages in life, will have new literacy needs. In other words, the debate must be broadened and everyone must feel concerned, but unfortunately, the pressure to speak simplistically is enormous.

That pressure has been felt at some time or the other by all literacy practitioners. On the one hand, teachers of children and adult educators are more concerned with identifying needs and responding to them, but the call for accountability and statistics is overwhelming. Funding agencies want to see how their money is being spent and evaluate the efficiency of their investment. As matters currently stand, however, there are simply no truly reliable statistics which can be used for cross-national comparison, let alone for ranking one country as more successful than another. Literacy acquisition is a more complex issue than is that of counting doses of vaccine made available in a particular country. Unfortunately, the language of international organizations, such as UNESCO, has in some ways contributed to the confusion. The work of UNESCO, as well as that of other providers, is frequently broken up into programmes or projects which may have a life-span of a few months or a few years. The first phase is usually called the 'literacy programme'. What comes next is called 'post-literacy'. Young people or adults who have participated in programmes or schooling and who do not sustain their skills are said to 'relapse into illiteracy' as if they had acquired a dose of knowledge and then lost it. This approach mystifies our understanding of what is really going on and, of course, contributes to blaming the victim. First of all, learning to read and write is a complex process which goes far beyond simply de-coding the alphabet. All individuals do not learn at the same speed or by the same methods. It is more accurate to speak of young people or adults who have school or literacy programmes with fragile basic skills. These skills are not sustainable for a variety of reasons, but there is no question of a 'relapse'. Second, what is readily called 'post-literacy' is really a provision of appropriate tuition or reading materials to enable the further development of basic skills. It is not, however, an autonomous state of being which can be objectively identified. This confusing language also plagues adult basic skill provision in countries where it is closely linked to labour market insertion initiatives. The unemployed are frequently entitled to a certain number of hours of training and that legal allowance tends to define the content of learning. Work-place programmes also tend to respond to other agenda than those which reflect a learner's aspirations or reality.

Perhaps, the most fundamental challenge of all during International Literacy Year was to ensure that interest and activity all over the world be transformed into long-term commitment. The Year was a call to action not to celebration. There has never been a realistic means to eliminate illiteracy by the year 2000, given present trends. Also, if we broaden our definition of literacy as suggested in this discussion, we shall always have literacy needs.

A final challenge needs to be mentioned before looking more closely at the literacy situation in the world. Among the objectives for International Literacy Year, a high-level national commitment to ensure a fully literate society was fore-most. It is essential that a long-term partnership be forged to keep literacy and basic education as human rights on national agendas around the world. That is not to say that the future is rosy and that an international year and major conferences, such as the World Conference on Education for All, have been valu-able in and of themselves. Advocacy and mobilization undertaken during 1990 will be judged by the kinds and quality of long-term commitment we have been able to ensure. In some countries, this commitment has taken the form of national legislation to ensure basic skill acquisition for all, children and adults alike. In other countries, where recognition of literacy needs and weaknesses in the formal education system is just emerging, progress has to be gauged in other terms. We judge ourselves by how adequately we have really analyzed specific contexts and taken a step forward. That step forward is necessarily different from group to group, from country to country and from one form of international co-operation to another. We can measure our success by our own flexibility in learning from settings in countries of the South as well as countries of the North; by recog-nizing that we can all learn from each other. Respect for diversity must be a long-term goal, even when immediate priorities have to be tailored to suit human and financial resources.

A last but critical element of International Literacy Year was the role of new voices. The aspirations of adult learners have been reflected for the first time in the international debate. A major example, the Book Voyage of learners' writing, has been both a symbolic gesture and a forceful statement in favour of the empowerment of all. There is now a collective responsibility to ensure that learners, young and older alike, have a voice in shaping their futures. We should

Table 2.1: Estimated World Adult Illiterates (1985, 1990 and 2000)

Adult Illiterates* (in millions)	1985	1990	2000
World total	965.1	962.6	942.0
Developing countries	908.1	920.6	918.5
in the regions of:			
Sub-Saharan Africa	133.6	138.8	141.1
Arab States	58.6	61.1	65.8
Latin America and the Caribbean	44.2	43.5	40.9
Eastern Asia	297.3	281.0	233.7
Southern Asia	374.1	397.3	437.0
Developed countries	57.0	42.0	23.5

* Adults = those age 15 and over

Table 2.2: Estimated World Illiteracy Rates for Both Sexes (1985, 1990 and 2000)

Illiteracy Rates** per cent Decrease	1985	1990	2000	1985–2000
World total	29.9	26.9	22.0	−7.9
Developing countries	39.4	35.1	28.1	−11.3
in the regions of:				
Sub-Saharan Africa	59.1	52.7	40.3	−18.8
Arab States	54.5	48.7	38.1	−16.4
Latin America and the Caribbean	17.6	15.2	11.3	−6.3
Eastern Asia	28.7	24.0	17.0	−11.7
Southern Asia	57.7	53.8	45.9	−11.8
Developed countries	6.2	4.4	2.3	−3.9

** Per cent of population over age 15 that are illiterate

Source: UNESCO Office of Statistics, 1990.

Notes: The foregoing are preliminary results. Countries and territories with less than 300,000 inhabitants have not been taken into account. Some countries are classified at the same time as Sub-Saharan Africa and as Arab States.

not submit to the discourse which argues that an increasingly technological world will require a flexible work-force able to adapt to its needs and requirements. Rather, we should provide educational opportunities which enable real choice as to whether specific technological innovation is really in the best interest of humanity.

With these policy and practice concerns in mind, we now turn to a more in-depth look at the literacy situation in the world and the debate which has surrounded it over the years.

The Literacy Situation in the World

The UNESCO Office of Statistics regularly analyzes the literacy situation in the world as well as a number of other indicators of participation in education. In November 1989, it completed such an analysis. Tables 2.1 and 2.2 above illustrate the major findings. The number of adult illiterates (15-years-old or above) in 1985 was estimated at 965 million, with the world-wide illiteracy rate 29.9 per cent of all adults. That figure was expected to decrease to 962.6 million by 1990. Thus, the numbers should continue to decline slowly. Yet if past trends continue, there will still be 942 million illiterates in the year 2000, representing 22 per cent of the adult population. In this same year, all but 23.5 million of the 942 million illiterates will be found in the developing countries. The decrease in the absolute number of illiterates will be observed only in developing countries of Eastern Asia (which includes China), in Latin America and the Caribbean, and in the industrialized countries.

The world illiteracy rates were also projected to decline from 29.9 per cent in 1985 to 26.9 per cent in 1990 and to 22 per cent in 2000. However, there is considerable variation in the extent of this decline between different groups of countries. For example, between 1985 and 2000, the rate in Sub-Saharan Africa is expected to drop 18.8 percentage points compared to 16.4 percentage points for the Arab States, 6.3 for Latin America and the Caribbean, and approximately 12 points for both Eastern and Southern Asia.

In the developing countries in 1990, adult illiteracy rates were highest in Southern Asia (53.8 per cent), followed by Sub-Saharan Africa (52.7 per cent), Arab States (48.7 per cent), Eastern Asia (24 per cent), and Latin America and the Caribbean (15.2 per cent). This ranking is expected to remain valid in the year 2000, although individual rates will probably decrease. In 1990 illiteracy rates were estimated to be higher than 40 per cent in forty-nine countries, thirty of them in Sub-Saharan Africa. If this trend is not modified, in the year 2000 there will still be thirty-three countries in the same situation, twenty-two of them in Sub-Saharan Africa.

These figures do not distinguish between men and women who are illiterate. Invariably, however, women have higher rates of illiteracy, and the differences in percentage points between the sexes are quite large in Africa and Asia (twenty-one points in 1985) but much smaller in Latin America and the Caribbean (four points). These figures on adult illiteracy in the world do not take account, of course, of the more than 140 million school-age children who have never attended any formal or non-formal educational institution. Nor do they take account of a similar number of children who drop out prior to completing four years of primary schooling. Further, they make no reference to the uncalculated numbers of children who have seen the quality of their primary schooling severely eroded as a result of persistent economic austerity.

A caution must be issued here. UNESCO statistics are based on figures provided by governments of its member states, and these are usually based on census data. Thus, the Office of Statistics may be using data collected at different times in different countries. The census information may be based on a simple question, such as 'How many people in your household can read or write?' What is meant by literacy and illiteracy may be different or unclear. Therefore, it is important to recall that these figures should be treated with caution. They do not provide a valid ranking of countries and are only roughly comparable. They indicate broad trends; the methodology to project these trends is constantly being refined.

The Changing Economic and Political Climate

This brings us to the political and economic climate world-wide and how it affects the quality and quantity of educational provision, the study of which helps us to situate efforts to ensure the development of a fully literate world. Looking back, we find the 1960s and early 1970s were a period of optimism concerning the value of education to enhance the life chances of all young people. The world enjoyed a period of enormous educational expansion as well as innovation in the form of compensatory measures to ensure equality of opportunity. The democratization-of-education movement guided major policy shifts in both in-dustrialized and developing countries. But with the onset of economic recession about 1974, governments began looking more closely at the social sector as a whole. Education loomed up as the most probable area for saving. Why edu-cation? As Keith Lewin of the University of Sussex (United Kingdom) in a study for UNESCO has pointed out:

> Social sector spending is more likely to be under domestic control than, say, debt servicing and is therefore more immediately susceptible to government action. Second, as one of the largest segments of social expenditure, it presents itself as having the greatest potential for substan-tial savings. Third, where economic policy favours a diminution in the role of the state and limitation in the service that it is responsible for, social services as a whole are likely to be vulnerable. Finally, where short-term planning horizons are dominant, it is those sectors which have long lead times and long-term benefits that appear least attractive. (Lewin, 1986, p. 223)

These views continue to dominate policy making in numerous industrialized and developing countries. The 1980s were particularly hard on the poorest countries, indeed on poor people everywhere. In more than half of the least-developed countries, per pupil expenditure on primary education declined in real terms to the point that the education systems are on the verge of collapse. A UNESCO study which appeared in 1990 showed that primary education enrolment is drop-ping in one out of every five developing countries. In some African nations, primary-school student numbers declined between 1980 and 1985 by as much as one-third. Policies to restructure economies, devised to deal with the debt crisis, are contributing to this educational deterioration. Even when inflation is taken into account, educational spending per primary school student has declined over the last decade in half of the world's countries.

The quality of education is also suffering. For example, two-thirds of the teachers in developing countries currently receive lower salaries than they did in 1980. Class sizes have expanded. It is more common to see sixty pupils in a class-room in Africa than the exception. In a number of developing countries, there is evidence that parents no longer perceive school attendance as valuable. This state of affairs was not the case during the 1960s and early 1970s, even in developing nations. In those earlier decades, Sub-Saharan Africa alone doubled its school enrolment from 20 to 46 million pupils.

The current climate has been described by Eric Hewton in *Education in Recession* (Hewton, 1986) as one in which a 'cutback culture' prevails in the indus-trialized countries. There is ample evidence to show that most of the support systems put in place in the 1960s have been seriously cut — remedial education, compensatory programmes, and school meals. Class sizes have increased in the industrialized nations, especially in the early elementary grades and lower secondary schooling. In effect, it is these critical years for basic-skill acquisition which have been most hard hit.

Each continent has a growing body of literature recording the waste of untapped human potential. In Latin America, structural-adjustment policies have led to what is called a 'lost generation'. Hence, it is not surprising that broad literacy projections reflect the fact that the world is not progressing at the same pace as in the preceding period. On the other hand, the geopolitical climate of the world is changing rapidly before our eyes. The growing trend towards co-operation between the United States of America and the Soviet Union opens up opportunities for governments to reconsider national priorities. The movement of Western Europe towards the elimination of many economic and legal barriers in 1992 and the rapid changes taking place in Eastern Europe are providing new possibilities to readjust national goals. Throughout the world, countries can now seriously consider reductions in arms expenditure and can place education back on national agendas for high-level public commitment. It is also timely that the United Nations declared 1990 International Literacy Year. UNESCO and the other agencies of the United Nations System, the World Bank, and numerous bilateral and multilateral aid agencies have prepared major strategies to assist countries in providing more and better educational opportunity.

Literacy/Illiteracy in International Perspective

Having set the stage, we should now look more closely at what the international literature tells us about definitions of literacy and illiteracy. The definitions can be grouped in three broad categories: those which view literacy as a set of basic skills; those which view literacy as the necessary foundation for a higher quality of life; and those which view literacy as a reflection of political and structural realities.

For the purpose of gathering the literacy statistics with which we began this chapter, UNESCO provided the following guidelines to its member states in the 1978 'UNESCO Revised Recommendation Concerning the International Standardization of Educational Statistics':

The following definitions should be used for statistical purposes:

(a) A person is literate who can with understanding both read and write a short simple statement on his (*sic*) everyday life.
(b) A person is illiterate who cannot with understanding both read and write a short simple statement on his everyday life.
(c) A person is functionally literate who can engage in all those activities in which literacy is required for effective functioning of his group and community and also for enabling him to continue to use reading, writing and calculation for his own and the community's development.
(d) A person is functionally illiterate who cannot engage in all those activities in which literacy is required for effective functioning of his group and community and also for enabling him to continue to use reading, writing and calculation for his own and the community's development.

This attempt to give some guidance to the international community in order to have globally accepted definitions has proved difficult to apply. The guidelines were intended to be used in the collection of statistics either through a national census or through a standardized test. In many countries, the guidelines have simply proven unusable. Countries such as Canada and the United States usually refer to grade-level or number of years of schooling as a reflection of literacy levels. Other countries, particularly in the developing world, look to school enrolment indicators to give some idea of how many people have been given at least some opportunity to learn to read and write. Each of these types of indicators has its shortcomings. When literacy skills are measured by grade-level, it is usually assumed that a standardized test can be used to evaluate a reading level associated with a particular grade. However, these tests have been strongly criticized as arbitrary and insufficient when they are the sole criterion for measuring attainment (Anderson, Hiebert, Scott and Wilkinson, 1985; Owen, 1985).

School-enrolment indicators also provide incomplete information. They do not adequately reflect how many children repeat a year of schooling, how many children drop out along the way, or anything about the quality of the instruction they receive (Coombs, 1985).

Another approach to defining literacy was introduced by UNESCO in the late 1960s and early 1970s with the Experimental World Literacy Programme (EWLP). The term 'functional literacy' became associated with work-oriented programmes. Indeed, the EWLP was conceived as a special programme for specific groups of adults in a number of developing countries. The idea behind the programme was that developing countries could usefully follow in the path of the industrialized nations. There were necessary stages of development in capitalist societies. When certain sectors of the economy reached what was called the 'take-off' stage, they were ready for special attention. If developing countries could not afford to educate all their adults, they should focus on those adults working in the productive sectors; to provide literacy instruction would make them even better workers. The net result of the programme in eleven countries was generally disappointing (UNESCO, 1976). One of the key ingredients of a successful literacy programme had been neglected, that of learner motivation. Workers in the sectors selected for the experimental programme could see no direct advantage to themselves in becoming more 'functional' to their employers. Hence, the term 'functional literacy' as used in such a context took on a specific ideological connotation. It was perceived as a method of creating a more efficient work force without concern for the needs and goals of individuals.

In the later 1980s, the term functional literacy/illiteracy led to another set of difficulties which illustrates the problem of discussing literacy in an international setting. A large number of industrialized countries have been reluctant to recognize that there are sizeable numbers of young people and adults in their populations who are either completely illiterate or who possess very little mastery of the written word. Countries such as Canada, the United States, and Great Britain have been addressing the problem in various degrees for many years (Hunter and Harman, 1979; Limage, 1986, 1990). Countries such as France, the Federal Republic of Germany, and the Scandinavian nations only officially recognized this issue in the early and mid-1980s. Indeed, many people in these and other industrialized countries have found it difficult to accept the idea that nations which have had obligatory schooling for more than one hundred years can possibly have illiterates in their populations (Limage, 1975, 1990). In addition, there is a strong reluctance for people to look at what is going on in schools which might affect children's learning, or that affect their not learning, as the case might be. In France, for instance, it was always assumed that the millions of immigrant workers who resided in the country provided the only possible illiterate population. Courses were created from the late 1960s onwards called '*alphabétisation de travailleurs migrants*'.[1] In reality, these courses were, and remain, 'French as a second or foreign language'. In many cases, the immigrants have been literate in their first languages but not in French. But to add to the confusion, when the French government officially recognized in an official report in 1984 (Espérandieu, Lion and Bénichou, 1984) that native French speakers might be illiterate, they used a newly-created word for the purpose: *illettrisme*. This new word was intended to distinguish French illiterates from immigrants and also to show that people who had been to school for some period of time had a different kind of illiteracy than those who had never attended schools. An enormous controversy continues in France as one vocabulary is used for French people and another for immigrants from the Mediterranean Basin countries and Africa.

The other French-speaking countries do not use separate words for literacy/illiteracy when referring to immigrants and nationals or when referring to literacy problems in the developing countries. Nonetheless, the issue has reached the forum of international organizations such as UNESCO. At the 1989 General Conference of UNESCO, many representatives from developing countries denounced the use of one vocabulary for the industrialized nations and another for their own country (Limage, 1990). They rejected the idea that it is more noble or different to be illiterate in an industrialized country than in a developing one. The term functional literacy/illiteracy (*illettrisme* in the French case) was being used in the General Conference documents to refer to the industrialized countries and illiteracy on its own referred to the developing nations. As a result, the author of this chapter, as a member of the International Literacy Year Secretariat of UNESCO, has been engaged in a systematic review of terminology to be used in the international discussions as an effort to produce terminology which will not prove insulting to individuals, communities, or groups of countries, a task necessary for making international comparisons fair and meaningful.

Another illustration of the complexity of talking about literacy took place among the four international agencies organizing the World Conference on Education for All (WCEFA), held in Thailand in 1990. UNICEF, UNESCO, the World Bank, and the United Nations Development Programme have sought to make education once more the national and international priority as mentioned earlier in this chapter. The four have been concerned both with improving and expanding primary education and providing basic skills for all adults. Literacy and numeracy are viewed as part of a larger concept — basic education — whose precise characteristics have continued under debate.

For the purposes of our discussion of literacy in this chapter, however, we propose one advanced by Hunter and Harman (1979) in *Adult Illiteracy in the United States*. Literacy, then, becomes:

> the possession of skills perceived as necessary by particular persons and groups to fulfil their own self-determined objectives as family and community members, citizens, consumers, job-holders, and members of

social, religious, or other associations of their choosing. This includes the ability to obtain information they want and to use that information for their own and others' well-being; the ability to read and write adequately to satisfy the requirements they set for themselves as being important for their own lives; the ability to deal positively with demands made on them by society; and the ability to solve the problems they face in their daily lives.

This type of definition leaves it to the individual to set goals and decide what role literacy will play in his or her life. It does not place in the hands of an employer or an institution the decision about what it is to be functional. The definition is very much in tune with successful literacy campaigns and classes. For example, the guiding principle behind most adult literacy provision in the United Kingdom since the 1975 awareness-raising campaign has been to let the learner set goals, pace, and content (Limage, 1975). Indeed, since examinations of all types can lead to stress for the learner, most perceptive adult educators have avoided testing when possible. When funding of programmes depends on such evaluation, however, programmes have had to compromise. As recently as late 1989, three British groups — the Adult Literacy and Basic Skills Unit, the Training Agency, and the British Broadcasting Corporation — created communications and literacy programmes leading to certification that required testing. The organizations proposed that the time was right for the certain groups of people with limited basic skills to undertake a course and obtain some kind of diploma which may help them find a job or improve their career opportunities.

Literacy Efforts: The Approaches

Our discussion of the implications of literacy definitions for international perspectives leads us to a brief overview of the kinds of efforts intended to reduce the illiteracy figures mentioned in the beginning of this chapter.

The Universal Declaration of Human Rights, adopted by the United Nations on December 10, declares in its Article 26:

Everyone has the right to education. Education shall be free, at least in the elementary and fundamental stages. Elementary education shall be compulsory. Technical and professional education shall be made generally available and higher education shall be made equally accessible to all on the basis of merit.

A number of other conventions, recommendations, and declarations have appeared since that time, attempting to further define the right to learn. Broadly speaking, however, literacy efforts have been two-pronged: the expansion and improvement of primary education and adult literacy provision. Although some countries have attempted to address the issue of illiteracy as a continuum for children and adults alike, many others have kept the discussion of schooling separate from that of adult education. In addition, international trends set by funding agencies which hold the debt of many developing countries prevent these countries from establishing their own priorities. When for example, funding agencies promoted investment in higher education rather than primary schooling or adult basic education, many developing nations placed their scarce resources in higher education (Coombs, 1985).

Setting priorities for investment has strong implications for the type of literacy effort which will be undertaken. The agencies that promote the improvement and expansion of only primary education consider that it is better to provide basic skills for the young. They contend that adults might not be successful learners, and eventually illiteracy will be eliminated by the passing of the older generation. But as we saw earlier in the chapter, the quality of primary schooling is in serious jeopardy as a result of deteriorating economic conditions. Even in the industrialized countries, expenditure per pupil is not increasing as it did during the 1960s and early 1970s.

A second strategy in literacy provision is the target approach which was illustrated earlier by the Experimental World Literacy Programme and its work-oriented plan. This approach is still used when adequate resources and high-level public commitments are lacking. Such is very clearly the case in industrialized countries which are increasingly turning towards the voluntary or private sector to fill in the gaps left by public provision. Countries with a strong history of charitable activity and volunteer work, such as the United States and United Kingdom, are quick to respond to this type of programme. But the ability of small-scale projects or programmes to deal with the complex problem of illiteracy is necessarily limited.

A third approach to eliminating illiteracy is the mass campaign. In the twentieth century, the Soviet Union undertook the first such programme. In general, with such a scheme, literacy is seen as a means to a larger set of political, social, and economic goals. As Harbans Bhola has put it, the mass campaign is a declaration of 'business not as usual' (Bhola, 1984). Entire populations are mobilized, so that all are involved in the learning process in some way. Literacy is presented as part of a package which promises tangible change in the quality of life for the entire society. In Cuba, the slogan was 'Each one teach one'. In Vietnam, the literacy campaign was part of the struggle for independence, first from France and later, in the war with the United States. In the Soviet Union, both social change and nation-building were involved. Hence, literacy instruction was carried out in more than fifty languages spoken there, and alphabets were created for a number of languages that had a purely oral tradition.

Future Prospects for Literacy

After the mobilization for advocacy and action during International Literacy Year and the long-term strategies called for in UNESCO's Plan of Action and the World Declaration on Education for All, what can international co-operation and national commitment hope to achieve in the near future? Perhaps, it is first of all necessary to admit quite realistically that, as long as economic conditions dominate educational planning, it is probable that choices regarding educational investment will continue to be made based on expediency rather than on lessons learned about effective instruction. In other words, a continued effort will be made to do more with less.

Nonetheless, the lesson to be learned from all literacy efforts — be they formal schooling, campaigns, or targeted projects — is that success is based on three crucial factors: high-level national commitment, mobilization of human and financial resources, and popular participation. High-level national commitment means that education is essentially a public responsibility and governments should give it the necessary priority. Mobilization of human and financial resources means that governments should be able to allocate resources to the social sector, including education, on a greater scale than has been the case throughout the 1980s. Popular participation means that literacy is everybody's concern. Once a major public commitment has been made, there is a role for voluntary and community initiatives, private and business involvement, the press and television, and international co-operation.

In conclusion, it is not necessary that everyone has the same view of what constitutes literacy or that we all have a single model of how to promote its acquisition. International comparisons will continue to provide a rich range of experience which can be adapted to local needs and aspirations. The inter-dependency of the world requires that we better be able to communicate with each other. Literacy is a key to the quality of that communication.

Note

1 *Alphabétisation* in French means 'literacy tuition'.

References

ANDERSON, R.C., HIEBERT, F., SCOTT, E.H. and WILKINSON, I.A.G. (1985) *Becoming a Nation of Readers. The Report of the Commission on Reading, National Academy of Education*, Champaign, IL, Center for the Study of Reading.

BHOLA, H.S. (1984) *Campaigning for Literacy*, Paris, UNESCO.

COOMBS, P. (1985) *The World Crisis in Education. The View from the Eighties*, Oxford, Oxford University Press.

ESPÉRANDIEU, V., LION, A. and BÉNICHOU, J-P. (1984) *Des illettrés en France*, Paris, La Documentation Française.

HEWTON, E. (1986) *Education in Recession*, London, Allen and Unwin.

HUNTER, C. and HARMAN, D. (1979) *Adult Illiteracy in the United States*, New York, McGraw-Hill.

LEWIN, K. (1986) 'Educational Finance in Recession', *Prospects*, **16**, 2, pp. 215–29.

LIMAGE, L. (1975) *Alphabétisation et culture: Etude comparative*, Cas d'études: l'Angleterre, la France, la République Démocratique du Viet Nam et le Brésil. Unpublished doctoral dissertation, Paris, University of Paris V.

LIMAGE, L. (1986) 'Adult Literacy Policy in Industrialized Countries', *Comparative Education Review*, **30**, 1, pp. 50–72.

LIMAGE, L. (1990) *Adult Literacy and Basic Education in Europe and North America: From Recognition to Provision. Comparative Education*, unpublished manuscript, UNESCO.

OWEN, D. (1985) *None of the Above*, Boston, Houghton Miffin.

UNESCO (1976) *The Experimental World Literacy Programme*, UNESCO, Paris.

UNESCO OFFICE OF STATISTICS (1990) *Compendium of Statistics on Illiteracy*, 1990 Edition, UNESCO, Paris.

Chapter 3

The Pen and the Sword: Literacy, Education and Revolution in Kurdistan

Amir Hassanpour

Though adored as the greatest achievement of human beings, literacy — the ability to communicate in writing — has been subject to strict monopolistic control throughout its 6,000-year history. Access to literacy has been denied to individuals, groups, social classes, women, tribes, territories and languages. Today, the great majority of the world's several thousand languages remain unwritten while the scope of writing is extremely limited in most written languages. In fact, only a few languages equal English in degree and variety of literate communication.

The unequal spread of literacy among the world's languages is rooted not in their linguistic structure but, rather, in the extra-linguistic, that is economic, social, political and cultural, conditions of the life of each speech community and its relationships with other communities. Far from being neutral or free, language use — especially in its written, scribal or print, form — is closely intertwined with the distribution of social, economic and political power. When individuals, social classes and nations are not equal, the languages they speak or write will also be unequal. Dichotomies such as language/vernacular or language/dialect are more than simple conceptual constructs; they express and reinforce relationships of dominance. Thus, 'language' is associated with civilization, high culture, high class and political power while labels such as 'dialect' and 'vernacular' perpetuate conditions of subordination, poverty, backwardness and helplessness.

Conditions of dominance breed resistance. The Latin language, an indispensable component of absolutist rule in medieval Europe, was the dominant vehicle of learning in pre-modern Europe. It was finally dethroned during centuries of conflict between absolutist monarchies and the peoples of Western Europe. Numerous forces including writers, scholars, political activists, and printers, were involved in difficult battles against absolutism and its official language. As a result, 'vernaculars' such as English, French and German were able to enter the domains of education, science, philosophy, commerce and administration and finally emerged as prestigious 'national languages'.

This chapter examines the role of literacy and education in the struggle of the Kurdish people to achieve independence from Arab, Turkish and Persian rule. Kurdish nationalists believed that the Kurds were enslaved because they lacked their own independent state. They argued that the state was founded on two

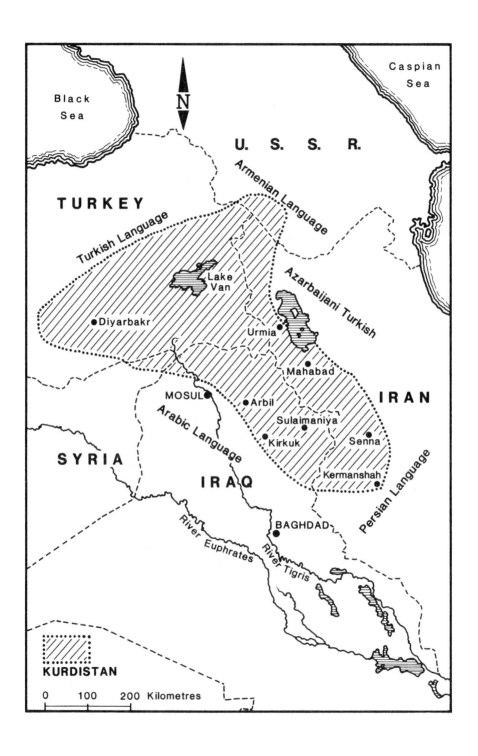

Black
Sea

Caspian
Sea

N

U. S. S. R.

TURKEY

Armenian Language

Turkish Language

Azarbaijani Turkish

Lake
Van

Diyarbakr

Urmia

Mahabad

IRAN

MOSUL

Arbil

Arabic Language

Sulaimaniya

SYRIA

Kirkuk

Senna

IRAQ

Kermanshah

Persian Language

River Euphrates

River Tigris

BAGHDAD

KURDISTAN

0   100   200 Kilometres

pillars, the *pen*, that is, literate use of language and the *sword*, that is, political power. This chapter examines the close relationship between state power and literacy in the process of nation-building and state formation.

The Kurds, their Country, Language and Social Organization

With a population of about 20 to 25 million, the Kurds are the fourth largest nation of the Middle East outnumbered only by the Arabs, Turks and Persians. For thousands of years, they have lived in their present homeland, Kurdistan, lying astride the Zagros mountains in Western Asia. The region is the birth-place of the world's written civilization, most of whose populations have disappeared.

The Kurds have outlived the rise and fall of numerous empires that ruled over (parts of) Kurdistan — the Seleucids (331–129 BC), the Parthians (247 BC to AD 226), the Sassanians (AD 226–636), the Arab Caliphate (AD 636–1258), the Mongols and Turkmens (AD 1258–1501). By the fifteenth and sixteenth centuries numerous Kurdish principalities emerged and ruled all over Kurdistan. However, Kurdistan was divided, in 1639, between two powerful empires. Ottoman Turkey and Persia. This division survived until 1918 when the Ottoman part of Kurdistan was redivided between the newly formed states of Iraq (under British Mandate until 1932), Syria (under French Mandate until 1946) and Turkey (1923), with small enclaves in the USSR. The Kurds were, thus reduced to minority status within countries that aimed at building nation-states in which ethnic and linguistic minorities were suppressed.

Contrary to a widespread image, Kurdish society is not tribal. While tribes constituted an important element of Kurdish social organization, settled agriculturalists, that is, the peasantry, formed the backbone of Kurdish people. The peasantry's pre-commercial and pre-industrial system of agrarian production supported a sizeable urban population within the limits of a feudal economy. The majority of the Kurds converted to Islam as a result of the Arab/Islamic conquests of the seventh century.

Literacy and Education in a Foreign Language

Little is known about the pre-Islamic language and religion of the Kurds. While the mountains of Kurdistan are adorned with inscriptions in numerous extinct languages and scripts, there is no reliable evidence proving the existence of literacy *in Kurdish* before the fifteenth century. The Arab conquerors had introduced into Kurdish society literacy in the Arabic language probably as early as the seventh century. It is well known that a number of Kurdish scholars have made important contributions to early Islamic learning.

Islam created the need for literacy *in Arabic* in all conquered lands. The practice of this religion requires the *written* use of Arabic. The Holy book, Koran, is in Arabic which is considered to be God's (Allah's) inimitable and untranslatable word. Literates and non-literates alike are required to conduct the obligatory daily prayers in Arabic. Other religious rites from the call to prayer from the mosque minarets, to religious ceremonies such as marriage and burial, and even conversations at the time of Resurrection, are all conducted in Arabic.

In order to convert the conquered peoples to Islam, Muslim rulers gradually established mosques everywhere in cities and sizeable villages. The mosques were, in the beginning, administrative and religious training headquarters. Later, they maintained their worship and training functions. In Kurdistan, the mosques have been used primarily for worshipping (daily prayers) and training clergymen, the mullahs.

Disintegration of the Islamic Empire and the Challenge to Arabic

The Islamic caliphate or empire which once extended from Spain and North Africa to China and India was a loosely integrated state structure. This empire ruled over a mosaic of widely divergent languages and ethnic peoples. While some Arab rulers were assimilated among the local population in many corners of the empire, a number of non-Arab peoples were gradually Arabized. In spite of the disintegration of the Islamic caliphate in mid-thirteenth century, Arabic remained the most prestigious language of religion, administration and scholarship much the same way Latin was in pre-modern Europe.

Esteemed as the language of God, Arabic was, however, gradually challenged throughout the Islamic empire. Two centuries after the Arab conquest of Persia, small dynasties came to power among the Persian-speaking peoples. With a modest beginning in court poetry, Persian emerged by the tenth century as a prestigious language of literature. After the disintegration of the caliphate in 1258 and the rise of powerful Persian states, the Persian language penetrated other domains such as administration, religion and science. While Arabic retained its sacred association with Islam, Persian became the second important language in much of Western Asia.

Another major development was the migration of Ottoman Turks to Western Asia where they formed the Ottoman empire (1281–1923) extending to North Africa and parts of eastern and south-eastern Europe. As a result of Ottoman rule, Turkish enjoyed royal patronage and was used, along with Arabic, in literary and administrative domains; but it never achieved the prominent position enjoyed by Arabic and Persian.

Under conditions of political and linguistic domination by the Arabic, Persian and Turkish states, peoples such as the Kurds, the Pashtun (now in Afghanistan and Pakistan), the Baluchi (now in Iran and Pakistan), lacking political independence, found it difficult to develop a literate tradition in their native tongue. Writing in a language such as Kurdish was in itself a political undertaking in that it involved a challenge to the established norms of linguistic and literary authority associated with the rule of the Arab caliphate and, later, its self-appointed successor, the Ottoman caliphate.

The Struggle for Native-tongue Literacy

The earliest known written texts in Kurdish were poems composed in the fifteenth century and Ali Hariri was probably the earliest poet. The sixteenth century produced two poets, Malay Jiziri and Salim Sleman, while four major poets including Ahmadi Khani, apostle of Kurdish nationalism, lived in the seventeenth century. Compared to Arabic and Persian with hundreds of poets, historians and scholars in each century, Kurdish literature and scholarship had a modest beginning.

All the early Kurdish poets were mullahs who received their religious education in Arabic and Persian languages in the mosque schools. The mullahs were professional clergymen who were supported by the constituency of each mosque in order to perform religious services. Writing poetry in Kurdish or in any language was not a requirement of the profession. While the two undertakings, religious service and literary activity, were not contradictory, a system of patronage which would allow the emergence of professional poets or scholars did not exist. One question to be raised, then, is the demand for literate communication in Kurdish in a society where these needs were limited and already met by the Arabic language.

State Power and the Monopoly of Literacy

The Mongol conquest of Western Asia in the thirteenth century put an end to the Islamic caliphate which had ruled over Kurdistan from the nearby capital of Baghdad. The post-Mongol period was characterized by the rise and fall of numerous large and small states. In Kurdistan, a number of principalities emerged in the fifteenth and sixteenth centuries. The rise of these principalities cannot be explained simply in terms of the political vacuum left by the disintegration of the Islamic and Mongol empires. The socio-economic bases of this development should be sought in the increasing detribalization, sedentarization and urbanization occurring in Kurdish society — a process that has not received any research attention.

The principalities had state structures that were similar to those of the larger, dominant empires. The main features of these mini-states were: (a) power was in the hands of the prince called Emir, Khan, Pasha, Beg or Agha whose rule was hereditary; (b) each principality had a territory whose borders were defined by custom and dictated through power; (c) an army with standing members and recruits from tribes was kept for purposes of defence and expansion; (d) the prince was the sole ruler of the whole territory and owned a considerable number of villages though there were many tribes and smaller feudal lords who were direct owners of the land where they settled and had to contribute to the treasury and army of the prince; (e) the more powerful principalities were independent and struck coins and the Friday prayer sermon, *khutba*, was read in the name of the prince; (f) the settled population was made up of serfs, *rei^cyet*, who were personally dependent upon the feudal lord and were tied to the land, and (g) the seat of government, including both civil and military bureaucracies, was usually the largest town in the principality.

It is not surprising, therefore, that the literary use of Kurdish coincides with the rise of Kurdish political power in the fifteenth and sixteenth centuries. Mosque schools and other religious institutions in flourishing towns and villages nurtured a sizeable population of religious scholars. Some poets enjoyed the patronage of the princes though on a very limited scale and an equally important factor was the nationalist awareness of the poets.

National Awakening

The social, economic and cultural development of Kurdistan was soon inhibited due to the rise of two powerful states, to the west (the Ottoman Empire) and to the east (the Safavid Persian Empire) of Kurdistan. Pursuing a policy of expansion and centralization, these two states engaged in a destructive war in Kurdistan, Armenia, and Azerbaijan that lasted until the mid-nineteenth century.

The Safavids tried to remove the Kurdish princes and replace them by governors appointed from the centre. This policy met stubborn resistance and the Safavids had to engage enormous numbers of troops in order to implement the policy of extending their control over Kurdistan. As a result, the populations of entire tribes, cities and principalities were massacred and many conquered tribes were forced into migration to the eastern borders of Iran. Shah ᶜAbbas alone deported 15,000 Kurds to Khorasan (Minorsky, 1927, p. 1143; cf. Eskandar Monshi, 1978, pp. 1010–19, official chronicler of ᶜShah Abbas, on the massacre of Mukri Kurds).

The Ottomans at first tried to profit by winning the support of the Kurds in their war with the Persians. They promised to respect the autonomy of the principalities in exchange for military support. After the defeat of the Safavids in the famous Chaldiran Battle (1514), in which the Kurds contributed, the Ottoman Sultan Selim officially recognized some sixteen 'Kurdish Governments', *Kürd hükumeti*, (see, *inter alia*, van Bruinessen 1978, pp. 181–94). The discordance between the princes, characteristic of feudalism, was skilfully utilized by both sides and a number of principalities fought on the Iranian side.

The wars brought incalculable devastation to Kurdistan; the destruction of agriculture, villages, towns, and numerous massacres profoundly retarded the process of social and economic development in Kurdistan and the unification of the Kurds into a nation (for an eyewitness account of the suppression of Bidlis principality and the destruction of the prince's unique library see Sakisian, 1937).

Kurdistan was finally divided into two parts by the warring empires. A treaty signed between the Ottomans and Persians in 1639 established a frontier that survived subsequent wars and other regional upheavals until 1918. The political and economic life of the Kurds has been profoundly affected by their position astride this international frontier (Edmonds, 1957, p. 25). 'Having no longer cause to fear the Persians, the Turks systematically undertook the task of centralization' (Minorsky, 1927, p. 1146). From 1650 to 1730, most of the autonomous principalities in the Diyarbakir-Van area were suppressed (Jwaideh 1960, p. 39), a process that was completed in the mid-nineteenth century.

The impact of the division on Kurdish society was analyzed by seventeenth century poet Ahmadi Khani (1962, couplets 220–5) who noted that the Kurds, stranded between the Turks, Arabs and Persians, had become 'targets of arrows of fate':

> Whenever the Black Sea [Ottomans] and the Caspian Sea [Persians]
> Flow out and agitate,
> The Kurds get soaked in blood

Similarly, the nineteenth century poet, Haji Qadiri Koyi wrote:

[Trapped] between Red-hats [Ottoman Turks] and Black-hats [Persians]
We are wrecked, and will be liked branded cattle.

The wars and the division of Kurdistan had two contradictory effects on the national development of the Kurds. On the one hand, they retarded the growth of the Kurds as a unified nation and inhibited the formation of a united Kurdish state. On the other hand, the enormous destruction and suffering caused by foreign domination resulted in the genesis of national awakening in a feudally organized society where loyalties were primarily to family, tribe and birthplace. The idea of nation and nationalism, historically anachronistic in this part of the world in the seventeenth century, did in fact develop in the particular circumstances of Kurdistan at this time.

Kurdish national feeling, distinct from tribal and local attachments, was voiced by both individuals and the masses of the people. The prince of Bidlis, Sharaf al-Din Bidlisi, wrote the first history of the Kurds in 1597 (in Persian) in order 'to save the story of the lives of great princes from oblivion'. A century later Ahmadi Khani, poet and mullah, formulated the idea of a Kurdish nation distinct from, and at war with, the ruling nations, Turks, Persians and Arabs (in his *Mem û Zîn* written in 1693–94). Also, popular ballads are carriers of nationalist attachment.

The revolts of the Kurdish princes against the two powers undoubtedly followed one single aim — to protect their autonomous hereditary rule. To achieve this purpose, they often fought each other and sided with one of the powers against the other. Under the circumstances a unified Kurdish state did not and probably could not emerge.

Sword and Pen

The most striking example of national awakening is Ahmadi Khani, a mullah who wrote a brilliant analysis of the political situation of Kurdistan in the late seventeenth century. Affected by the suffering of the Kurds at the hands of the two powers, Khani tried to understand the reasons behind their misery and proposed a solution.

In the introduction to his narrative poetic work, *Mam and Zin*, he asked, 'I wonder why in this world . . . the Kurds have become deprived and are all subjugated?' Answering the question, he first rejected the argument of those who claimed that the Kurds were inferior because they were 'uncultivated, without origins and basis . . . that all nations possessed books, the Kurds alone had none'. Khani argued that the Kurds were more valiant, more hospitable and more munificent than their neighbouring peoples, the Arabs, Turks and Persians. In spite of this, the Kurds were enslaved not because they were 'without perfection . . . ignorant and unknowing' but, rather, because they were 'orphans and without a chance'; they were, in fact, 'distressed and without a protector'.[1]

The absence of a 'protector', i.e., a Kurdish state which could enhance the Kurds to an independent nation, was, itself, the result of disunity among the princes. The solution was to have a Kurdish king who would unite the discordant princes, protect the Kurds and promote Kurdish language and learning. Would it ever be possible, he asked, that a 'king may appear among us, so that the sword of our art becomes distinguished, the value of our pen be appreciated, our pain finds a cure, our science gains currency?'

The 'pen' and the 'sword' were, for Khani, two necessary conditions for statehood. State power, that is, the patronage of kings, was necessary for the enhancement of language. This was certainly true in a society where literary creation was not regulated by market forces.

A king could serve the language by (a) giving it official status; Khani expresses this idea repeatedly by, among other things, comparing Kurdish with a coin that would gain currency through the king's minting; much in the same way a heap of worthless metal turns into valuable coin, words, phrases and sayings transform into precious pieces of poetry if approved by the king, and (b) providing for the 'perfection of religion and state', access to 'science and philosophy', and encouragement of science, the arts, poetry, and books. Khani, thus, underlined the role of a sovereign state in the ascendance of language to a position of prestige. Calling on all the princes to unite, he warned them that the protection of Kurdistan's sovereignty was the responsibility of the princes not of 'the poets and the poor'. 'Subordination' to the Persians and the Turks was a shame on the ruling nobility, he said.

The second effective means of elevating the position of Kurdish was, according to Khani, the efforts of men of learning, especially poets and educators, who would use the language for literary, scientific, religious and other scholarly purposes, compile books, and raise the intellectual level of the nation.

The two tasks, political (i.e., formation of a Kurdish state) and literary (i.e., writing and compiling in the native tongue) were considered by Khani to be two sides of the same coin. He did not view language cultivation as an end in itself. A prestigious literary language, together with a sovereign king, was the hallmark of a civilized and independent Kurdish nation.

The political conditions during Khani's lifetime were, however, far from conducive to the unification of the principalities and officialization of the language. Not surprisingly, a powerful prince apparently did not respond to the poet's call and was, as a result, criticized by Khani: the 'knowledgeable ruler of the time' who could, in a glance, turn a heap of worthless coin into gold, and attended a thousand destitute people every day . . . 'did not listen',

> If he had once given us a look
> From the elixir of his blessed attention,
> These sayings would all change into poems . . .

Literary Use of Kurdish

Khani could not wait for the unified Kurdish state to emerge and used his 'pen' in the absence of 'the sword'. Without court patronage, he moved to develop his native tongue by using it in literary and educational domains. His main contribution to literary Kurdish was a narrative poetic work, *Mem û Zîn* (Mam and Zin), which has become the national epic of the Kurds.

The love story of Mam and Zin is not borrowed from the rich repertoire of Arabic and Persian literature. It was, rather, adopted from a Kurdish folk ballad called *Mem û Zîn* or *Memê Alan* which is still recited by Kurdish troubadours today. The details of the plot, names, characters and setting are all Kurdish. Mam and Zin are two lovers whose union is destroyed due to the discord sown by Bakir. Mam dies first; then, while mourning the death of her lover on his grave, Zin falls dead of grief. Zin is buried next to Mam's grave. Bakir's role in the tragedy is then revealed. Fearing his fate, Bakir runs away taking refuge between the two graves. Bakir is, however, killed there, out of revenge. Out of Bakir's blood, grows a thorn-tree which sends roots deep into the earth separating the two lovers even after death.

Khani's message is clear. Mam and Zin represent the two parts of Kurdistan divided between the Ottoman and Persian Empires. Bakir personifies the 'discord' and disunity of the Kurdish princes which Khani considered to be the main reason for the failure of the Kurdish people to achieve sovereignty. In spite of the divisive thorn-tree, it seems that the poet hoped that disunity would finally come to an end.

Education in Kurdish

Khani was aware that literary composition alone could not enhance the status of Kurdish. Introducing an uncultivated language such as Kurdish into an educational system where 'the language of Allah', that is, Arabic, was the medium of instruction was a serious innovation (*bid'et*) which Khani dared to commit. He compiled a brief, easy-to-copy, Arabic-Kurdish lexicon, written in verse, which proved to be well-suited to the learning system based on rote memorization.

Khani wrote another short work intended for use by mosque school students. Known as *ᶜEqîda aman* (Belief in Faith) the work explains, in verse, the principles of Islamic doctrine; it is of special importance in sanctioning the use of Kurdish in religious education. Khani's educational work was continued by Mala Yunis Halkatini who composed an Arabic grammar in Kurdish and a short work on the birth of prophet Mohammad.

The Pen Without the Sword: Opposition to Native-Tongue Literacy

Before the downfall of the principalities in mid-nineteenth century, the Ottoman and Persian states were not able to exercise effective control over the mosque schools in Kurdistan. Opposition to the literate use of Kurdish came, therefore, not directly from the state but, rather, from the well-established tradition of religious education in Arabic and Persian.

Khani's aim was to enhance the status of Kurdish to that of the Arabic and Persian languages. Obviously, because of the divinity associated with Arabic, he did not compare Kurdish to Arabic. Writing about his purpose in composing *Mem û Zîn*, Khani said:

> Whether a product of obstinacy or injustice
> He [=Khani] made this innovation against tradition,
> He cleared from its dregs,
> The Kurdish language, [and put it] on par with Persian,
>   Put it into order and system,
> Tolerated much suffering for it.

The 'innovation' (*bidᶜet* or *bidea*) Khani refers to

> means some view, thing or mode of action the like of which has not
> formerly existed or been practised, an innovation or novelty... [T]he
> word ... came to suggest individual dissent and independence, going to
> the point of heresy although not of actual unbelief (*kofr*). (*Encyclopaedia of
> Islam*, Vol. 1, 1913, pp. 712–13)

Since Khani was not the first person to compose in Kurdish, one may ask why he
considered *Mem û Zîn* a *bidᶜet*? Among the innovations introduced, the poet
emphasized the originality of the work — it was a product of his own 'mind',
having borrowed nothing from Arabic and Persian literatures. The originality
was obvious in both linguistic features, 'words, meanings, phrases', and the literary component, 'subjects', 'stories', 'content'.

The major *bidᶜet* of Khani was, however, in the content and the message
of *Mem û Zîn*. In this work, Khani 'preceded his era by several centuries by
proclaiming, in a time when nationalism was unknown in the Islamic lands, the
individuality of the Kurds and their right to independence' (Lescot, 1977, p. 801).

In the absence of political and moral support by a sovereign, Khani expected
resistance of his *Mem û Zîn* from several sources: (a) *Ehlê halan* ('sufis'), who
might condemn it, (b) 'self-interested persons' and 'intriguers' who would dis-
credit or disgrace him, (c) the 'jealous and zealous' who would slander his work,
and (d) 'inharmonious people'.

Khani asked the 'self-interested' people to listen to him and to generously
conceal his shortcomings. He appealed to other groups, well-wishers, not to
be persuaded by adversaries and to try, instead, to neutralize their opposition.
He asked (a) 'learned men' not to slander like the jealous but rather correct
his mistakes; (b) 'accomplished people', to gloss over his faults, and (c) 'men of
secrets', not to scoff.

These pleas, appeals and prohibitions were accompanied by a defence of his
work, the Kurdish language, and himself. Khani argued that *Mem û Zîn* was an
infant — innocent, modest and noble; that it was destined to grow and have a
bright future — whether sweet or bitter, it was *nûbar*, first picking of fruit, and
was to ripen. This line of argument is similar to du Bellay's 1549 defence of the
French language against Latin. Though his Kurdish was not as 'juicy' as ripe fruit
(referring to Arabic and Persian), it was strong just because it was written in
Kurdish. His self-defence is humble, yet proud. He called himself a peddler, not
of noble origin, self-grown not educated, and a Kurd from the mountains and
distant lands.

In the educational field, too, Khani anticipated opposition from conservatives
who did not regard Kurdish as suitable for Islamic religious education. He did,
therefore, justify his Arabic-Kurdish lexicon by emphasizing that it was intended
to help the beginning students not the learned men (Khani, 1979, pp. 28–9):

> These words of the [two] languages
> Are compiled by Ahmadi Khani
> who named it *Children's Nubar* [first picking of fruit]
> It is not intended for the learned men
> But, rather, for Kurdish children

who, after finishing Koran,
should become more literate . . .

Opposition to the lexicon was probably stifled because, in the tradition of mosque school education, the native tongue had always been used, orally, to explain to the beginning student the meanings of Arabic words. The significance of the two works lies in institutionalizing the use of written Kurdish in the religious educational system.

The Fall of the Principalities

In spite of the unceasing centralizing efforts of the two states, several principalities were able to survive into the nineteenth century. After much resistance, however, these principalities were all suppressed in the 1840s and 1850s and all parts of Kurdistan fell under the direct control of the two central governments of Turkey and Persia. These states were now in a position to extend their military and administrative system together with their languages, Turkish and Persian, to all the urban centres as well as to parts of the countryside. Another important development, in the latter part of the nineteenth century, was the turning of Kurdistan into an arena of conflict for the economic and political interests of the European powers, especially Russia and Britain.

Haji Qadiri Koyi (1817–97)

Thus, by the end of the nineteenth century, Khani's vision for the advancement of the Kurdish nation through the acquisition of the pen and sword had not materialized. Indeed, the last vestiges of Kurdish political rule, the principalities, had been overthrown. Neither had the literary language achieved any degree of popularity or elaboration beyond the use of an Arabic-Kurdish lexicon and one Arabic grammar (in Kurdish) in the mosque schools and in certain poetry-reading assemblies of the clergy and the feudal aristocracy.

Among the Kurdish intelligentsia in the Ottoman empire, Haji Qadiri Koyi (1817–97), a poet, mullah and religious teacher, emerged as the second apostle of Kurdish nationalism. Like Khani, he argued that without the sword, the pen could not lead to emancipation of his people. Haji was well aware that Kurdish was not a language in vogue but he rejected the idea that, in terms of literary value, it was inferior to Persian:

> Do not say that Kurdish is not as eloquent as Persian!
> It possesses such eloquence unmatched by any language,
> It is [only] due to indifference of the Kurds that it is not fashionable.[2]

Elsewhere he addressed the clergymen who did not want to use Kurdish in religious education and in other functions:

> Tell [us], what is wrong with Kurdish?
> It is only the word of God [i.e., Koran] that is faultless.

> Why is it [Kurdish] different from Persian,
> Why is one fine, the other debased?

Haji, complained about two sources of backwardness. First, the majority of *shaikhs* (heads of religious orders) and mullahs who had a monopoly over the religious educational system wrote and taught in Arabic and Persian and were not interested in the fate of their native tongue. Second, the general backwardness of the Kurds as manifested in the lack of scientific expertise and techniques, and, most important, the absence of political unity in the form of a Kurdish state.

Angry at the clerics' indifference to their native tongue, Haji devoted much of his poetry to point out how the religious educational system had hampered the development of the Kurdish language: to cite one example,

> Now all the nation knows that
> O, you mullahs who teach, you *muftîs* [judges] of people
> That texts, elucidations, expositions, and commentaries
> Have all become obstacles to Kurdish learning (*me^carif*)

He even declared that the clergy were all traitors. In an angry expression of his dissatisfaction, Haji castigated those who refused to read and write in Kurdish. The following couplets have become clichés in Kurdistan:

> If a Kurd does not know his/her language,
> Undoubtedly, his/her mother is infidel and father adulterous

> If a Kurd does not like his/her language, do not ask, 'why?' or, 'how?'
> Ask his/her mother where she got this bastard!

Haji was even more critical of the *shaikhs* and exposed their demagogy, greed for accumulating wealth and property, laziness, lack of training in any practical art, parasitic dependence on their followers and, most important, their lack of interest in the use and promotion of the Kurdish language.

Like Khani, Haji proposed two interrelated solutions. The primary one was simply to compose, translate and write in the native tongue:

> Why is it blasphemy to write in our language?
> A nation without books and writing,
> There is none on earth but the Kurds

Elsewhere,

> Books, notebooks, history and letters,
> Had they been written in Kurdish,
> Our mullahs, learned men rulers and kings,
> Would have become immortal names

The two most frequently used words in his works on the Kurdish language are, in fact, 'writing' (*nûsîn*) and 'book' (*kitêb*). Though Haji never failed to denounce the clerics for neglecting their native tongue, he held a high opinion of the literary achievements of both past and contemporary poets. In a lengthy eulogy, he extols the works of twenty-five poets who wrote in three Kurdish literary dialects. He also glorified the popular ballads (*beyts*) and called upon the literati to learn them and put them into written form.

The poet spent the last years of his life in cosmopolitan Istanbul and became familiar with developments in the modern world. He argued that countries such as Japan had achieved progress because they translated the sciences into their languages and then learned the applied sciences in their native tongue.

> It is only the Kurds, among all nations,
> Deprived of reading and writing.
> By translating into their own languages, the foreigners
> Became familiar with the secrets of other peoples' books
> None of our scholars/clergymen (*ᶜulema*), great or small,
> Has ever read two letters in Kurdish . . .

The second important factor in the advancement of the Kurdish language was, for Haji, state power. He compared the Kurds with other advanced nations and pointed out that the Bulgars, the Serbians, the Greeks, the Armenians and others were all on their way to independence though their numbers were smaller than even those of the Kurds of the Baban area of Kurdistan. He called on the people to take up arms, 'cannons and rifles', in order to achieve sovereignty. It should be noted that Haji, unlike Khani who relegated the task of political unification to the princes, found no place for them in this cause. Like Khani, however, Haji established a clear relationship between the two necessary elements in language cultivation — state power symbolized by *sword* (*sîr*) and the literary use of the language represented by *pen* (*xame*). Like Khani, he noted that without the sword the pen could not go far:

> Sword and pen are companions in this age; Alas,
> My sword is a penknife and its scabbard is a pen-case!

Haji felt at rest, however, that he had fulfilled his commitment to his nation through writing in Kurdish as much as he could. He reminded the Kurds, however, that the 'sword' was lacking:

> The state is founded on sword and pen,
> I have the pen, [but] there is no trace of the sword.
> He [Haji] has neither a flag, nor kettle-drums
> The helpless [Haji] wrote as much as he could.
> I fulfilled all my duties,
> The nation's order depends [however] on the sword . . .

As can be seen from the above quotations, Haji did not consider the enhancement of the Kurdish language an end in itself. A prestigious developed language was, for both Khani and Haji, the mark of a civilized, sovereign nation.

This view of language development was based, apparently, on their knowledge and experience of the two major languages of the Muslim world, Arabic and Persian, which had enjoyed the patronage of powerful dynasties ever since they were put to written use.

The Second Division of Kurdistan: The Nation State and Linguistic Genocide

By the end of World War I, Kurdish neither enjoyed state support nor was on a par with Arabic, Persian or Turkish. The publication of the first Kurdish journal in 1898–1902 greatly enhanced the status of the language among the Kurds. It also promoted prose writing in Kurdish. However, this publication, like other Kurdish language printed works, was subject to persecution by the Ottoman state and had to migrate to Cairo, Geneva, London and an unlikely place, Folkstone in Kent, England.

During the War (1914–18), Kurdish leaders were seeking independence from Turkey. Defeating the Ottomans, the victors of the War, France and England, carved up the empire into smaller states. The Treaty of Sèvres signed in 1920 provided for the creation of a Kurdish state in what is now eastern Turkey but this treaty was never implemented. Instead, the Ottoman part of Kurdistan was redivided between the three newly created states of Iraq under British Mandate, Syria under French Mandate and Republican Turkey under nationalist Turkish rule.

Turkey, where the majority of the Kurds live (about 10 million now), pursued a policy of building a Turkish nation-state in which non-Turkish peoples were to be either Turkified or physically eliminated. If the loosely integrated Ottoman state was unable to Turkify its non-Turkish peoples, its centralist and statist successor did attempt Turkification by proscribing not only writing in Kurdish but also speaking the language. The educational system, the mass media and the repressive state organs, the army, rural police and police were used to suppress any manifestation of Kurdish ethnic identity.

Propaganda against the Kurds and their language is a very important part of the genocidal policy of Turkey. In the vast propaganda literature produced by academics and army generals, the existence of a separate Kurdish identity has been denied. The Kurds are said to be 'mountain Turks' and their language is called a Turkish dialect corrupted by the neighbouring Persian language. Kurdish was claimed to possess only 8,428 words of which only 200 are original Kurdish words (Hassanpour, 1989, pp. 124–29; Helsinki Watch Committee, 1988).

In Syria under French Mandate (1920–46), the Kurds were allowed to engage in limited publishing activity in the early 1930s and during World War II. Kurdish demands for native-tongue instruction in primary schools were, however, rejected because it was considered to contravene France's commitment to Middle Eastern states (Zaza, 1982, p. 81). In other words, Kurdish language education would encourage Kurdish nationalism in Syria which, in turn, would encourage separatism in the neighbouring pro-Western states of Turkey, Iran and Iraq. Syria has followed, since 1963, a policy of genocide of the Kurdish people similar to that of Turkey. Of much interest is a secret government document outlining a plan to eliminate Kurdish ethnic identity in which the mosque schools were rated as 'literary Kurdish assemblies' serving the Kurdish nationalist cause. The plan called for the replacement of Kurdish mullahs by Arab clergymen (Hassanpour, 1989, pp. 130–31).

In Iran, a genocidal policy similar to that of Turkey was adopted under the first Pahlavi monarch (1925–41). While all manifestations of Kurdish language and culture were proscribed, the propaganda machinery of the government called the Kurds an Iranian 'tribe' of 'pure Aryan blood' who speak a pure Persian 'dialect'. The last Pahlavi monarch (1941–79) implemented a relaxed version of this policy.

More recently, the policy of the theocratic Islamic Republic is a replica of the secular, national chauvinistic approach of the former monarchist regime. The 1979 Islamic constitution declares Persian as the only 'official and common language and script of the people of Iran'. It decrees that 'official documents, correspondence and statements, as well as textbooks, shall be written in this language and script. However, the use of local and ethnic languages in the press and mass media is allowed. The teaching of ethnic literature in the schools, together with Persian language instruction, is also permitted' (*Constitutions of the Countries of the World*, 1980, p. 24). While the existence of 'local and ethnic languages' is admitted, so far no steps have been taken towards the teaching of 'ethnic literature'. The adoption of the Arabic/Persian script as an official one is meant to prevent the change of the alphabet to Roman or other systems as was done in the secular, Western-type Republican Turkey (Hassanpour, 1989, pp. 117–24).

In the USSR, the almost entirely illiterate and small population of Kurds, scattered in four republics, acquired literacy in their native tongue by the early 1930s. Kurdish became the language of instruction in schools and was used in publishing and radio broadcasting which flourished, especially in the Armenian Socialist Republic. During World War II, however, the policy changed, publishing in Kurdish stopped and the central government forcibly moved many Kurds from Armenia and Azerbaijan to central Asian republics. The Soviet government was apparently concerned that the Kurds and a number of ethnic minorities might be used by the Germans who were planning to occupy the strategic oil fields of Azerbaijan.

After World War II, the deportees were not allowed to return to their homes and Kurdish was no longer used as the language of instruction though Kurdish grammar and literature continued to be taught. The Soviet government was apparently concerned about the impact of Kurdish nationalism of the greater Kurdistan on Soviet Kurds. In spite of these concerns, the USSR was ahead of Iraq and Iran in terms of Kurdish language book publishing, journalism and radio broadcasting as measured in per capita terms (Hassanpour, 1989, pp. 133–5).

Iraq was created by Britain at the end of World War I when Britain defeated Ottoman Turkey and occupied Baghdad. As a means of fighting the Ottoman army with limited forces, Britain supported Kurdish nationalism and allowed the use of Kurdish in journalism and primary education. Turkey continued to fight British occupation forces over the oil-rich Mosul province which was populated primarily by the Kurds. The League of Nations awarded the Mosul province to Iraq in December 1925 on the condition that the Mandate authorities and the Iraqi government pay regard

to the desire expressed by the Kurds that officials of Kurdish race should be appointed for the administration of their country, the dispensation of justice, and *teaching in the schools, and that Kurdish should be the official language of all these services* (League of Nations, 1925, p. 89, emphasis added).

A conflict over the extent of 'teaching in the school' ensued between the Kurds on the one side and the British Mandate authorities, the Arab government of Baghdad, the League of Nations and the neighbouring countries on the other. Kurdish political and intellectual leaders regarded full native-tongue education as an indispensable tool of national consolidation and a sure way to resist the assimilation efforts of the Arab regime installed in Baghdad by the British. For their part, the central government considered education in Arabic a necessary means of integrating the independence-seeking Kurds. This battle took many forms ranging from petitions to parliamentary debates to armed struggle.

The Kurds demanded native-tongue education on all (that is, primary, secondary and higher) levels, enough schools in all parts of Iraqi Kurdistan proportionate to their population in Iraq, together with a general directorate of education for all Kurdish provinces. Iraqi Government policy was to limit Kurdish education to the primary level, to limit the number of schools and the number of courses taught in Kurdish, to reduce the territory of Kurdistan to half its size and to encourage Kurdish students to attend Arabic language schools.

The British Mandate authorities supported the policy of restricting Kurdish education and helped to justify it at the Permanent Mandate Commission of the League of Nations where the practice of the Mandatory power in Iraq was reviewed annually. Britain did, in fact, mislead the League whose Permanent Mandate Commission was not in a position to visit the country or directly get in touch with Kurdish leaders (for more information and documentation see Sluglett, 1976, pp. 182–95, 199–206, 211–16; Hassanpour, 1989, pp. 274–84). A typical example is the 1929 annual *Report by His Majesty's Government in the United Kingdom of Great Britain and Northern Ireland to the Council of the League of Nations on the Administration of 'Iraq for the Year 1929*:

> The opening of three new Kurdish elementary schools has not appeased the discontent of the Kurds with the general educational policy of the Government. This discontent takes the form of complaining:—
> (a) that there are not enough Kurdish elementary schools,
> (b) that there is no Kurdish training college,
> (c) that there are not enough school books in Kurdish,
> (d) that the Kurdish schools are handicapped by not being under a separate Kurdish education area.
> A fair answer to these complaints is that (a), if true of Kurdistan, is equally true of the Arab speaking areas; (b) that a separate training college is neither practicable nor in the interests of the Kurds themselves; that (c) is true, but is becoming less true every year; that (d) is a reasonable complaint which certainly should be redressed. If it were redressed probably all the other grievances would disappear. (1930, pp. 139–40)

Indeed Baghdad had already begun the Arabization of the existing thirty-one Kurdish schools with the complicity of the Mandate authorities (Sluglett, 1976, p. 184; Hassanpour, 1989, pp. 280–82). While Britain justified the Arabization policy by claiming, among other things, that 'the Kurdish language alone provides too narrow a basis for secondary and higher education' and that emphasis should be on studying in the Arabic language (Sluglett, 1976, p. 184;

Hassanpour, 1989, pp. 280–82), the main objective of the policy was to under-mine and finally eliminate Kurdish education in order to integrate the Kurds in Arab society and thereby weaken Kurdish nationalism. This policy was in full accord with that of Syria, Turkey and Iran. All these pro-Western regimes considered Kurdish nationalism ('separatism', 'secessionism', 'communism', in official political discourse) a threat to their 'territorial integrity'.

Kurdish response was dismay and anger. Many Kurdish nationalists argued that it was better to remain illiterate than become educated in Arabic. They believed that both Britain and the League of Nations had betrayed the Kurds.

While opposition to Kurdish national rights was the cornerstone of British/ Iraqi educational policy, it must be emphasized that the British government pursued a general policy of restricting the 'spread' of modern education through-out Iraq. Responding to the general demand for more education, the British government warned the League of Nations, in a remarkable statement published in an official document, about chief dangers in the way of a proper educational development in 'Iraq:

> The increasing control of education, as of other activities of the govern-ment, by 'Iraqis makes it necessary to dwell chiefly on those dangers of which 'Iraqis themselves are least aware. One danger is the belief held by nearly all, except of most obscurantist, that there is no limit to what education can do, and no limit to the money that might profitably be spent on education. There is no risk of too much money being spent on education, but there is real danger in the belief in unlimited education as the cure for every ill. Education is one of the influences, perhaps the most important influence, in the creation of sound citizenship and morals, and of industrial efficiency. But even the best educational system in the world cannot produce results immediately, and must therefore conform to the real, and not to the imaginary, economic, political and social needs of the country.
>
> *The overcrowding of the clerical profession and consequent unemployment in a class productive of political agitators, is one of the results which may follow the uncontrolled spread of education* . . . (Colonial Office, 1925, pp. 214–15, emphasis added).

It is clear from this statement and similar pronouncements in other official reports that both sides, the ruling regime and the Iraqi people, were aware that education and educational policy were both tied to the structure of political power. Education, including literacy, can be regulated to either perpetuate or overthrow the existing power structure.

In spite of a heap of constitutional and legal guarantees, the right of the Kurds to native-tongue education was not respected in Iraq. By the end of the monarchical regime in July 1958, less than a dozen Kurdish schools were operat-ing in Iraq. Kurdish education flourished in the first two years of the Republican regime of 1958–63. Soon, however, repression began, and also the autonomist armed resistance that has continued since 1961 and was able to wrest from the Iraqi government secondary education in Kurdish. Although secondary school books were translated into Kurdish in the 1980s, they were not used in all the schools of Kurdistan. The Baᶜth regime has, in fact, followed the policy of the

Mandate period — officially accepting the right of the Kurds to native-tongue education and practically limiting the exercising of this right to a few schools useful for propaganda purposes. It remains to be seen whether, in the aftermath of the 'Gulf War', the promised protection of Kurdish people in Iraq by Western powers will change this situation, and, if so, to what extent.

Conclusions

This survey of the struggle of the Kurdish people to enhance their status as a sovereign nation has demonstrated the close ties that bind political power to education. The experience of the Kurdish people in the last several centuries supports the idea that without the 'sword', a dominated people will not be able to achieve national emancipation by upholding the 'pen'. In fact, the 'pen' itself becomes an arena of struggle between two unequal sides. The despotic state, especially in its modern form, is in control of the colossal social institution of formal education which is used as a tool of assimilation and repression.

Ranking fortieth among the world's languages in terms of numerical strength (Leclerc, 1986, pp. 55, 138), Kurdish is one of the most threatened languages of the world. It is subject to various forms of linguicide or linguistic genocide in all the five countries where it is spoken. The threat to the Kurdish language is political, coming primarily from the despotic states of Turkey, Iraq, Iran and Syria. In countries where political freedoms such as the right to read and write in one's language exist, the threat to less powerful or minority languages comes primarily from the unequal distribution of social, economic and cultural power as dictated by the forces of the market. The ongoing and speedy death of aboriginal languages in North America, Australia and elsewhere in the Western world is rooted primarily in the equally oppressive rule of the market. It is relatively easier to point to the anti-democratic constitutional proscription of the Kurdish language in Turkey than to the economic failure of a small linguistic community in Canada or the United States to sustain a native-tongue school system, and print and electronic media.

Students of language planning are just beginning to see the connections between power and language use (see, especially Luke, McHoul and Mey, 1989). The recent distinction between 'status planning' and 'corpus planning' is a step in this direction (Cobarrubias, 1983a, 1983b; Fishman, 1989). The Kurdish nationalists of the seventeenth and nineteenth centuries, Khani and Haji, had a clear idea of not only this distinction but also the dialectical relationships governing their interaction. It is relatively easy, in countries where linguistic pluralism is tolerated, to 'reduce a language to writing', to compile dictionaries and textbooks, to write grammars, to create tens of thousands of scientific terms. In other words, it needs a handful of experts to develop the *corpus* of a language. It requires, however, a revolution, a centuries-long struggle to enhance the *status* of a language.

In the emerging 'global village' dominated by a handful of media empires, we will witness numerous language deaths. The dictatorship of the market together with the dictatorship of despotic states will claim more lives in the near future. We rarely take notice of the fact that a number of African states are not rich enough to have a daily paper; we also forget that thousands of languages throughout the world find access to the industrially-based electronic media as difficult as to the print media.

Our understanding of the life and death of languages has been hampered by a social science that persuades us to be 'objective', 'neutral', 'value-free' and quantitative. This social 'science' has robbed us of conceptual tools such as 'repression', 'oppression', 'struggle', 'emancipation', while it has not, for the same reasons, allowed us to even quantify the number and scope of language deaths occurring in front of our eyes. We will indeed benefit from the insights of our predecessors of past centuries, educationalists and language planners such as Khani and Haji, who could see the close connection between power and literacy, between 'the pen' and 'the sword', and who did their best to raise the banner of the pen.

Notes

1 Quotations from Khani's work are from the 1962 Moscow edition of *Mam and Zin* unless otherwise indicated. Also, see Hassanpour (1989) for the Kurdish text of the quotations.
2 Quotations from Haji Qadiri Koyi are from Mala Karim (1960). See, also, Hassanpour (1989, pp. 87–91).

References

COBARRUBIAS, J. (1983a) 'Language planning: The state of the art', in COBARRUBIAS, J. and FISHMAN, J. (Eds) *Progress in Language Planning: International Perspectives*, Berlin, Walter de Gruyter and Co, pp. 3–26.

COBARRUBIAS, J. (1983b) 'Ethical issues in status planning', in COBARRUBIAS, J. and FISHMAN, J. (Eds) *Progress in Language Planning: International Perspectives*, Berlin, Walter de Gruyter and Co, pp. 41–85.

COLONIAL OFFICE (1925) *Report by His Britannic Majesty's Government on the Administration of 'Iraq for the Period April, 1923–December, 1924*, London, HMSO.

DU BELLAY, J. (1549) *Deffence et Illustration de la Langue Francoyse (English translation: The Defence and Illustration of the French Language)*, London, J.M. Dent.

EDMONDS, C.J. (1957) *Kurds, Turks and Arabs*, London, OUP.

ESKANDAR [BEG] MONSHI (1978) *History of Shah ᶜAbbas the Great (Tarak-e alam ara-ye ᶜAbbasa)*, 2 volumes. Translated by R.M. SAVORY, Boulder, CO, Westview Press.

FISHMAN, J. (1989) 'Status planning for endangered languages', in I. FODOR and C. HAGEGE (Eds) *Language Reform*, Vol. IV, Hamburg, Helmut Busk Verlag, pp. 1–11.

HASSANPOUR, AMIR (1989) 'The Language Factor in National Development: The Standardization of the Kurdish Language, 1918–1985', PhD dissertation, University of Illinois at Urbana-Champaign.

HELSINKI WATCH COMMITTEE (1988) *Destroying Ethnic Identity: The Kurds of Turkey*, New York, Helsinki Watch Committee.

JWAIDEH, W. (1960) 'The Kurdish Nationalist Movement: Its Origins and Development', PhD dissertation, Syracuse University.

KHANI, AHMAD (1962) *Mem û Zîn/Mam i Zin* (Mam and Zin), edited and translated into Russian by M.B. RUDENKO, Pamaatniki Literatury Narodov Vostoka, Teksty, Malaia Seriia, Moscow, IVL.

KHANI, AHMAD (1979) *Nûbihara Seydayê Mezin Ehmadê Xanî* (Back cover: *The Nobihar of Learned Ahmad Khani*, collected, scrutinized and verified by Sadiq Baha al-Deen Amaidi), Baghdad, KZK Press.

LEAGUE OF NATIONS (1925) *Question of the Frontier Between Turkey and Iraq*, report submitted to the Council by the Commission instituted by the Council Resolution of September 30th, 1925, Lausanne, League of Nations.

LECLERC, J. (1986) *Langue et société*, Laval, Canada, Mondia Éditeurs.

LESCOT, R. (1942) *Textes Kurdes. Deuxième Partie: Mamé Alan, Collection de Textes Orientaux*, Vol. I, Beyrouth, Institut Français de Damas.

LESCOT, R. (1977) 'Littérature Kurde', in *Histoire des Littératures. I. Littératures Anciennes, Orientales et Orales*, Paris, Editions Gallimard, pp. 795–805.

LUKE, A., McHOUL, A. and MEY, J. (1989) 'On the limits of language planning: Class, state and power', in BALDAUF, R. and LUKE, A. (Eds) *Language Planning and Education in Australia and the South Pacific*, Clevedon, UK, Multilingual Matters, pp. 25–44.

MacKENZIE, D.N. (1959) 'The Language of the Medians', *Bulletin of the School of Oriental and African Studies*, XXII, 2, pp. 354–5.

MALA KARIM, M. (1960) *Hacî Qadirî Koyî* (Haji Qadir Koyi), Baghdad, al-Najah Press.

MINORSKY, V. (1927) 'Kurds', in *Encyclopaedia of Islam*, Vol. II, pp. 1132–55.

SAKISIAN, A. (1937) 'Abdal Khan: seigneur Kurde de Bitlis au XVIIᵉ siècle, et ses trésors', *Journal Asiatique*, CCXXIX, pp. 253–70.

SLUGLETT, P. (1976) *Britain in Iraq, 1914–1932*, London, Ithaca Press.

VAN BRUINESSEN, M.M. (1978) *Agha, Shaikh and State: On the Social and Political Organization of Kurdistan*, Rijswijk, Holland, Europrint.

ZAZA, N. (1982) *Ma Vie de Kurde ou le Cri du Peuple Kurde*, Lausanne, Editions Pierre-Marcel Favre.

Chapter 4

Aboriginal Education in Northern Australia: A Case Study of Literacy Policies and Practices

Christine Walton

This paper describes the context of literacy education in the Northern Territory, Australia, examining particularly structural and institutional constraints on Aboriginal access to education. It does this by providing an overview of the current rhetoric surrounding access and equity issues in Aboriginal education in the Northern Territory from early childhood to tertiary education. It raises the issue of whether inequalities of access and participation reflect underlying institutional racism, and considers the constraints on effective teaching and learning that are built into both policy discourse and pedagogical practices. Suggested changes in policy and practice are also discussed. While the discussion is focused primarily on the Northern Territory context, many of the issues raised are relevant to the broader Australian context and may well have their parallels in other 'Fourth World' indigenous societies.

After a brief demographic description of Aboriginal people in the Northern Territory, the first section of the paper critically examines literacy-related pedagogical issues in the Northern Territory context; the second section examines the gap between the state and rhetoric in Northern Territory Aboriginal education. It is argued that these pedagogical and structural issues are interrelated. Both of these sections are framed in part by examinations of those discourses dealing with Northern Territory Aborigines that are found in official policy documents and more popularly accessible media statements.

Aborigines in the Northern Territory

The Northern Territory, as its name implies, is a territory not a state. The small and sparse population of 154,848 people, according to the 1986 Census, comprised 22.4 per cent Aborigines (34,739). The high proportion of Aborigines in the Northern Territory contrasts with the national level of about 1.5 per cent. Most Northern Territory Aborigines (93 per cent) live in communities other than the main urban centres (*A Social Atlas of Darwin: 1986 Census*, 1989).

Most Northern Territory non-urban Aborigines speak traditional Aboriginal languages and/or Kriol, which is derived from English and Aboriginal languages. Varieties of Kriol are spoken over a large area of the top end of Australia, from

Western Australia, through the Northern Territory, to parts of Queensland. Most Northern Territory Aboriginal people are multilingual, speaking traditional Aboriginal languages, Kriol and English. It is estimated that out of the 200 to 250 Aboriginal languages in existence at the time of initial European colonization, only about fifty remain in a 'relatively healthy state', mostly in central and northern Australia (Lo Bianco, 1987, p. 34). As a response to this particular linguistic context, bilingual education programmes have been implemented in twenty-one non-urban community schools in the Northern Territory, using seventeen Aboriginal languages, including one with a Kriol/English programme.

Darwin, the capital city, is situated in the north of the Territory and is close to Indonesia. Darwin has a total population of 72,937, of which 7.6 per cent are Aborigines. The 1986 Census found that 45.5 per cent of Darwin Aborigines were not in the labour force; in the terms of census, 'not looking for work'. Presumably many of these would be accounted for by their relative youth, as 40.3 per cent of Aborigines were under fifteen years of age at that time. However, 12.9 per cent of Darwin Aborigines were unemployed, using their definition of 'looking for work', with the figure reaching 30 per cent for one particular Aboriginal community in Darwin. Interestingly, the Census also found 14.6 per cent of Darwin's total population consisted of speakers of languages other than English in the home.

The Northern Territory economy has in the past been dependent upon the pastoral industry. However, more recently there has been an expansion of the mining and tourism sectors. There is little manufacturing. In the past Aborigines played a significant role in the development of the pastoral industry. Darwin, as the administrative centre for the region, has a high proportion of people employed in the public service. While the ethnic and linguistic diversity of the Northern Territory is one of its most attractive features, there is also a sense of cleavage between the urban, mainly non-Aboriginal centres and the Aboriginal communities scattered throughout the Territory. A complete historical account of dispossession would be necessary to understand the contemporary scene; however, suffice to say that dispossession occurred this century and is still strongly contested in current debates about land rights and other issues.

The Australian bicentennial activities in 1988 focused Australians' attention on reconciling Aboriginal and non-Aboriginal Australian interests. International Literacy Year, two years later, to some extent further developed that focus on Aboriginal education. *The Report of the Aboriginal Education Policy Task Force* (1988), informally known as the *Hughes Report*, documented the structural inequalities in access to education experienced by Aboriginal Australians. This report was compiled by an Aboriginal task force, which reported to the relevant Federal Ministers. The *Hughes Report* describes the situation in terms of a 'crisis in the provision of education to Aborigines' (1988, p. 7). While the authors of the *Hughes Report* wrote of a 'crisis', it will be evident from analysis of local policy and media documents that the crisis is down-played, even written out of these public discourses, through the strategy, now almost clichéd, of 'blaming the victims'.

In terms of national policy outcomes, the *Hughes Report* was extensively drawn upon in the creation of the *National Aboriginal and Torres Strait Islander Education Policy* (1989), which in turn has led to negotiated agreements to achieve the goals of the national policy at the state and territory levels. The second section of this paper uses the *Hughes Report* and other related documents to provide information about the current participation of Aboriginal people in education. Before examining that participation, it is useful to situate the local scene in an historical and international context.

Historical Overview of Minority Education

Historically, minority education has provided a litmus test of prevailing ideologies. Theories that try to account for educational inequalities or differences in outcomes between different groups such as social classes, ethnic groups, or sexes have changed over the years. As Baker and Luke (1990, in press, p. 3) suggested, the field known as the sociology of schooling has had a longstanding concern with 'the production and reproduction of systematic inequalities among categories of students'. Early theories have relied on presumed genetic differences. At the turn of the century Social Darwinism, colonialism, and genetic explanations of educational outcomes interlocked to create a climate in which certain distinctive cultural and linguistic groups (those being colonized or invaded) were educationally isolated and the device of schooling functioned to destroy their culture and language.

There can be no question about the overt racism of this culturally genocidal phase in Australian history. Education in general and the related area of language policy were integral components of colonial policy. Penalosa (1981, p. 169) described the role of language in colonization 'as an instrument of colonial policy'.

In the 1950s and 1960s environmental explanations predominated: the child's home, parents and language, were said to cause the 'problems' some children experienced in schools. This problematization was effected through the use of the notion of 'cultural deprivation'. Such an account represented an improvement, of sorts, on earlier genetically-based theories. The following Native American illustration has many parallels to the Australian Aboriginal context:

> Carried far enough, this ideology of cultural deprivation leads to characterizations of Sioux life which are deplorably fallacious ... [which] places responsibility for scholastic defeat on the Indian home and the Indian child, ... justifies almost any activity ... as being somehow 'educational' ... [and] ... justifies the educators in their isolation from and ignorance of the Indian Community. (Wax, 1973, p. 217)

There are a number of interesting aspects to this statement. The first is Wax's depiction of the environmentalist position; and the second the pedagogical implications of such a position. This will be taken up again later in this chapter. For our purposes it is sufficient to alert us here to the practice of creating what Bourdieu and Passeron (1977, p. 174) have called 'dumping grounds' which institutions and their agents are able to present as leading to 'alternative achievements'. Bourdieu and Passeron suggested that these 'dumping grounds' help explain drop-out rates, which they re-name as the 'differential educational mortality rate' (1977, p. 154).

More recently, differences between the language and culture of the home and the school are receiving more attention along with detailed studies of what happens inside classrooms (McDermott and Aron, 1977). Recent explanations have come to incorporate into the discourse and elaborate upon broader social, political and ideological dimensions. Thus, over the last three decades, 'cultural deprivation' has given way under an onslaught of 'cultural difference' explanations of educational disadvantage, at least in the public rhetoric of educators, if not fully in their practice. Researchers (particularly linguists) were in a position to prove that the majority view of Native Americans and blacks was fallacious. Baratz and Baratz (1970) argued that both the genetic and the 'social pathology' models were ethnocentric examples of an institutionalized racism that wrongly equated 'equality with sameness' (1970, pp. 31–2). They argued the failure was 'in the schools, not the parents' and that it was the educative process not the goals of education that should be changed (1970, p. 41):

> The goal of such education should be to produce a bicultural child who is capable of functioning both in his (*sic*) sub-culture and in the mainstream. (Baratz and Baratz, 1970, pp. 42–3)

The cultural and linguistic rights of minority groups began to play a role in conflicts over the 'curriculum agenda' in schools. Penalosa (1981, pp. 199–200) argued that the linguistic conflicts that emerged in the 1960s and later were manifestations of other conflicts, language rights issues being the symbolic focus of political conflict.

In examining current practices, we encounter inflections of all of these earlier discourses and their underlying ideologies, echoed in contemporary contestations between and even within groups. While the 'difference' position is dominant in the literature, there is a tendency for it to be co-opted by those in power to justify policies and practices that continue to disadvantage minority groups. When 'cultural difference' is co-opted to excuse discriminatory policy and practice by teachers and policy makers, a new level of covert institutionalized racism is attained, with clear continuities with the past. Historically it was necessary to argue the case for 'difference' in order to overcome the 'deficit' position.

There are interesting parallels between the history of sexism and racism. For instance, Eisenstein (1984, p. 25) has traced the swings of the pendulum in the feminist debate. Initially, men viewed women as fundamentally different from themselves, good at interpersonal particularism, but not at universal generalizing, concrete rather than abstract. 'Female difference was the primary source of women's oppression' (Eisenstein, 1984, p. 45). Having focused on the sources of this difference and separated out the concepts of gender and sex role, it then became possible for differences that had been described as deficits 'to be viewed in a new light, as elements of strength' (Eisenstein, 1984, p. 46). In the case of Aboriginal education, the difference between poverty and culture may be analogous to these distinctions.

In the subsequent development of feminist theory it was logical that a separatist branch emerged believing that 'one could begin to consider the possibility that femaleness was normative, while maleness was a deviation' (Eisenstein, 1984, p. 47). Eisenstein names the third section of her book 'Beyond the impasse of difference'. Similarly, in cross-cultural education the need arises to go beyond the impasse of difference so that the trap of a new form of paternalism is avoided

— one that uses the discourse of 'cultural differences' as excuse for not providing basic educational services. This 'hands-off' approach is an over-reaction to the colonial-style imposition of Western education that ignored differences, and thus felt able to trample them with impunity.

When groups, whether defined in terms of gender, race or class, are labelled as outsiders by those in power, a discourse is available that not only rationalizes the process but proceeds to turn a difference into a deficit. The victims of unequal distribution of power in our society, rather than the structural features of the society itself, can thus be blamed.

When these groups begin to develop a power base, the emphasis shifts to one of difference; differences are capable of being considered as sources of strength in the re-negotiation of the balance of power. Without a reconsideration of universals that underlie the differences, the least powerful group is capable of being checkmated in the game for power. This is the point now reached in Aboriginal education in the Northern Territory, as I will develop further in this chapter.

One of the current dilemmas in Aboriginal education is that the work of linguists and anthropologists (e.g., S. Harris and M. Christie) that highlighted cultural and linguistic differences, is now used by some to justify and to rationalize aiming for other than equitable educational outcomes or goals, in much the same way in which genetic theories were used earlier. The task is to develop alternatives that build on existing cultural and linguistic repertoires, in which minority cultures and languages are genuinely valued and politically assertive, options that are foreclosed by the discourse of 'choice' as an explanation of history and location, just as surely as they are foreclosed by the discourse of cultural 'blame'.

Bacchi (1989) recently discussed this impasse in terms of 'the inclusion solution' with regard to the feminist debate. She suggested that 'differences' has become a problematic term as it masks women's differential social location. Affirmative action legislation should address the inequality, rather than the differences. 'Difference' has become a loaded term used against women. For example, her 'inclusion solution' with regard to women and work rules was that 'women's specific needs need to be included in the standards by which work rules are set'. If we were to extrapolate her argument to the Aboriginal education context, we might conclude that she was suggesting:

1. Aborigines need equal treatment in the sense that they do not want to be discriminated against.
2. They need Affirmative Action to compensate for differential social location.
3. Their specific needs have to be included in the standards by which services are provided.

The 'benevolent inertia' intrinsic in the liberal/progressive educational position has been described by many commentators (e.g., Martin, Wignell, Eggins and Rothery, 1986, p. 1) as valuing differences in a way that leaves people and social relations as they are. By taking this position, the culturally different are still left without expanded options. Such a position recognizes differences without intervening to expand people's options. Countering this position, Freire suggested critical literacy as a necessary form of intervention (Freire and Macedo, 1988).

The realities of racism and sexism are no less real for having become largely covert in the discourse.

Differential educational access and outcomes are manifestations of those social practices that disempower groups defined by race, sex or class. Much of the debate about minority group educational outcomes has been driven by the competing discourses of individualism versus socio-cultural, economic, political, and ideological factors. In relation to literacy research in particular, there has been a shift from a focus on the individual learner to a focus on literacy in social contexts. These issues will be addressed in more depth in subsequent sections of this chapter.

Pedagogy

Over and above policy decisions at government and departmental levels, constraints and inequalities are built into pedagogical practices. I will argue that there are inherent misconceptions in contemporary thinking about literacy, and teaching and learning, that compound the already difficult position in which Aboriginal students find themselves.

The connection between pedagogical issues and institutional racism can be further developed by focusing on the ideological processes of schooling. Fairclough (1989, p. 33) suggested examining 'institutional practices which legitimize existing power relations by appearing to be "universal and common-sensical"'. He argued that this process of 'naturalizing' the discourse and practices of the dominant group served to maintain their dominance, and functioned 'ideologically'. Similarly, Giroux (1981, p. 24) suggested that in schools 'the production of hegemonic ideologies' is dependent upon the 'presentation of specific forms of consciousness, beliefs, attitudes, values and practices as natural, universal, or even eternal'.

The ideological content of reading lessons has been recently analyzed by Baker and Freebody (1989) in their discussion of 'talk around text' in classrooms. Their analysis of classroom discourse revealed the authority assigned to teachers and texts. They argued that students receive 'a lesson in the politics of school knowledge', in the authority of teacher and text along with their reading lesson (1989, p. 278). A common theme of such critiques is that ideology works most effectively when implicit and seen to be grounded in 'common sense'; it functions to disguise social problems as individual problems (Fairclough, 1989, pp. 77–85).

Luke (1989) examined the ideological positions underlying current literacy theories and practices, suggesting that technicist theories and practices are grounded in the mistaken assumption that developing better pedagogical programmes can fully address the literacy crisis. Other criticisms of technicist discourse have focused on its interpretation of the nature of knowledge as narrow, closed and non-negotiable. Luke (1989, p. 9) questioned the assumptions of progressivist discourse on the basis that its 'emphasis on self-expression and self-disclosure, self-selection of literature and activities can just as effectively lead to cultural reproduction as elitist classicism'. Both technicist and progressivist pedagogy are ethnocentric in that the social context of literacy education does not figure in substantial or theorized ways in their discourse.

Emerging from the work of Fairclough, Baker and Freebody, Luke, Martin,

Freire and others is a contrasting discourse about literacy, one that moves beyond technicist and progressivist discourse. They share a concern with developing critical social literacy necessary for active participation in post-industrial society. Fairclough (1989, p. 241) proposed the development of 'critical language study', which would include a 'metalanguage' or way of talking about language. Similarly, Freebody, Luke and Gilbert (1991) have suggested that the capacity to interrogate texts is an important feature of critical literacy that can be used to unmask the ideological operation of texts.

Literacy learning and teaching are the most fundamental tasks of schools. As Olson puts it, schools are there 'to mediate the relationships between children and the printed text' (Olson, 1977, p. 66). A group without access to literacy in our society is relatively powerless, unless trusted 'brokers' are available to act on their behalf. While it can be argued that literacy is useful or even necessary to enhance participation in the social, cultural, and economic life of the community, this should not be confused with the literacy myth — the suggestion that literacy inevitably leads to changes in cognition, economic independence, political emancipation, and social justice (Graff, 1979).

Implicit or Explicit Teaching?

Coming from a number of disparate sources is the theme of practices and beliefs that keep 'outsiders' excluded from valued knowledge. For instance, Bourdieu and Passeron (1977, p. 72) hypothesized that the greater the cultural and linguistic distance between the home and the school, the less successful will be the learning/teaching of the school. They also argued that the more implicit the school's pedagogy, presupposing prior understandings and attainments, the more locked-out will be the outsiders. This enables the 'possessors of the prerequisite cultural capital to continue to monopolize that capital' (Bourdieu and Passeron, 1977, p. 47).

Atkinson (1985, p. 57) developed Bernstein's (1975) distinction between 'visible' and 'invisible' pedagogies, suggesting that there has been a shift from visible to invisible pedagogies 'associated with the rhetoric of "progressivism"'. Atkinson (p. 166) claimed that teacher control is a feature of both pedagogies, merely realized differently in each. The significance of these analyses of pedagogy to the argument here is in the suggestion that invisible or implicit pedagogies work least effectively with students whose cultural and linguistic backgrounds are most different from that of the schools. The ideological workings of 'invisible' pedagogies are clearly related to Fairclough's (1989, p. 91) contention that dominant discourse types come to be seen as natural, common-sensical, and universal.

Applying pedagogies developed in one socio-cultural context to other contexts is problematic. For instance, research by Walton (1986) considered young Northern Territory Aboriginal children learning to write in an urban English-medium programme. The children's first languages were Kriol and other Aboriginal languages. They were from an oral cultural tradition. That study raised questions about the application of a model of teaching and learning, developed from research with literate culture English-speaking children (e.g., 'process writing' and other 'experience based' pedagogies) to cross-cultural contexts. The model was ethnocentric as it assumed all children came to school from a literate cultural background.

When applied to a cross-cultural context, the implicit model of teaching disadvantaged the Aboriginal children. The consequence was that literacy learning was differentially available to children under the same regime. Walton's (1986) study supports Kress' 'hunches' about the process writing approach:

> [it] has worked in those classrooms where children come with much knowledge of written texts . . . the approach does not work precisely in those classrooms where the children cannot draw on their experience: classrooms with a preponderance of non-English-speaking background children, classrooms where Aboriginal children are in the majority . . . (Kress, 1988, p. 15)

Implicit models of learning/teaching, do not take sufficient note of the complexity of the task facing the young Aboriginal child who is coming from an oral Aboriginal cultural tradition.

Not surprisingly, Walton (1986) found a strong relationship between teaching practices and learning outcomes. Individual student's difficulties were socially induced. The students were not responsible for the constraints placed on their learning. In particular, there were instances of constraints on learning that could be traced to particular pedagogical practices. That is, all students in the class shared limits to the 'discoveries about print' that they could make. While each child's learning can be said to be individual, it is also the case that learning is socially constructed. Process writing has tended to work from an implicit model of learning that under-emphasized the social construction of learning, the role of interaction with mature language users, and presupposed prior experience of the nature and uses of literacy.

In addition, Walton's (1986) findings suggested that there is a real danger of creating prolonged periods of stagnation in children's learning if teachers are not familiar with the developmental sequence of children's literacy learning. A pattern of forces contributing to lowered expectations was in evidence, not unlike that found in the classrooms studied by Christie (1985), in which there was an over-use of low-risk mechanical 'busy work' such as copying and colouring. These studies raise issues about pedagogical practices in terms of the need for 'purposeful learning' via more purposeful teaching. Urban Aboriginal ESL students may be disadvantaged by placing them in special classes, often with non-Aboriginal teachers with little specialized training. Sometimes these classes seem not to be doing much for the students' Aboriginal identity, while minimizing their access to English speaking peers, and becoming dead-end tracks reminiscent of Bourdieu and Passeron's 'dumping grounds' (1977, p. 174).

As an example of a more effective model of intervention (other than isolation in special classes or 'sink and swim' in mainstream classes) we may consider the Traeger Park School model, developed by Brian Gray, as an alternative to withdrawal or special classes. In the early 1980s Gray worked at Traeger Park School in Alice Springs, which had a majority of Aboriginal pupils for whom English was a second language or dialect. Gray developed an integrated approach to language teaching, around the relationship between text and context, which became known as Concentrated Language Encounters (1985). All of the students and their teachers, from school commencement to Year 3, were catered for daily, in small group interactional settings. Compared to a withdrawal model, this strategy required few additional resources; and further, the approach avoided stigmatizing students, a problem associated with withdrawal models or special classes, and also provided classroom teachers with models of exemplary practice they could use in their teaching.

More generally, in the Northern Territory, while a small body of research has existed for some time about cultural differences — Aboriginal 'world view' (Harris 1979); traditional learning styles (Harris, 1980); and the perceptions of Aboriginal children about schooling (Christie, 1985) — there has been a tendency for such findings to be used to rationalize what Christie (1984, p. 372) called 'educational pantomimes' in which the students and teachers negotiate coping strategies that are dysfunctional in terms of academic goals. Tyler's (1988, p. 136) interpretation of Christie's thesis describes the 'mutually reinforcing coping strategies which render classroom life bearable':

> Aboriginal children respond to the teachers' demands through retreatism (truanting, sulking, crying), or, more commonly, through ritualism (preference for rote work, copying, from the blackboard, judicious following of classroom ceremonies). (Tyler, 1988, p. 136)

This observation appears to parallel the American experience described by Massey, Scott, and Dornbusch (1975), in which teachers, even with the intention of 'being nice', had actually stopped teaching black children.

'Other Australian researchers and educators are coming to terms with the need for explicit teaching, without being caricatured as part of the 'back to the basics' movement. For instance, Martin and others have argued for the explicit teaching of 'Secret English', which they describe as a 'collection of specialized registers' of English. Teaching 'Secret English' to empower 'means giving students conscious control over its technologies' (Martin, Wignell, Eggins and Rothery, 1986, p. 13). Martin (1987, p. 3) argued English in Aboriginal Australia is needed for negotiating with non-Aboriginal Australia. Martin also suggested that some current teaching practices (e.g., 'process writing') were not achieving the level and kind of literacy in English that would lead to being able to use English to negotiate with non-Aboriginal Australia.

In New South Wales the work of the Social Literacy team is along the same lines. Kalantzis and Cope have argued that, while traditional pedagogy was flawed in its over-emphasis on explicit teaching of content rather than learning processes, progressivist pedagogy is similarly flawed by its over-emphasis on process and implicit learning models. They are developing an orientation to pedagogy that improves on both models by combining the strengths, and avoiding the excesses of each (Kalantzis and Cope, 1987, p. 20). Their educational goals are expressed in the following terms:

> We need to maintain the strength of progressivist learning theory: active rather than passive learning. . . Yet at the same time, knowledge also needs to be presented in the form of generalizations, rules, hypothesis, . . . learning should be both deductive and inductive. . . The dilemma is to create curriculum which is both open to difference but

which is based upon clearly articulated common linguistic-cognitive ends and standards. (Cope, 1988, p. 23)

Cope and Kalantzis (1985) have posed the question of whether the academic curriculum has failed or just never been offered — a significant point in the light of later discussions in this chapter about secondary education in the Northern Territory:

> Cultural diversity is not a diversity of equals. This is admitted in the hidden agenda of activism about class, sex and ethnicity. The job is not merely to respect the divisions for what they are, but to right the injustices of everyday lack of power. How, then, will diversification of curriculum, in order to meet the diversity of needs, avoid reproducing social stratification at the same time? ... It might not be the case that the academic curriculum has failed the working class; rather, the work-ing class have never had academic curriculum. (Cope, 1985, p. 12)

Cope argued that the 'skills of western industrialism' are 'socially inherited' not 'spontaneous' and that schools should equip all students with these skills (Cope, 1985, p. 19). In addition, he asserted that 'curriculum should operate to common social ends' (Cope, 1985, p. 34). If we extrapolate again from the feminist position presented by Bacchi (1989), her 'inclusion solution' suggests that there should be ways of negotiating common social ends in relation to curriculum that provide for the special needs of particular client groups. Building variety and flexibility into curriculum development would facilitate this process.

There is another version of the implicit/explicit debate about teaching language and literacy evident in the USA, with the same potential for being assimilated into either liberal-progressivist discourse or technicist 'back to basics' discourse. One of its best spokespeople is Delpit, an American black researcher schooled in the 'skills and drills' days, and professionally trained under progress-ivist, 'process' approaches. Like Cope, Kalantzis, Martin and Kress in Australia, Delpit makes connections between the reproduction of inequality and implicit pedagogical practices and has consequently come to question teaching based on implicit principles. She discussed five aspects of power in classrooms:

1. power is enacted in classrooms,
2. there are codes or rules for participating in power — that is, there is a 'culture of power',
3. the rules of the culture of power are a reflection of the culture of those who have power,
4. if you are not already a participant in the culture of power, being told explicitly the rules of that culture makes acquiring power easier,
5. those with power are frequently least aware of — or least willing to acknowledge its existence — those with less power are often most aware of its existence. (Delpit, 1988, p. 282)

Delpit has worked in a variety of cross-cultural situations. She argued that 'members of any culture transmit information implicitly to co-members'. How-ever, she suggested that communication breakdown often occurs when 'implicit codes are attempted across cultures'. Immersion works when learners have a life-time to master the implicit codes (1988, p. 283). She did not advocate a return to decontextualized skills and drills, but rather that teachers teach the codes of power within 'meaningful communicative endeavours'.

'Natural' Language Learning

A key organizing concept for progressivist pedagogical discourse is 'natural learn-ing'. It is this 'naturalness' that sanitizes the moral force of pedagogy and serves to by-pass the critique of knowledge-content by focusing on the 'naturalness' of interpersonal relations — under the heading of 'process'. Progressivist thinking has contributed a great deal to our understanding of how literate-culture child-ren learn literacy before schooling. However, the use of the term 'natural' in this context has been unfortunate, enforcing a dichotomy between 'natural' and 'con-trived' learning. For instance, Cambourne (1985, p. 78) distinguished 'natural' and 'contrived' learning in terms of the role of the teacher/parent in children's learn-ing; natural learning being mistakenly seen as child-controlled; contrived being teacher-controlled.

Neither extreme is substantiated by the child language research. The role of mature language users, in interaction with children, is that of guiding the nego-tiation of meaning, through strategies described by Bruner as scaffolding (1986). Bruner provides the following example of scaffolding:

> In general, what the tutor *did* was what the child could *not* do. For the rest, she made things such that the child could do *with* her what he could plainly not do *without* her. And as the tutoring proceeded, the child took over from her parts of the task that he was not able to do at first but, with mastery, became consciously able to do under his own control. And she gladly handed these over. (Bruner, 1986, p. 76, emphases in original)

The use of the term 'natural' for literacy learning is problematic because it masks the social and cultural nature of literacy, implying universality. It is clear that 'what is learned' and 'how it is learned' vary a great deal depending on cultural, historical, class, gender and other factors (Gilbert, 1989; Scribner and Cole, 1981). Further, the discourse of 'naturalness' conceals the differences between oral and written language and learning, disguising the fact that unlike oral language, literacy is not universal; even today in literate cultures there are children who are not as successful learning literacy as they are at learning oral language. Learning to listen and speak is imperative in ways that learning to read and write may not be and may involve linguistic strategies that are, in no genuine sense of the word, 'natural'.

Luke, Baty and Stehbens (1989, p. 47) critique 'natural language learning' theories, suggesting that naturalizing what are 'historical and cultural phenomena' is part of the 'workings of modern ideologies' that put them beyond scrutiny. Research by Graff (1986) supports the view of literacies as culturally and histor-ically diverse. Graff argued that it is a common misconception to think of literacy as a singular entity or thing that is a prerequisite for modernization. Graff's

(1986) historical studies of literacy suggest that a simple, linear, modernization model of literacy is not sufficient.

Teaching in cross-cultural settings tends to present distinctive challenges to assumptions about what is 'natural'. Bourdieu and Passeron (1977, p. 13) questioned assumptions about 'universals' and 'myths of non-directive' or 'natural' teaching.

> The agents produced by pedagogic work would not be so totally the prisoners of the limitations which cultural arbitrary imposes on their thought and practice, were it not that, contained within these limits by self-discipline and self-censorship ... they live out their thought and practice in the illusion of freedom and universality. (Bourdieu and Passeron, 1977, p. 40)

We have already explored challenges to universalist claims in the discussion of minority education: here in the context of 'natural' language learning, it is again an issue. Universalistic discourses about 'natural' language learning and minority education combine to doubly disadvantage minority students, necessarily marginalizing them.

Relationships of Power

The issue of power in the terms provided by Delpit (1988) requires further discussion at this point. It is one of the recurring themes, of course, in contemporary discussions about minority education, both in Australia and overseas. As we have seen, for many years researchers have been looking for plausible explanations for minority students' successes and failures. Cummins (1986, p. 21), while maintaining a role for 'cultural mismatch' theories and the quality of the education provided, argued that 'status and power relations between groups' is the key to explaining differential academic success. This dimension helps to explain the variety of responses, between ethnic groups, in terms of educational outcomes. Three sets of power relationships are central to his analysis:

1. The classroom interactions between teachers and students;
2. relationships between schools and minority communities; and
3. the intergroup power relations within the society as a whole. (Cummins, 1986, p. 19)

Cummins' analysis points to broader structural issues that must be dealt with if existing trends of minority group exclusion and failure are to be reversed. Power relations are diffuse and ubiquitous, and according to Cummins (1989) need to be addressed concurrently along four dimensions:

1. cultural and linguistic incorporation (subtractive or additive);
2. community participation (exclusion or inclusion);
3. pedagogy (transmission or interactive);
4. assessment (legitimizing or advocating);

The first dimension deals with the quality and quantity of the incorporation of the minority group's language and culture into the school; whether educators see themselves as eliminating the mother tongue and culture or adding to the linguistic and cultural repertoire of the students.

Along each of these dimensions, Cummins argues for fundamental changes in teachers' roles. By actively incorporating students' language and culture, schools and teachers can build on the students' strengths, while avoiding the chain reaction from difference to deficit. For instance, incorporation of vernacular literacy into the school could provide a role for the school in Aboriginal culture and language maintenance. Martin (1987, p. 3) interpreted the social function of Aboriginal vernacular literacy in terms of Aboriginal aspirations to *conserve* their language and culture.

The second dimension deals with the relationships between the school and the minority community; whether educators' policies and practices work toward the inclusion or exclusion of community members in the processes of decision-making that affects their children's education.

The third dimension suggests that an 'interactive-based' pedagogy is more useful than a transmission-based or technicist model. Like others in this field, Cummins is trying to avoid a return to the past, while being influenced by progressivist pedagogy. The choice of 'interactive' in Cummins' 1989 paper was deliberate. The teacher's role is to become a cross-cultural broker, consciously seeking ways to turn differences to the child's advantage, while maintaining pedagogical goals that maximize students' literacy learning.

In the fourth dimension, Cummins suggested that assessment has played a major role in disadvantaging minority students; that it has been used to 'legitimize' institutionally racist practices. He did not suggest there is no role for assessment, but rather that it should be used with a view to 'advocacy' on behalf of minority students. Cummins (1984) has researched extensively in the area of inappropriate assessment practices in Canada and the USA. There is a place for advocacy-oriented assessment, particularly in relation to gathering data about system-wide outcomes, but it needs to be consistently put that this is a qualitatively distinct enterprise from system-wide assessment of individual student outcomes.

In the Northern Territory Department of Education there is an assessment programme in Primary English and Mathematics. This programme can be analyzed to establish the position of Aboriginal students at various year levels. Many teachers involved in the programme in recent years have been critical of the validity of the tests developed. However, if valid assessment tools were developed, they could be used in Cummins' 'advocacy' sense, that is, to monitor more closely the overall academic development of Aboriginal students.

Access, Participation and Retention

In examining Northern Territory Aboriginal Education, I will use data from the *Hughes Report* and other documents. By focusing on the location of Aboriginal people in this section, I intend to illustrate some of the themes already addressed in earlier sections of the chapter. The discussion will provide exemplification of current discourses concerning minority education and pedagogical issues.

Primary/Elementary Education

Turning to primary education, according to the *Hughes Report:*

> In Australian society it is generally expected that every child between the age of five and fifteen years should receive an education, and that every Australian child has the right to a school place provided by State education systems, unless families choose to send their children to non-government schools. (1988, p. 10)

It might seem odd that in 1988 the *Hughes Report* felt the need to remind the Australian community of this expectation. However, there is a substantial number of the primary school age Aboriginal population with no automatic or ready access to schooling. The mainly non-Aboriginal Northern Territorian students who are in isolated locations are provided with extensive and expensive services through special provisions such as 'School of the Air', which delivers services to students on isolated cattle stations, using a sophisticated range of media. The question posed for non-Aboriginal Territorians seems to be 'How can a service be provided for all school age children?'; while for Northern Territory Aborigines it is more like, 'If they request a service, what is the minimum that might be provided?'

There are a number of estimates of enrolment figures for the whole of Australia. According to the *Hughes Report*:

> 13 per cent of five- to fifteen-year-old Aboriginal children and young people — those of compulsory school age — do not participate in schooling. (1988, p. 7)

According to the report, this means that about 8,500 Aboriginal children, mainly in Western Australia and the Northern Territory, do not have access to schooling (*Hughes Report*, 1988, pp. 10–2). This is partly explained by the geographic isolation of 'homeland centres'. These homeland centres are usually small communities, many of which have been formed in recent years as families move from the larger settlements to return to the country with which they have traditional ties. Clearly, geographic isolation is, *per se*, not an explanation since it usually is not an impediment to providing services to non-Aborigines living in such small and isolated communities.

In the Northern Territory, homeland centre schools are included in the Aboriginal enrolment figures. For example, in 1987 there were about 800 students being serviced by homeland centre schools. Of these 800 students, 583 were of compulsory school age (Crawford, 1989). There are many homeland centres without schools of any kind. The following extract from the *Report of the House of Representatives Select Committee on Aboriginal Education* (1985, p. 114) gives a clue to the situation:

> at the end of 1983, there were sixty-three homeland centres in the Northern Territory being provided with an education service. This represents only a small proportion of the estimated 400 homeland centres which exist in the Northern Territory.

While 1983 data is not complete or totally reliable, it does allow us to estimate how many children live in homeland centres without schools. For instance, if we were to estimate that each centre had five children of school age, that would put the 1983 figure of children not receiving schooling at 1,685. Given the relative youth of the Aboriginal population, we could expect about 30 per cent of the Northern Territory Aboriginal population to be of compulsory school age. So another way to check the above estimate is as follows: The Northern Territory Department of Community Development informed the House of Representatives Standing Committee on Aboriginal Affairs that there were 416 homeland centres, with a population estimate of 6,715 people (*Return to Country*, 1987, p. 28). If we were to estimate that 30 per cent of the 6,715 people were of compulsory school age, then about 2,000 compulsory school age 'potential students' existed, at a time when we knew 583 were actually enrolled in homeland centre schools. That method of estimating the number of students of compulsory school age without access to schooling would give us the figure of 1,417.

Neither of these estimates is particularly sound. However, they do point to a significant number of Northern Territory Aboriginal children with no access to school. In 1989 a Northern Territory newspaper, the *NT News*, reported a story about a Federal Government grant of $101,500 'to count the number of Aboriginal children in the Territory who are not being educated'. The research was proposed by Feppi, the Northern Territory Aboriginal Education Consultative group. However, a spokesperson for the then Minister for Education (Mr Harris), was reported in the *NT News* as commenting that:

> We acknowledge that some children are not being educated, but if people choose to go bush, there's not much we can do about it. (*NT News*, 7th June 1989, p. 3)

Thus, the rhetoric of personal choice acts as a framework in which to account for differential treatment of Aboriginal and non-Aboriginal people. Non-Aboriginal families on isolated cattle stations expect and receive educational services. The current policy of waiting for Aboriginal communities to submit formal applications for educational services is probably, in effect, deterring people from obtaining educational services which are the government's responsibility to provide. Meanwhile Northern Territory Government Policy stated:

> Aboriginal children should have educational opportunity equal to that of other Australian children. (*Information Statement No 6*, p. 2.)

Note that such a statement avoids the imputation of responsibility for providing educational services — they are to 'have it', but the agency of provision is omitted from the statement, rendering it merely an expression of governmental desire. Strategies developed in the Information Statement included implementing 'the compulsory education provision of the Education Act'. These policy statements raise a number of questions: why have the compulsory education provisions not been implemented for these children? If the provisions of the Education Act were to be implemented, would the government be bound actually to provide the service to all school-age children?

Not surprisingly, the *Hughes Report* makes a number of recommendations in terms of setting targets, to begin to overcome this exclusion of Aborigines from educational services. For example:

> Recommendation 4:
> That all governments adopt a participation target in early childhood education of parity for Aboriginal children with all children in Australia by 1992. (1988, p. 22)

In order to achieve this target the Northern Territory will need to change its existing policy with regard to providing education services for homeland centres. It will have to mount or support a major research project to establish the magnitude of the problem and, in consultation with communities, establish a range of options for the provision of services in communities currently not served.

There are many contradictions in current policy and practice. There are reasoned, articulate arguments used against universal educational services. Some use the discourse of 'self management' as a justification for allowing the situation to continue. Some commentators imply that the children on outstations do not need educational services. Evidence suggests many outstation communities do want educational services, but that it is made difficult for them to obtain them. The onus is placed on Aboriginal people to demand basic educational services; no other group in Australia is placed in such a situation. Even the most isolated, mainly non-Aboriginal, students on cattle stations are provided for through expensive and sophisticated arrangements such as School of the Air.

Two recent interviews with prominent politicians provide examples of contemporary discourse about the provision of education for Aborigines in isolated locations. Firstly, Bob Collins, a Labor Party Senator in the federal parliament, (*ABC Radio*, 14 October, 1988) expressed this view in a recent exchange:

> Collins: Bill Baird's figure of about 2,000 kids (with no school) is about right.
> Interviewer: Does it matter?
> Collins: If there is no real threat to the security of title over their land . . . then no need to worry. They are being educated for the lifestyle they have chosen to lead — traditional.

Note again the recurring theme of 'self-determination', linked in this case, as a corollary, to the Aboriginal peoples' right to land ownership. Secondly, the Northern Territory Education Minister, Tom Harris, had this to say (*ABC Radio*, 8 June 1989):

> Interviewer: On the face of it, it would seem that you would want to deprive Aborigines of education, by criticizing this expenditure of $100,000.
> Harris: Not at all . . . the inference of that press release is that there are 7,000 odd students out there that don't have access to education. That is completely wrong . . .
> Interviewer: What are the figures of Aboriginal children who don't have access?

Harris: ... there was found that there was something like 600 that didn't have access to education. There are however, many other Aboriginal children who are not attending school. That is the real problem.

Interviewer: What does it mean by saying not having access to education?

Harris: ... scattered ... people have access to the ... schools that are established ... 162 schools scattered throughout the Northern Territory ... we are in fact able to provide education, but the real problem is the social concerns ... the drinking, the kava consumption, the alcohol abuse ... the students don't get fed correctly, the student don't get their sleep.

We can note the shift away from the issue of access, which Harris interprets in terms of an 'attendance' problem and which is quite a different issue, to an imputation of 'choice' in the matter. It is this imputation, put as an unproblematic link in the apparently explanatory chain, that maintains the discourse of 'blaming the victim'.

While the rest of Australia, non-Aboriginal Australia, is concerned about how to increase secondary and tertiary access and retention, Aboriginal education in the Northern Territory has not yet dealt with primary education provision adequately. Improved retention rates of Aboriginal students need to be viewed in terms of national trends. While there have been increases in Aboriginal education access and retention rates in the primary, secondary and tertiary sectors over the last ten years, it is also the case that the non-Aboriginal population's participation has not remained static.

The inequitable differential in participation rates cannot allow the 'increase' to be discussed as an 'improvement'. For example, nationally, Year 12 retention rates have increased from 41 per cent in 1983 to close to 70 per cent in 1991. The *Hughes Report* suggested that the national Aboriginal retention rate for Year 12 is 17 per cent (1988, p. 7). Achieving equitable outcomes by the year 2000 in these circumstances will require extraordinary changes and will clearly necessitate the use of an affirmative action framework.

Secondary Education

In 1984, the Northern Territory Government Policy Statements on Aboriginal Education (*Information Statement No 6*, p. 2) set targets for the 'production' of Aboriginal matriculants, that is students who complete Year 12 and gain entry to tertiary studies — by 1984, five matriculants and by 1988, twenty-five. How close did the NT system come to achieving these admittedly modest matriculation targets?

Crawford (1989) documented that in 1987 there were 212 Aboriginal students in senior secondary school; that is while Aborigines make up about 30 per cent of the school age population, they have only 7 per cent representation in Northern Territory senior secondary courses. Within the rural Aboriginal communities of the northern region of the Northern Territory (excluding major rural towns) there is currently, in effect, no 'state' provided secondary schooling. 'Post-primary education' is, as its name suggests, a continuation of primary education.

Indeed, there is no choice but to keep secondary-age students at home in post-primary education, or to send them away from home to private schools, thereby 'off-loading' the cost burden onto the Commonwealth and off the Territory governments. Additionally, in Central Australia, Yirara College (a 'state' boarding school) is precluded from offering secondary education (JSSC, Junior Secondary School Certificate). This Central Australian issue is, at the time of writing, being contested by 'The Aboriginal Parents and Friends Support Group', who were reported in a local Alice Springs newspaper as suggesting that the current policy is a 'fundamental denial of human rights'. They are seeking a public hearing through the Human Rights and Equal Opportunity Commission (*Centralian Advocate*, 29 August 1990).

The *Hughes Report* (1988, p. 25) recommended that the Federal Government should provide funds for initiatives in this area, including 'adding one or more secondary classes to existing primary schools' and creating 'specialized learning centres' in Aboriginal communities. The report set ambitious national targets aimed at increasing Aboriginal retention rates to Year 12, from 17 per cent to 65 per cent by the year 2000 (*The Hughes Report*, 1988, p. 27).

We need to examine critically those policy initiatives designed to address this issue. The main policy initiative, endorsed by the Aboriginal consultative group Feppi, is the development of Community Education Centres (CECs). There are four main areas of concern with the proposed CECs. Firstly, comparable non-Aboriginal students would be in secondary schools and programmes, staffed by trained secondary teachers, working to secondary curricula (accredited locally through the Northern Territory Board of Studies), while the Aboriginal students would be offered courses that are not accredited secondary courses with teachers that are primary-trained.

Secondly, CECs seem partly designed to help avoid the Northern Territory paying for secondary education for Aborigines even though in Australia pre-tertiary education is explicitly the responsibility of State or Territory governments. Rather, the Commonwealth is being persuaded to pay for the development of 'alternative tracks', with different goals or end-points for Aboriginal and non-Aboriginal secondary-aged students.

There are plans for eight CECs. John Boveington (Principal, Northern Territory Open College) suggested on radio (*ABC Radio*, 14 September 1988) that the CECs were 'linked to the Feppi 12 point plan, to maximize post year 7 opportunities'. Further, it is probably the case that Aboriginal parents believe they are about to get secondary schooling for their children:

> Interviewer: What do you think Aborigines expect of CECs?
> Boveington: Equality of opportunity is the main message. (*ABC Radio*, 14 September 1988)

There are about eighty schools in predominantly Aboriginal communities in the Northern Territory, about thirty of them relatively large schools, with enrolments of between fifty and 400 students. One cannot help wondering about the other schools. Would it be more equitable to look at creating area schools

(Transition to Year 10) in the larger communities as is the norm in predominantly non-Aboriginal communities? Area schools exist in a number of larger, mainly non-Aboriginal communities. For instance, Jabiru School, with an enrolment of about 300 primary students and seventy secondary students, is an area school; and Alyangula with 211 primary students and forty-two secondary students is an area school.

However, relatively large Aboriginal community schools remain primary only (some have post-primary) or are designated Community Education Centres. For instance, Angurugu CEC, enrolment 232 students; Maningrida CEC, enrolment 366 students, Milingimbi CEC, 344 students, Oenpelli Primary School, 280 students, Shepherdson College (Galiwin'ku CEC) 406 students, Yirrkala CEC, 295 students (Northern Territory Department of Education, *Schools Directory*, 1989).

CECs are an expensive option, the cost of which would need to be compared with providing secondary education locally. In such an exercise the cost of sending students away to boarding school would need to be accounted for. In implementing the CEC policy, primary schools' names have been changed, but as yet there is little going on in them that is substantially different from what was offered before the name change. There is a need to develop policies about the creation of area schools, using equitable criteria, including a minimum number of secondary-age students, and to develop creative approaches to distance secondary education for those students in the very small communities.

Tertiary Education

Having described the primary and secondary scene, it is not surprising to find that in the tertiary sector the relative figures for access, participation, and retention are even more dismal for Aboriginal students. Nationally, Aboriginal participation in TAFE (Technical and Further Education) and Higher Education 'is about 1/3 of the mainstream figures' (*The Hughes Report*, 1988, p. 8).

Given the situation in primary and secondary education it should again come as no surprise to find that in the Northern Territory University (NTU) only 1.8 per cent of the Higher Education student body is Aboriginal (*ABC Radio*, Peg Havnen, Head of Aboriginal Task Force, NTU, 21 October 1988). Havnen suggested the aim should be to achieve broad equity in educational outcomes by the year 2000. Meeting the goal will be dependent upon improvements at NTU, in addition to improvements in the primary and secondary sectors. The other main provider of Technical and Further Education (TAFE) and Higher Education, Batchelor College, has been successful in developing a range of innovative, nationally accredited courses, using a mixture of delivery models, including that of studying at home with local support. However, even combining the current student intakes at NTU and Batchelor would not substantially alter the overall Northern Territory picture.

Institutional Racism

There is enough evidence in the data presented so far to convince us of the reality of structural inequality in terms of access, participation and retention rates. In contemporary western societies, factors such as class, ethnicity, language, and gender form the basis of the unequal distribution of knowledge, which determines differential access to power. As argued in earlier sections of this chapter, inequality is a function of dominant/dominated group power relations, manifested and maintained equally through both technicist and progressivist discourses.

Turning now to some of the specific mechanisms that perpetuate inequality, what are the policies and practices that can be said to contribute to inequality of outcome, and are the outcomes documentable as manifestations of institutional racism? In this respect, some considerations about institutional racism are in order. The *Harvard Educational Review* recently devoted a volume to issues of Black Americans (1988). In the introduction to that volume, the Advisory Board felt it necessary to explain why the volume focused on these issues. They argued that there was a new mythology, which 'postulates the death of racism' and that in 1980s double-speak we now use the notion of 'at-risk, which serves to mask the concept of race'. Echoing the voices of the 1960s they suggested we should stop talking about 'dropout rates' and begin to talk about 'the failure of schools' (1988, p. v).

The articles in that volume described and analyzed many manifestations of overt and covert institutional racism. The issue of race and racism is still with us despite the rhetoric of a 'multicultural Australia' and pride in the ethnic diversity of the Northern Territory and Australia generally. It is the metaphor of a 'web' of institutional racism that best suits the Northern Territory situation: while we can rationalize our way out of each part of the picture, when we put something close to the whole picture together, it becomes clear that the patterned distribution of 'life chances' is not random. If we were to add information about the relative position of Aborigines with regard to health, housing, employment and so on, there is no doubt that the 'web' would be strengthened rather than weakened. One definition of institutional racism used in England states that it is:

> a web of discriminatory policies, practices and procedures whose consequence is that black people have poorer jobs, health, housing, education and life chances than do the white majority and less influence on the political and economic decisions which affect their lives. (*ILEA Policy for Equality*, in Jeffcoate, 1985, p. 55)

Two Australian commentators put it this way:

> Institutional racism refers to a pattern of distribution of social goods, including power, which regularly and systematically advantages some ethnic and racial groups and disadvantages others. It operates through key institutions . . . [for example] the education system. (Chambers and Pettman, 1986, p. 7)

The web of policies and practices are manifest in the differential distribution of access to valued goods, services and life chances — what Bacchi has described as 'differential social location' (Bacchi, 1989). Cowlishaw described in these terms:

> The existence of racism does not depend on expressed hostility but on the consequences of actions and beliefs. Further the actions and beliefs of

individuals need to be seen as a part of a series of processes whereby racial inequality is structured into the whole social matrix. (1988, p. 6)

So racism exists on at least two levels, individual and social. It can be intentional or unintentional, overt or covert. Cummins (1989) has traced the history of racist educational policies and practices in the USA and Canada, arguing, for instance, that Canada had a history of racism, and that under the 'veneer of multicultural-ism today very little has changed'. In fact the kind of multiculturalism that considers racism as primarily an individual pathology, working on affective change at the level of the individual, rather than as a set of social/historical processes, can mask or even exacerbate existing inequalities (Kalantzis and Cope, 1984, p. 4).

Cummins (1989) suggested that racism has become covert rather than overt and that there was thus a growing disjunction between rhetoric and reality. What he called the 'disabling structures' had remained intact. Cummins used as American examples the public debate (backlash) raging about bilingual education; and the re-appearance of minority children in classes for the mentally disabled, once their over-representation in classes for the retarded was challenged. He suggested we needed to look at the 'entire context of the school's relationships with the community'. This implies change would need to be more group than individual oriented. He argued that:

> groups that tend to experience the most pronounced education failure are those that have historically experienced a pattern of subjugation to the dominant group, over generations . . . the relationship between the majority and minority group is one which historically has led to an ambivalent and insecure identity among native minorities. (Cummins, 1989)

The rhetoric about Aboriginal Education in the Northern Territory is often accepted at face value. Recently the Northern Territory Minister for Education, Tom Harris, suggested the Northern Territory 'led the way' in Aboriginal education and that the 'real issues are poor nutrition, . . . drinking . . . not a matter of lacking in what we are providing' (*ABC Radio*, 5 May 1989).

Once again the rhetoric ascribes or invites the ascription of blame onto 'endemic' long-term features of Aboriginal culture (poverty, drunkenness, going bush) such that government policies remain unchallenged. This quotation provides us with an illustration of 'blaming the victims' which is characteristic of the ideology of racism. While there are some positive policies such as bicultural education, there is still a wide gap between the policies and the practices. For instance, most Northern Territory Aboriginal students are not in bilingual/bicultural programmes. The programmes that do exist are always precariously resourced and staffed.

Most innovations in Aboriginal education in the Northern Territory have been either community or federally driven, and have achieved results despite the Territory government, not because of it. Bilingual education was foisted onto a reluctant Northern Territory Administration in 1972. As the bilingual pro-gramme developed, it became bicultural as well as bilingual, reflecting changes from assimilationist policies of the past. S. Harris described bicultural education as:

the teaching of two ways of life. A Bicultural school is one where at all levels, the Aboriginal to non-Aboriginal staff ratios, classroom subject content, languages of instruction, teaching styles and sources of decision making, significantly represent both cultures. (1978, p. 1)

This quote has the seeds of contemporary thinking by Aboriginal educators concerning 'Two Way' or 'Both Way' education. However, the point is that while the current developments in Aboriginal education are exciting, they are usually not led in any sense by the current Northern Territory Government; consequently their funding support is uncertain and their futures are precarious.

The Northern Territory Education Minister is, at the time of writing, under-taking 'a major review' of Aboriginal Education, which is of course laudable, given the extent of educational inequality (*Education NT*, 1989, p. 1). Feppi had input into the *Hughes Report*. The next step may be the development of federal and territory policies to implement changes, both of course dependent on the will to allocate funds and examine current discriminatory practices. However, that will does not appear unequivocal in official discourse. In the same issue of *Education NT* (1989, p. 8) there was an article that made the claim with regard to excellence, that 'the opportunity is certainly there for all students'.

Consider the recent policy document *Towards the Nineties* (1988). The policy direction set by this document did not address equity issues at all. Indeed it did not even acknowledge the cultural and linguistic diversity of the Northern Terri-tory population, except by reference to the earlier policy document, *Direction for the Eighties* (1983), which 'expected that the education system . . . provide educational opportunities for all Territorians' and 'meet the special needs resulting from isolation or language barriers' (1988, p. 5). *Towards the Nineties* focused on 'excellence' as its main ideological platform. While at the rhetorical level 'excel-lence' was emphasized, at the same time the Northern Territory Department of Education was making cuts to bilingual schools staffing, and ESL provisions. The document certainly represented policies that were a long way from the equity recommendations that later came from the *Hughes Report*.

I now turn to some specific examples of discriminatory policy. One example, is the current policy of staffing schools. Staffing is 'adjusted' according to a formula which discriminates against community schools with poor attend-ance. This has the effect of understaffing the community schools, while also 'blaming the victims' for the different level of resources. Aboriginal attendance averaged 71 per cent in 1985. The Minister for Education, Tom Harris, recently argued [in relation to a particular bush school with 150 students and four staff]:

Harris: I would query the actual number of children . . . there's a wide difference between attendance and enrolment.
Interviewer: So what you're saying is you're going to staff the school on attendance. Doesn't that preclude those children from attending?
Harris: You can't staff schools on enrolment. (*ABC Radio*, 5 May 1989)

While there are many rationalizations for this policy, the fact remains that it makes teaching and learning more difficult in these schools for the staff and students. Again, enforcing a separation of 'attendance' and 'enrolment' (as with 'have access' and 'go to school') permits the institutionalization of punitive measures that compound the disadvantages.

In urban schools many Aboriginal students find themselves placed in special all-Aboriginal classes (Walton, 1986). Does this practice reflect affirmative action or apartheid/segregation; the first achieving improved options, the second limiting options? In special education circles for the last ten years or so, there has been a major reassessment of minority student placement procedures. The Northern Territory's version of streaming is comparable to the American strategies, that were found to close off options for American blacks and others. For example, a study by McDermott (1978) on the inbuilt failure mechanisms operating in streamed reading classes, reported that, unconsciously, teachers systematically deprived students in the lowest stream of active engagement with reading. Another study by Rist (1970, p. 411) described 'how the school helps to reinforce the class structure of the society' by imposing subjective criteria on the stratification of children into different groups in the first few weeks of school.

The following recent interview with Tom Harris, the Northern Territory Minister for Education, indicates his interpretation of 'affirmative action' measures being sought by some Aboriginal groups by way of independent Aboriginal schools. If the local schools were perceived by Aboriginal parents to be adequately meeting the needs of their children, no doubt the push for independent schools would not have emerged.

Interviewer: You have also said Federal Government policies in this area are creating racial disharmony.

Harris: Well I say that, not to take away from those people who really do have good intentions in setting up Aboriginal schools, but the Federal Government seem to be bending their rules. For example they're looking at establishing a school in Tennant Creek . . . there is spare capacity in the Primary School . . . it's irresponsible for the Federal Government to be talking about setting up a black school in Tennant Creek . . . it's best to have a special unit in the local school. The Northern Territory government is about integration, not segregation.

Interviewer: Are you opposed generally to Aboriginal schools?

Harris: I'm opposed to having separate schools . . .

Interviewer: But these schools are being established following a demand by these communities themselves?

Harris: It's not a demand generally . . .

Interviewer: Yipirinya was though . . .

Harris: Yipirinya was set up to look after the town camps. (*ABC Radio*, 8 June 1989)

Harris' discourse highlights a number of issues that have been developed in this discussion: He misrepresented affirmative action as apartheid, appropriating 'racial harmony' and 'integration' along the way; his argument is based on the 'choice', as in earlier discussions, apparently expressed by Aboriginal parents (via the interviewer), who have shown their preference for an independent school.

To conclude this discussion, this examination of educational and, more specifically, literacy policy and practices illustrates the nexus between practices and the maintenance of those legitimizing discourses that serve to maintain relationships of power. By examining pedagogies, based on both technicist and progressivist discourses, it has suggested both are flawed as they ignore or mask the social, political, and ideological contexts of literacy learning and teaching. Considering a range of particular policies and practices within Aboriginal education in the Northern Territory, it is evident that institutional racism and invisible pedagogies are a powerful combination in maintaining inequality.

In terms of pedagogy, there are alternatives emerging in the form of various interpretations of critical social literacy. One of the strengths of such alternatives is the importance placed on understanding literacy teaching and learning in context, thus avoiding ethnocentric naturalizing and universalist discourses, which are features of progressivist pedagogy serving to affirm existing power relationships.

References

ABC Radio, Annie Warburton and Senator Bob Collins (14 September 1988) *'How many are missing out?' Response to Bill Baird's evidence to the House of Representatives Standing Committee on Aboriginal Affairs*, Darwin.

ABC Radio, Peg Havnen and Clare Collier (21 October 1988) *About NAEC Report (Hughes Report)*, Darwin.

ABC Radio, John Boveington (Northern Territory Department of Education) and John Loizou, (14 September 1988) *About CECs*, Darwin.

ABC Radio, Gerry Gannon and Tom Harris (Northern Territory Education Minister) (8 June, 1989) *Referring to the Federal Government grant to investigate the numbers of Northern Territory Aboriginal children without access to school*, Darwin.

Atkinson, P. (1985) *Language, Structure and Reproduction: An Introduction to the Sociology of Basil Bernstein*, London, Methuen.

Australian Bureau of Statistics and North Australian Research Unit (1989) *A Social Atlas of Darwin: 1986 Census*, Darwin.

Bacchi, C. (1989) *Do Women Need Equal Treatment or Different Treatment?* Paper presented at the Northern Territory University, Darwin.

Baker, C. and Freebody, P. (1989) 'Talk around text: Constructions of textual and teacher authority in classroom discourse', in De Castell, S., Luke, A. and Luke, C. (Eds) *Language, Authority and Criticism: Readings on the School Textbook*, London, Falmer Press, pp. 284–90.

Baker, C. and Luke, A. (1990, 1991) 'Chapter 11 postscript: Discourses and practices', in Luke, A. and Baker, C. (Eds) *Towards a Critical Sociology of Reading Pedagogy*, Amsterdam, John Benjamins.

Baratz, S. and Baratz, J. (1970) 'Early childhood intervention: the social science base of institutional racism', *Harvard Education Review*, **40**, 1, pp. 29–49.

Bourdieu, P. and Passeron, J-C. (1977) *Reproduction: In Education, Society and Culture*, London, Sage Publications.

Bruner, J. (1986) *Actual Minds, Possible Worlds*, Cambridge, MA, Harvard University Press.

Cambourne, B. (1985) 'Change and conflict in literacy education: What it's all about', *Australian Journal of Reading*, **8**, 2, pp. 77–87.

Chambers, B. and Pettman, J. (1986) *Anti-Racism: A Handbook for Adult Educators*, Human Rights Commission Education Series, No 1, Canberra, AGPS.

CHRISTIE, M. (1984) 'The Classroom World of the Aboriginal Child', Unpublished PhD thesis, University of Queensland.

CHRISTIE, M. (1985) *Aboriginal Perspectives on Experience and Learning: The Role of Language in Aboriginal Education*, Geelong, Deakin University Press.

COPE, B. (1985) *The Reality of a Term: 'Racism' in Social Analysis*, Social Literacy Monograph 19, Stanmore, Social Literacy.

COPE, B. (1987) *Traditional Versus Progressivist Pedagogy*, Social Literacy Monograph 11, Stanmore, Social Literacy.

COPE, B. (1988) *Facing the Challenge of Back to the Basics: An Historical Perspective*, Social Literacy Monograph 28, Stanmore, Social Literacy.

COWLISHAW, G. (1988) *Black, White or Brindle: Race in Rural Australia*, Cambridge, Cambridge University Press.

CRAWFORD, A. (1989) Personal communication.

CUMMINS, J. (1984) *Bilingualism and Special Education: Issues in Assessment and Pedagogy*, San Diego, College Hill Press.

CUMMINS, J. (1986) 'Empowering minority students: A framework for intervention', *Harvard Educational Review*, **56**, 1, pp. 18–37.

CUMMINS, J. (1989) *Language Teaching for Student Empowerment and Social Justice*, (From notes taken.) Plenary address, ATESOL Conference, Sydney.

DAWKINS, J. (1989) *Research in Australia: Higher Education's Contribution*, Canberra, AGPS.

DELPIT, L. (1988) 'The silenced dialogue: Power and pedagogy in educating other people's children', *Harvard Educational Review*, **58**, 3, pp. 280–298.

DEPARTMENT OF EMPLOYMENT, EDUCATION AND TRAINING (1988) *Report of the Aboriginal Education Policy Task Force*, Canberra, Department of Employment, Education and Training ('The Hughes Report').

DEPARTMENT OF EMPLOYMENT, EDUCATION AND TRAINING (1989) *National Aboriginal and Torres Strait Islander Education Policy*, Canberra, Department of Employment, Education and Training.

EISENSTEIN, H. (1984) *Contemporary Feminist Thought*, Great Britain, Unwin Paperbacks.

FAIRCLOUGH, N. (1989) *Language and Power*, London, Longman.

FREEBODY, P., LUKE, A. and GILBERT, P. (1991) 'Reading position and practices in the classroom', *Curriculum Inquiry*, **21**, pp. 455–77.

FREIRE, P. and MACEDO, D. (1988) *Literacy, Reading the Word and the World*, London, Routledge and Kegan Paul.

GILBERT, P. (1989) *Writing, Schooling and Deconstruction: From Voice to Text in the Classroom*, London, Routledge and Kegan Paul.

GIROUX, H. (1981) *Ideology, Culture and the Process of Schooling*, London, Falmer Press.

GRAFF, H. (1979) *The Literacy Myth*, New York, Academic Press.

GRAFF, H. (1986) 'The legacies of literacy: Continuities and contradictions in Western society and culture', in DE CASTELL, S., LUKE, A. and EGAN, K. (Eds) *Literacy, Society and Schooling: A Reader*, Cambridge, Cambridge University Press.

GRAY, B. (1985) 'Teaching oral language', in CHRISTIE, M. *Aboriginal Perspectives on Experience and Learning: The Role of Language in Aboriginal Education*, Geelong, Deakin University Press.

GRAY, B. (1987) 'How natural is "natural" language teaching — Employing holistic methodology in the classroom', *Australian Journal of Early Childhood*, **12**, 4, pp. 3–19.

HARRIS, J. (1979) *Ethnoscience and its Relevance for Education in Aboriginal Communities*, Unpublished PhD thesis, University of Queensland.

HARRIS, S. (1978) *Traditional Aboriginal Education Strategies and their Possible Place in a Modern Bicultural School*, Keynote address, Third National Conference of Teachers of Aboriginal Children, Darwin, Northern Territory.

HARRIS, S. (1980) 'Culture and Learning: Tradition and Education in North-east Arnhem Land', Abridged PhD dissertation. Darwin, Northern Territory Department of Education.

HARVARD EDUCATIONAL REVIEW ADVISORY BOARD (1988) 'Introduction', *Harvard Educational Review*, **58**, 3, pp. v–vii.

HOUSE OF REPRESENTATIVES COMMITTEE ON ABORIGINAL AFFAIRS (1987) *Return to Country: The Aboriginal Homelands Movement in Australia* Report of the House of Representatives Standing Committee on Aboriginal Affairs. Canberra, AGPS.

JEFFCOATE, R. (1985) 'Anti-racism as an educational ideology', in ARNOT, M. (Ed.) *Race and Gender: Equal Opportunities Policies in Education*, Oxford, Pergamon Press and the Open University.

KALANTZIS, M. and COPE, B. (1984) *Head or Heart? Strategies for Combating Racism*, Social Literacy Monograph No 9, Stanmore, Common Ground.

KALANTZIS, M. and COPE, B. (1987) *Social Literacy: An Overview*, Stanmore, Common Ground.

KRESS, G. (1988) 'Barely the basics? New directions in writing', *Education Australia*, **1**, pp. 12–5.

LO BIANCO, J. (1987) *National Policy on Languages*, Canberra, AGPS.

LUKE, A. (1989) 'Literacy as curriculum: Historical and sociological perspectives', *Language, Learning and Literacy*, **1**, 2, pp. 1–17.

LUKE, A., BATY, A. and STEHBENS, C. (1989) '"Natural" conditions for language learning: A critique', *English in Australia*, **89**, pp. 36–49.

MARTIN, J., WIGNELL, P., EGGINS, S. and ROTHERY, J. (1986) *Secret English: Jargon and Bullshit in a Secondary School*, Plenary address, Language in Education Conference, Macquarie University, Sydney.

MARTIN, J. (1987) *Language and Control: Fighting With Words*, Plenary address, Cross-Cultural Issues in Educational Linguistics Conference, Batchelor College, Northern Territory.

MASSEY, G., SCOTT, M. and DORNBUSCH, S. (1975) 'Racism without racists: Institutional racism in urban schools', *The Black Scholar*, **7**, 3, pp. 2–11.

McDERMOTT, R.P. and ARON, J. (1978) 'In the classroom: On the possibility of equal education opportunity in American culture', in REYNOLDS, M. (Ed.) *Futures of Education for Exceptional Students: Emerging Structures*, Reston, VA, CEC.

NORTHERN TERRITORY DEPARTMENT OF EDUCATION (1983) *Direction for the Eighties*, Darwin, Northern Territory.

NORTHERN TERRITORY DEPARTMENT OF EDUCATION (1983) *Information Statement No 6. Strategies for Improving the Academic Performance of Aboriginal Students in Primary and Secondary Education*, Darwin, Northern Territory.

NORTHERN TERRITORY DEPARTMENT OF EDUCATION (1986) *Feppi's 12 Point Plan*, Darwin, Northern Territory.

NORTHERN TERRITORY DEPARTMENT OF EDUCATION (1988) *Towards the Nineties, Volume 2*, Darwin, Northern Territory.

NORTHERN TERRITORY DEPARTMENT OF EDUCATION (1989) 'Spotlighting Aboriginal education', *Education NT*, Darwin, Northern Territory, Community Relations Unit.

NORTHERN TERRITORY DEPARTMENT OF EDUCATION (1989) *Schools Directory*, Darwin, Northern, Territory, Community Relations Unit.

OLSON, D. (1977) 'The languages of instruction: On the literate bias of schooling', in ANDERSON, R., SPIRO, R. and MONTAGUE, W. (Eds) *Schooling and the Acquisition of Knowledge*, New Jersey, Lawrence Erlbaum Associates, pp. 65–90.

PENALOSA, F. (1981) *Introduction to the Sociology of Language*, Massachusetts, Newbury House.

REPORT OF THE HOUSE OF REPRESENTATIVES SELECT COMMITTEE ON ABORIGINAL EDUCATION (1985) Canberra, AGPS.

RIST, R. (1970) 'Student social class and teacher expectations: The self-fulfilling prophecy in ghetto education', *Harvard Education Review*, **40**, 3, pp. 411–51.

SCRIBNER, S. and COLE, M. (1981) *The Psychology of Literacy*, Cambridge, MA, Harvard University Press.

TYLER, W. (1988) *School Organization: A Sociological Perspective*, London, Croom Helm.

WALTON, C. (1986) 'Aboriginal Children Learning to Write: Kriol and Warlpiri Speakers in an English-Speaking Classroom', unpublished MEd thesis, University of New England, Armidale.

WALTON, C. (1987) 'Learning to write: A case study', *The Aboriginal Child at School*, **15**, 5, pp. 3–32.

WAX, M. (1973) 'Cultural deprivation as an educational ideology', in BENTLEY, R. and CRAWFORD, S. (Eds) *Black Language Reader*, England, Scott Foresman.

Chapter 5

Rights and Expectations in an Age of 'Debt Crisis': Literacy and Integral Human Development in Papua New Guinea

Naihuwo Ahai and Nicholas Faraclas

To analyze the discourses surrounding 'solutions to the problem of illiteracy' in Papua New Guinea (PNG), it is necessary first to understand the contexts and causes of illiteracy — the economic, social, and political features of neo-colonialism in PNG, and the failure of an education system that is both founded upon and consistently undermined by these features. In many industrialized countries, the 'blame the schools' and the accompanying 'back to basics' rhetoric concerning literacy standards have served to divert attention from underlying political, social and economic problems, and to buttress regressive social and economic orders. Issues that underlie 'the illiteracy problem' in PNG are social, economic, and political; education systems do not exist in isolation, but are themselves a manifestation of and an instrument used to perpetuate those systems. In the case of PNG, the education system plays such a vital role in creating and maintaining neocolonialist domination that it must serve as a major focus of critical debate and radical reconstruction before the more specific issue of literacy can be addressed in any meaningful way.

The education system in PNG, through its enforcement of the 'English Only Policy', the levying of school fees, and the use of 'eliminatory' examinations, has managed to produce for the neocolonialist system the two classes upon which it thrives: a very large number of losers or 'School Leavers' ('pushouts' — who are alienated and powerless in the context of industrial society) and a very small number of winners or 'Elites' (graduates, who are alienated but powerful in the context of industrial society). In overview, the pattern of participation in PNG looks like this: 34 per cent of school-aged children never attend school in the first place. These children usually grow up to become 'well-adjusted' community members in villages that are marginal to the 'modern' economy. Of the remaining 66 per cent, less than 25 per cent will attend high school (Grades 7–10) and less than 17 per cent will complete Grade 10, the minimum legal gradet which students may leave school in most industrialized countries.

Icons of the Products of the Educational System

The products of the PNG education system are popularly conceived of in terms of images or icons. The many who fail in school are usually dissatisfied with traditional life and often leave their villages to become plantation workers or low-skilled wage earners (Icon Number One: the School Leavers). Many find themselves among the unemployed, some of whom make their living illegally (Icon Number Two: the Rascals). Because so few Papua New Guineans are given the opportunity to get a formal education, vast numbers of expatriate skilled labourers, professionals, business-people, and consultants are imported into PNG at an astronomical cost to the PNG Government (Icon Number Three: the Experts). The few Papua New Guineans who do graduate usually join the small and relatively privileged group of indigenous business-people, professionals, and senior public servants (Icon Number Four: the Elites). Each of these icons has the force of a guiding myth in educational discourse in PNG, and thus each deserves some elaboration.

Icon Number One: The 'School Leaver'

In PNG society, the 'School Leaver' is typically a young person in a rural area who has had some formal schooling but has 'left' school because he or she couldn't cope with the English Only curriculum or the eliminatory examinations, or because his or her parents could not find a classroom space and/or could not afford to pay school fees. School Leavers are often viewed as misfits who have learned neither the skills that they need for well-paid work in the towns nor the skills that they need for work in the village. Because they cannot survive in the industrial economy and because they often lack the desire and the skills needed to contribute to the traditional economy, they are seen, and often see themselves, to be 'useless' individuals, who represent a bad investment of their parents' hard-earned school fee monies.

In a few years' time, if not already, School Leavers will constitute the majority of the population of PNG. For most of these school leavers or 'pushouts', school has been an experience of progressive alienation from their traditional way of life. We prefer the term 'pushout' to 'dropout' because the former term appropriately allocates the agency for the phenomenon. In place of this traditional way of life, little in the way of skill-acquisition has been provided that might help the student to cope with the industrialized society for which the school has simply whetted the appetite.

Despite the newly adopted National Language and Literacy Policy (described below), the great majority of school students in PNG are still expected to learn to read and write in a language that most of them do not know in its oral form — English. Attempts by teachers and students to use languages with which the students are familiar — to lessen the confusion resulting from giving lessons in English — have been and continue to be vigorously repressed. Confusion builds on confusion and the toll is devastating, both in terms of rates of school leaving and declining standards for the few who manage to continue. Parents' inability to find classroom spaces or to pay school fees for their children, which may amount to over 50 per cent of their earnings, and students' inability to pass eliminatory examinations in Grades 6 and 10 make it impossible for some of even that group of students who have managed to cope with the English Only curriculum to stay on.

Along with English language comes European culture. Students see Europeans in the pictures in their school-books, and they learn about European culture, history, science, and literature. Although the use of English in schools makes it almost impossible for most students to learn much of the content of their lessons, one lesson comes through loud and clear: European language, culture, and way of life are superior to Papua New Guinean languages, cultures, and ways of life. Very few primary school students in PNG can read or write or achieve basic mathematics with confidence, but nearly all of them have cultivated a taste for European culture, European dress, European food, 'town life', and a corresponding distaste for their own culture and village life.

When they are finally pushed out of primary school the great majority of PNG students lack both the skills needed to do town work and the desire and many of the skills needed to do village work. Defeated and frustrated, many 'pushouts' stay on in the rural areas, trying to integrate themselves into traditional life or just hanging on as perpetual misfits. Others travel out to find low-paid wage work. Some, however, join the ranks of the Rascals.

Icons Number Two and Three: The 'Rascal' and The 'Expert'

In PNG society, a 'Rascal' is typically a young School Leaver who has turned to criminal activities to make enough money to survive in town and enjoy what is euphemistically called 'town life' — a life largely imported from Europe, and characterized by such activities as drinking beer, driving an automobile, and gambling. Rascals are perhaps the most despised members of PNG society and they are the target of constant and intense criticism and invective in the media as well as in common conversation; it is the Rascals who are deemed to have caused the 'law and order problem' or 'law and order crisis' in PNG.

The crime rate in PNG is not nearly as great as in the United States, Europe, or Australia, yet the international media and international agencies have characterized PNG as one of the most dangerous and crime-ridden countries in the region. What makes the 'law and order problem' in PNG so much more unacceptable to expatriates in PNG than the more serious law and order problems in their own countries? Why are Papua New Guinean Rascals so much more dangerous than Australian, American, or European criminals?

'Racism' is perhaps one obvious and justified answer to these questions, but a careful analysis of the economic realities reveals that the basis for rascalism in PNG is quite different from that of criminality in, for example, Australia or the US. The average Papua New Guinean does not yet believe, as do the average Australian and American, that the few deserve to have most of society's resources under their control, while the great majority have little or no power over those resources. When this strong sense of justice and equality is confronted by the extreme inequalities and injustices produced by the economics of neocolonialism and the neocolonial education system, Rascalism becomes not only understandable but may even be considered 'positive social action'.

An illustration is in order here to support this claim — an archetypal narrative icon to be deconstructed, but also a genuine case: a security guard works twelve hours a day, ten days on and four days off every fortnight to protect the tenants of one of the luxury apartment buildings in Port Moresby against intrusions by Rascals. The tenants of this building include an Australian 'Expert' who has been hired by the PNG Government to help solve the 'law and order problem' in PNG. The Government pays over K1,000 per week (in 1990, 1 PNG Kina roughly equals 1 US Dollar) for the rental of the Expert's apartment, as well as K600 per month for the Expert to send his three children to private schools. The Expert also receives a salary of K2,000 per week plus paid home leave, with air tickets, for himself, his wife, and his children. The Expert enjoys a much higher standard of living in PNG, often including luxury automobile, maid service, yacht club membership, than he would in Australia, where he might not have been able to find work at all.

Despite the long hours and the risk of being attacked by Rascals on the job, the security guard's salary of K72 per week is not enough to pay even the least expensive private rental, which averages about K100 per week in Port Moresby and the other major towns of PNG. Such rental costs are indeed themselves related to the large numbers of well-paid expatriates competing for limited housing with Papua New Guineans. The security guard therefore lives in an illegal settlement house made of bits of timber, tarpaulin, and discarded building materials with his wife and three children. He finds it nearly impossible to find places for his children in the government primary schools and to save the K150.00 each year that it costs to pay his children's school fees. The number of available places in government schools and hospitals has been reduced and the school fees and medical fees have been increased as part of the International Monetary Fund/World Bank (IMF/WB) 'restructuring' package imposed on PNG to deal with the 'debt crisis'. As his eldest son completes Grade 6, there is no money to pay the even more expensive high school fees.

The security guard's son goes out to find work, but there are no jobs, since the IMF/WB imposed cuts have caused extensive retrenchments in the public sector, with ripple effects into the private sector. There are relatively well-paid jobs in the Defence Force, but many soldiers are, at this time, engaged in battles against fellow Papua New Guineans in order to protect the interests of an Australian-owned mining company in Bougainville. The son disappears for some time but is later found beaten to death by security guards who caught him trying to steal an expatriate Expert's automobile.

Rascals are often the School Leavers who refuse to define their condition in terms of defeat and frustration. They are the ones who are not willing to become security guards, work long hours, and live in distress and without hope for their children so that an expatriate can be sure that his or her automobile will be in the garage the next morning to take his or her children to private school at the PNG government's expense. Their sense of justice and equality is too strong, to allow them to accept this state of affairs.

Rascalism is one of the most dramatic expressions of the threat that a country like PNG, where most of the land is still communally owned by the people, poses to the neocolonial order. This is why the 'Rascal problem' and the 'law and order problem' are constantly being discussed and deplored in the media and among expatriates. This is also why Port Moresby is alive with expatriate Experts from the most lawless countries in the world who have been hired by the PNG government to solve the 'law and order problem' in PNG.

Icon Number Four: The 'Elite'

The 'Elites' are typically the few people who manage to graduate from the PNG education system. Their success is often due either to the fact that they come from one of the few homes where English is commonly used in everyday activities, or to the fact that they were willing to so thoroughly reject their own culture and so thoroughly adopt European culture that they were able to succeed against all odds in a European education system. The Elites may be thought to be the winners in the system, and take on the highest-paying jobs available to Papua New Guineans, usually alongside expatriates who are making double or triple the salary for the same work.

In a fundamental way, however, the Elites are the biggest losers of all. They are completely alienated from their languages, their cultures, their people, and themselves. Most Papua New Guineans live with the security of guaranteed work, housing, and food on their traditional lands. This sense of security and identity, long lost by the peoples of Europe and the industrialized countries of the world through a long history of expropriation and exploitation, is the basis for the considerable power that the people of PNG have compared to their counterparts in other countries, both industrialized and non-industrialized. The Elites in PNG pay the highest price possible for their 'success' — the complete loss of their traditional cultural-economic power base.

Elites are often reluctant to return to their villages, because they are ashamed of their inability to speak the languages of their origin or to participate in traditional ways of living. Elites are not so reluctant, however, to enter into deals with plantation owners or with international logging and mining companies to sell their traditional lands, often without the informed consent of their own blood relatives still living on these lands. The alienation of the Elites is so complete that many are willing to sell the present and future well-being of their immediate and extended families for the possibility of securing the trappings of affluent European society.

The Discourses Surrounding Literacy in PNG: Technicism Versus Integral Human Development

There are two major competing discourses concerning literacy work in PNG today. One may be termed a 'technicist' discourse, a variant of the 'back to basics' discourse found in other countries. This discourse has been adopted by many of the governmental and non-governmental agencies traditionally engaged in literacy work in PNG over the past century. Despite the efforts of these agencies, the literacy rate in PNG remains one of the lowest in the Asian Pacific region and the education system remains fragmented and incoherent. The discourse that has recently come to contest the field of literacy in PNG has thus far defined itself in terms of 'Integral Human Development', a form of words enshrined in one of the goals of the Constitution of PNG, and the fundamental principle upon which the Government's Official Philosophy of Education, formulated by Sir Palias Matane (1986), is currently based.

The discourse of Integral Human Development as it relates to literacy in PNG is related but not equivalent to the discourse of 'empowerment through literacy' developed in countries such as Nicaragua and Cuba. Empowerment discourse arose to challenge the conditions of people who were powerless and dispossessed. Conditions of comparable distress are not yet evident in PNG, but economic circumstances appear to be changing for the worse at a rapid rate. For example, while IMF/WB consultants are recommending and indeed forcing cutbacks in health and education services, they are engaging in substantial investment in so-called 'Land Mobilization Schemes', which involve, among other measures, land registration programmes, making it possible for traditional lands to be delineated, taxed, bought, and sold. Extensive expropriation has not yet occurred in PNG, a fact that makes effective exploitation of labour at neocolonial wage rates difficult. This may explain why 'Land Mobilization Schemes' are being given top priority by the IMF/WB consultants, along with increased development of defence and police forces, which will be needed to contain the inevitable popular reaction against the expropriation scheme.

These two competing discourses of literacy — Integral Human Development versus Technicism — imply distinctive forms of literacy. These in turn have their distinctive relationships with or correspondences to the larger discourses that embed PNG culture in the world economy. Our position is that they are not merely contesting theories of learning to read and write but rather embody nothing less than contesting positions on the issue of material and cultural control — on the one hand a drive to preserve and develop democratic power bases and structures, and on the other a drive to deprive the people of the sources of their present identity and power: their land, their control over their means of production and reproduction, their traditional economic bases, and their languages.

So, whereas in countries like Nicaragua and Cuba, literacy is viewed as a process of empowering the dispossessed in society, the discourse of Integral Human Development in PNG views literacy as a process of reinforcement and expansion of the considerable power that already lies in the hands of the great majority of Papua New Guineans, who still communally own 97 per cent of the land in the country.

By the same token, however, these differences can be exaggerated. The discourse of Integral Human Development in literacy work in PNG explicitly and forcefully asserts that, as in Nicaragua and Cuba, learning 'one's letters' is not enough, that learning how society operates and how certain groups come to be dispossessed is firmly on the agenda. But the context in PNG in which this learning takes place is radically different from those obtaining in Nicaragua or Cuba. Thus, strikingly different literatures and forms of literacy have been necessary to accommodate these differences. If there is any place on earth where the myth of a monolithic and formally-universal literacy can be dismissed at a glance, it is PNG, where 869 languages, many contrasting learning styles, and several radically different modes of literate production coexist.

Integral Human Development and the PNG Constitution

Another major distinction between PNG and other developing countries revolves around the fact that the constitutional and legislative impetus for the directing of literacy work away from the confines of the technicist approach and toward the globalism of the Integral Human Development approach is explicit. The

Constitution of PNG, in its outline of the duties of government, includes the commitment that all PNG citizens become literate first in their own 'tokples' (a term deriving from 'talk-place', and referring to any particular local indigenous language), and literate second in one of the three national languages: English, Hiri Motu, or Tok Pisin. Moreover, the five National Goals of the Constitution are an attempt to provide a set of motivating principles for work generally, including literacy work. Our position is that, were these principles fully understood and implemented by literacy workers, literacy would become more than learning to read and write, and would begin to constitute a significant factor in equitable social change. The five National Goals as stated in the PNG Constitution are:

1. Integral Human Development, rather than conventional, economically or technically driven development. Integral Human Development includes:
    a) Political Development
    b) Social Development
    c) Economic Development
    d) Spiritual Development;
2. Equality and Participation;
3. Sovereignty and Self-Reliance;
4. Protection of the Environment and Natural Resources;
5. Preservation and Development of PNG Ways.

Finally, several of the National Objectives outlined in the Constitution have a bearing on the way literacy work is conducted and the nature of materials used in literacy programmes. These include: helping people to understand the changes that are occurring in contemporary society (Objective 13, see below for further discussion); actively supporting the participation of women in social, political and economic activities (Objective 6); ensuring that basic human needs are met (Objective 16); promoting community and family self-reliance (Objective 19); reducing inequalities, especially with regard to access to land and other basic goods and services (Objective 20); and developing processes for public feedback into government decision-making by private citizens (Objective 22).

The main problem with the goals and objectives of the Constitution is that they have yet to receive the monetary and institutional support necessary for their successful realization. In fact, the social programme outlined in the goals of the constitution not only clashes with but is directly undermined by the social programmes being implemented by many companies and government agencies, especially since the arrival of the IMF/WB 'Razor Gang' (another popular icon) in PNG (while directing the PNG government to direct money into 'Land Mobilization Schemes', the police and the defence forces, IMF/WB advisors have engineered drastic cuts in health, education, and job-creation programmes for women and youth, thus earning for themselves the title 'Razor Gang' in the media). Between the onset of independence from Australia (September 1975) and June of 1989, the date that the National Language and Literacy Policy was signed, the Department of Education universally enforced the English Only Policy in direct contradiction to the Constitutional mandate for 'local language literacy first'. The National Language and Literacy Policy (discussed below) has finally given those communities that wish to do so the option of bringing their children to literacy first in their own language, but it does not and has not prevented the continuation of the English Only Policy in most classrooms around the country.

Integral Human Development and the National Philosophy of Education

In 1988 a new 'philosophy of education', formulated by Sir Palias Matane and based on the notion of Integral Human Development, was adopted as the official philosophy of the National Department of Education. At the abstract level, the document stated unequivocal support for initial literacy in local languages (pp. 12, 37), and for those literacy workers and other educators who address political, social, economic, and spiritual issues in their classes, rather than focusing narrowly on 'reading and writing' or even 'basic skills' (p. 28). Matane success-fully shattered the popular icon of education, and by extension, literacy, as the 'passport' to a good job and the 'good life', interpreted as a 'European lifestyle' in town and away from traditional village life.

Matane urged educational administrators to 'Put the last, that is, least advantaged students first'. In the areas of curriculum and standards, he proposed the following motto: 'Aim for less and do it better'. These two mottoes sum up a major contradiction, not only in Matane's position, but in the National Consti-tution itself: Matane's basic priorities are self-evidently appropriate to the PNG condition in terms of ensuring that disadvantaged groups such as women and children in remote areas have access to education (p. 3), advocating Universal Primary Education (p. 4), reducing dependence on eliminatory examinations (p. 39), and so on; but Matane can be seen to have sometimes fallen into a moral-istic trap when it comes to the implementation of his strategies. 'Aim for less' im-plies that Papua New Guineans must have been aiming 'too high'. To further add to the iconic force of this virtually content-less metaphor, its dubious assumption is echoed in National Objective 2 of the Constitution, which implies that high expectations on the part of Papua New Guineans constitute a major national problem, a point we discuss further below. Are Papua New Guineans' expecta-tions really too high? To whom might this statement be meaningful? What specifically might it be taken to mean? Whose interests are maintained or devel-oped by continued or expanded participation in the discourse of more modest goals? Most expatriate Experts, especially those from the IMF/WB Razor Gangs, participate in and proclaim this discourse, but at least in the area of education in general, and literacy in particular, there is little documentable evidence of counter-productively 'high aim' — indeed, if the metaphor is to be relentlessly pursued, it seems that the sights could be lifted dramatically.

In urging greater community contribution to education, Matane not only expected people to participate more in their own and their children's education, he also advocated an increase in school fees at the secondary level (p. 34). Did Matane really believe that Papua New Guineans' expectations are too high, when they spend major proportions of their incomes on providing primary education to their children and at the same time they see thousands of expatriate children being sent to private schools or abroad to boarding schools at their own government's expense? The travel, tuition, and boarding costs of these expatriate students and a few expatriate education consultants' salaries could probably cover the cost of school fees for much of the national cohort of primary school students. Papua New Guineans may well ask: 'How low do we have to aim in trying to secure literacy?'.

Papua New Guineans have stood by and watched their school fees being wasted and their children being systematically deprived of literacy and other skills due to an English Only Policy, yet they have held firmly to the popular belief propagated by a neocolonial administration that 'English is the only language worth studying'. They have accepted quietly the massive failure rates that have resulted from such a policy. When India became independent in 1947, one of its first acts as a sovereign state was to ban the use of English as a medium of instruction in primary schools. In 1990, this one basic step has not yet been taken in PNG, but still Papua New Guineans are being accused of expecting too much from their government and their education system.

In his work, Matane failed to conceptualize crucial socio-economic aspects to the point of writing out of the problem such central issues as school fees. Because of this, his philosophy of education, while providing an appropriate theoretical foundation for major advances in literacy work and other educational areas, is inadequate: its most gross misinterpretations appear precisely at the point of practice. This gap between progressive theories and policies on the one hand and regressive practice and implementation on the other hand is a consistent theme that characterizes literacy education in PNG.

National Language and Literacy Policy

The National Department of Education endorsed a new Language and Literacy Policy in June of 1989. This policy states that the department will encourage and support those communities that wish to: (1) start local language literacy pre-schools or convert Grade Ones into 'Local Language Year'; (2) convert Grade 1 into a Transitional or 'Bridging' Year from local language literacy to literacy in English; (3) have non-core subjects (all subjects except language, mathematics, science and social studies) taught in the local language in all primary grades; (4) promote local language and culture at the secondary or tertiary levels; (5) establish local language literacy programmes for adult men and women or adolescents.

This Language and Literacy Policy represents the first attempt by a government department in the country's independent political history to act on the constitutional mandate for universal literacy in local languages. The implementation of the policy, however, is left to the promoting agencies, who have received no substantial allocation of new resources to realize the goals of the policy. As of the time of writing, the nature of the encouragement and support promised in the policy has been less than the levels required for effective implementation. In contrast to the English Only Policy, the National Language and Literacy Policy has little or no budgetary or executive force behind it.

The Literacy And Awareness Programme

The Literacy and Awareness Program (LAP), which was approved by the government in 1990, has as its principal aim the realization of Objective 13 of the Constitution of PNG, 'to help people understand the changes occurring in contemporary PNG society and to improve their ability to maintain and enhance their awareness of and their participation in development through the improvement of basic literacy and access to development information'. Just what this statement means is not clear until the social, economic, and political contexts of its production are understood. An initial observation is that the 'people' and the 'changes' are clearly separated in this discourse — the people are not discursively positioned as the agents of these changes, in their own society, but rather as observers of the changes. We can explore further aspects of this context by posing a few key questions:

What Changes Do People Need to Understand?

The societal impact of currently rapid technological and scientific advances is more acute in the newly developing countries than in the industrialized countries. In developing countries like PNG, the technological jump experienced from about 1960 to the present has not simply been a transition from stone axes to metal axes and machetes, but has rather been a leap from stone axes to the latest computer and space-age technology. The impact of Westernization has been felt in all spheres of Papua New Guinean society.

The basis for social value and action is changing from humanized, traditional wisdom to dehumanized commodity-oriented calculations of loss and benefit. In traditional societies, for instance, the obligation to help others was an expected service whether one liked to give it or not. In modern life, there is no such obligation and a decision to do so is usually decided by a cost-benefit analysis. The Melanesian Way (Narakobi, 1980), based on co-operative and communal values gives way to individual-centred competitive attitudes through Western education, which inculcates in learners a taste for urban life — the recurrent complaint about the 'Coca-Cola culture'.

Traditional economic activity and its supporting organizations and institutions also give way to the cash-crop economy, the manufacturing industry and the depletion of the natural resources through foreign-owned mining, logging, fishing and oil ventures, which provide the traditional land owners very little in the way of lasting benefit. The outcome is that a land or sea based self-reliant economy is in the process of being transformed into an import-dependent economy.

Traditionally, the political bases of PNG society centred around tribal elders or chiefs, who exercised a 'consensus jurisdiction' over all socio-economic and political matters as an expression of their obligation towards the welfare of their society. Increasingly, this political organization has been replaced by political entities defined by foreign parameters, for example, geographic surveys, language groupings, census groupings, and even religion. Leadership is now determined by economic power, educational background and political affiliation. The larger the political organization, the more remote it becomes from the people, the more specialized its political and economic discourse, and hence the decrease in any feeling of obligation or accountability to the people.

Culturally, traditional PNG society presented an intricate set of linkages among songs, chants, and dances and the planting of crops, the harvesting of yams, the catching of fish, and the paying of homage to ancestral guardians. There were few dances that were purely of entertainment value. The current spread of electronic media and the pop-cultural contents stereotypically associated with them have little in common with the spiritual bases of traditional society; indeed the attendant values which have developed militate against and implicitly deride traditional forms of expression. Since these realities are not explicitly or implicitly challenged in any form in the language and literacy policy documents, the conclusion to be read is that the kind of societal changes that the LAP programme is going to help the people understand is essentially the eventual transformation of a Melanesian Papua New Guinean society into a society dominated by Western values.

Why do the People Need to Understand These Changes?

This question is partially answered by National Objective 13, which plays such a major role in defining the LAP. It is expected that learners will not only understand the changes but will also inform others about these changes and the reasons behind them. This maintenance and enhancement operation might be carried out by means of village seminars and discussions or by the production and use of literacy materials.

A more complete, but ominous answer to this question, however, appears once again in the form of National Objective 2, one of the less progressively oriented passages in the Constitution which sounds frighteningly similar to Matane's misguided or at least misinterpreted motto: 'Aim for less, but do it better'. Objective 2 is also cited in the official LAP documents as an objective of the programme. Objective 2 aims: 'to reduce the disparity between the expectations of families/individuals and the real prospects that they face'.

What is this disparity in expectations? And what are the real prospects that Papua New Guineans face? Again these concepts are not defined in the LAP document. However, it is clear from events in the last few years just what these so called high expectations are.

Unemployment is high and the associated law and order problems are also on the increase. People want to get paid employment to buy the imported material goods that they have recently learned to appreciate. Increasingly, landowners are asking for more compensation for their land — land that was either compulsorily acquired by the Crown or bought for a few beads, sticks of tobacco or some farming or fighting implements. Papua New Guineans are increasingly expressing the need for an equitable distribution of their resources through increased equity in logging, fishing, mining, and agricultural ventures. Is this the disparity in the expectations of the people? Is it wrong for Papua New Guineans to expect these things in their own country and out of their own land and resources? What are the real prospects that they face? Are the real prospects that they face the denial of their expectations while foreign-owned multinationals exploit the natural resources and pollute the rivers and seas?

A further answer to the question of why the people need to understand these changes can be found elsewhere in the LAP document (p. 2) where the role of LAP is said to include the function of helping people: 'to make sense of their lives . . . and feel part of development'. It is implied here that the reason why the people do not participate in development is because they do not know what is happening in their lives. The break-ins, the road-blockades, the militant activities by landowners are some manifestations of their lack of understanding and their reaction to their exclusion from 'development', or perhaps derive from their unwilling inclusion in a process that is destroying the familiar contexts of their lives.

In the absence of any clear definitions of what societal changes the LAP programme is expected to help people understand, we can conclude that the LAP envisages a form of development which includes the restrictive set of societal changes described above. Furthermore, we have little choice but to conclude that the LAP aims to ensure that the people will more readily accept these changes and offer less resistance to the type of development strategy now being pursued by the government, the companies, and the international agencies. An honest analyst is forced to come to such strong conclusions because nowhere in the policy statement is it stated, or even implied, that it is the system or the type of development that needs to be modified rather than the attitudes and thinking of the people.

The LAP policy does not define the type of development that it has in mind. However, it can be safely argued from current development activities and discussions in the media that the type of development which the LAP will be used to facilitate is the type of resource exploitation characterized by large scale transnational owned open-cut mines, clear-fell logging operations, gill net fishing fleets, and oil fields. In the agricultural sector, the type of development envisioned is that which aims to supplant small-scale farms and the traditional land tenure system, that has given virtually every Papua New Guinean a secure economic base, with large foreign or Papua New Guinean Elite owned plantations and estates.

The deployment of the defence forces by the state to crush landowner demands for fairer rewards from the Bougainville Copper Mine shows clearly the type of role in development that Papua New Guineans are increasingly being expected to play. The compulsory acquisition of traditional land by the state, announced in 1990, in spite of landowner protests, and its subsequent transfer to a foreign company for the Hides Natural Gas Project (which will provide energy for the foreign-owned and run Porgera Gold Mine) shows that government and company practices have changed little since the colonial era when the Bougainville landowners were forced from their land.

Icons of the Learner in Literacy Programmes

Icon Number Five: The Passive and Ignorant Learner

The LAP document policy constructs and problematizes a learner whose passivity and ignorance are the roots of the social disharmony between the rural populace and the agencies of the government and the private sector. These traits of passivity and ignorance are also seen as the causes of the lack of participation by the learner in the 'developmental' process.

What the LAP documents overlook is the fact that in PNG, most people do in fact understand many of the changes going on in their lives — they simply do not endorse or actively participate in these changes because they do not consider them to be in their best interests. Landowners do not simply want to be peripheral recipients of royalties but actually want to have equity in any developmental project that is to take place on their land. Furthermore, in the kind of developments that are promoted by the government and the international agencies — developments that are heavily capital-oriented and dependent on Western technology — the learners have very limited avenues for participation. Perhaps their only means of participation, besides making available their land or sea, would be to provide low-paid manual labour.

So, at work in the discourse of the LAP documents, is the strong implication that the attitudes of the learners need to be changed to conform to current developmental strategies. Further, such a paternalistic administrator-citizen relationship squares well with some clauses in the PNG constitution, while directly contradicting others.

Icon Number Six: The Literate 'Participant in Development'

Implied in the objectives of the LAP programme is the belief that literacy will pave the way for the people's participation in development. Literacy will certainly enable the learners to have access to new information and make them aware of what is happening around them. But it is a myth to think that literacy alone will lead to increased participation in development, let alone acceptance of developmental trends.

Newly literate subsistence farmers may not have the initial capital to put into practice the new farming skills they have acquired, partly through their access to literature on the topic, for a cash-crop venture. The banks might refuse to lend them the initial capital because they have no collateral. The efforts of literacy programmes in encouraging people's participation in development must be supported by structural changes in the economic and social institutions of the country. If these institutions continue to be of service only to the well-to-do, then literacy can do little besides add to the ever increasing population of critically aware and dissatisfied people.

Administration and Implementation of the Literacy and Awareness Programme

The Literacy and Awareness Programme suffers from the same lack of financial and executive muscle as the National Language and Literacy Policy. The LAP must restrict its activities to co-ordinating all government and non-government literacy activities and acting as an information clearing-house. The government has two administrative mechanisms for literacy, both being housed within the National Department of Education — The Literacy and Awareness Secretariat (LAS) and the Literacy Section (LS) of the Curriculum Development Division.

The LAS was created through the parliamentary endorsement of the LAP programme in February 1990 but has remained an unfunded entity and will not receive any direct funding for the foreseeable future. For part of its first year the Secretariat was staffed by only one person.

The Literacy Section has a staff of four expatriate officers and has a budget of about K230,000 (0.5 per cent of the total Education Budget). The terms of all the four officers expire at the end of 1991 and to date there are no plans to hire Papua New Guineans to understudy the expatriate officers. This is in spite of the fact that there are many qualified and experienced Papua New Guineans available.

Most government initiatives in literacy have thus far been geared toward supporting literacy activities of communities, provincial governments and non-government organizations. This is a commendable way of encouraging community involvement in literacy. The danger with such a practice is that in the name of promoting community involvement, the responsibilities of government to the people in the areas of literacy and awareness are often abdicated. Some government and missionary literacy workers who once opposed community-based approaches (because of their former distaste for a Papua New Guinean solution to 'the illiteracy problem') currently justify their lack of initiative and support for community efforts precisely because they have been 'converted' to the community-based approach, which, according to their interpretation, limits their role to an extremely passive one.

The Ideological, Social, Economic, and Political Parameters of Literacy Work

Given the social, economic, and political realities of PNG, one of the key tasks of literacy planners and implementers is to define the parameters for literacy work. Such a definition must instance and build a definition of 'development' in which Papua New Guineans are the central agents and not merely bit-players or spectators in a foreign dominated theatre.

The technicist discourse on literacy work generally avoids an explicit position on politics, society, and ideology in the name of 'objectivity' or 'neutrality'. This is in fact a posture — a public stance that works to conceal its convert position: the consistent inability of technicist literacy workers to implement the constitutional mandate for literacy, the Philosophy of Education, the Language and Literacy Policy, and the Literacy and Awareness Programme graphically illustrates the fact that those who fail to define the ideological, political, social, and economic parameters of their work are merely allowing the prevailing ideological, social, economic, and political discourse of IMF/WB, the foreign companies, the foreign Experts, and the Papua New Guinean Elites to shape and mould their 'non-aligned' work by default.

We can expect little in the way of results for villagers and settlement dwellers from the work of the technicists. In the short term, the major beneficiaries will be foreign consultants and foreign computer and publishing operations, who will get the major share of literacy funds for the implementation of the technicists' Western oriented high-technology literacy training and materials production schemes. In the long term, the major beneficiaries will be the foreign companies and neocolonial powers who will continue to profit from the high illiteracy and school 'pushout' rates which will be perpetuated by the inevitable and functionally necessary failure of the technicists' culturally inappropriate programmes.

The discourse surrounding the Integral Human Development trend, on the other hand, contests the definition of critical parameters of literacy work and confronts the social, economic, and political features of current PNG society. This task has not been as difficult in PNG as it might have been in other developing countries, because the Constitution and the Philosophy of Education provide a strong, comprehensive, and an explicitly Melanesian framework within which to establish key definitions and parameters for literacy work that accurately build and reflect the needs and aspirations of the majority of Papua New Guineans. The definition of the ideological parameters of literacy includes explicit positions on the following issues.

Who Needs Literacy?

Obviously it is the majority rural (village) and semi-urban (settlement) sectors of the population of PNG that have the greatest need to be mobilized for literacy. They need to become literate not only as individuals but as communities within a given socio-economic context. These potential target communities are clearly identified in the LAP document.

The more public proponents and disseminators of technicist discourse have not actively engaged in the targeting of key populations for literacy work, claiming that because they advocate 'community based literacy' their help must be specifically requested by provincial governments or communities before they will commit any of their resources. The result has been that the technicists typically spend more time with consultants, politicians, and aid agency representatives than they do with villagers or settlement dwellers. When the technicists receive a request for help, it tends to come from communities where they have historical or personal ties, reinforcing the insular, individualist, if at times haphazardly applied, ideology which underpins their work.

The rhetoric developed by those working from within an Integral Human Development framework has played a major part in the development of community-based literacy programs in PNG (see Stringer and Faraclas, 1987). It seems a strange turn of events that the Integral Human Development discourse now places itself in direct opposition to technicist discourse, when the latter has only recently endorsed a community-based approach. But this ironic set of circumstances actually sheds light on a consistent illogicality in technicist discourse: the Technicists, as the nomenclature indicates, believe that the key to success in their work is attention to and perfection of the techniques of reading and writing. Fundamental principles and long term socio-cultural goals for literacy work do not form part of their professional discourse or indeed their explicit practice. In a stereotypically Western way, the 'means of transport' is all important, while the origin and the destination are ignored. When the Technicists finally adopted the community-based approach to literacy, they ignored the original reasons for the community-based approach or the eventual objectives for which the approach was formulated.

The Integral Human Development discourse explicitly problematizes the notion that community-based literacy projects are more difficult to establish and in the short term require a greater investment of time and energy by literacy workers than do non-community-based programmes. The Integral Human Development perspective has played a major role in localizing literacy expertise in PNG through programmes that take as part of the training exercise the targeting of key literacy workers and key constituencies. Rather than justifying a more passive involvement in the organization of literacy programmes, the community-based approach requires active and highly creative strategies for mobilizing communities to take control over their own programmes.

What Needs to be Done?

Statements about 'national aspirations' are often made by urbanized Expert or Elite planners with little knowledge of, or respect for, rural life or the interests of villagers and settlement dwellers. In the case of the LAP programme a conscious choice faces literacy workers. Literacy *will* transform the thinking and attitudes of the people of PNG, whether it be to accept the current lines of socio-economic and socio-cultural 'development', or to cultivate and develop the ability to transform social-economic features according to their own needs and aspirations. Is a literacy programme to address explicitly the political, social, spiritual, and economic features of its context, or are these features to be occluded by omission in the name of a mythically neutral literacy — 'just' the skills of reading and writing? These skills alone are inadequate and offer little improvement in the living standards of people if they are not accompanied by socio-economic structural change.

In the Integral Human Development schemes literacy workers are also trained to be awareness workers. They are introduced to techniques that assess the needs and aspirations of target communities before community organizing for literacy begins, so that these needs and aspirations can be incorporated into the literacy programme at every stage, including community organization, training, materials production, and maintenance classes.

Who Does the Literacy Work — Who Owns Literacy?

This is a very important issue, because if literacy is to meet accurately the needs of the people, it should be Papua New Guineans themselves who do the bulk of literacy work at all levels, from the top down. The failure to localize literacy expertise, especially at the highest levels, has been a consistent and serious flaw in most of the work carried out by (mainly Technicist) missions and non-governmental organizations in the past and by governmental organizations at present. Recently, however, significant efforts have been initiated to reverse this tendency — more Papua New Guineans are now being trained to take over literacy work. Note that by strictly Technicist criteria, comparatively few indigenous PNG people would be systematically recruited into the literacy education programme. It is only if the work is defined as essentially cultural that the criterion of indigenization becomes even relevant.

The education department, however, is dominated by a Technicist orientation and is therefore still slow in recruiting Papua New Guineans. Because of the Technicist bias, education department sponsored literacy work in PNG can still very much be said to be conducted by foreign 'Experts', especially at the highest administrative levels. This can only mean a continuation of the high rate of failure that literacy programmes have experienced in PNG over the past decades.

The question of ownership also determines responsibility, control, and participation. As such, literacy should be 'owned' and co-ordinated as much as possible by communities with strong government support in funding, training, and the provision of technical advice. The national government, through the claims central to its own discourse, has a political, legal, and moral obligation to fulfil the constitutional goal of universal literacy in all of Papua New Guinea's 869 languages. The national Department of Education is not living up to this obligation, because of its fascination with computer-developed materials which are difficult for villagers to participate in and control, and its reliance on foreign Experts, who tend to discount and overlook community members' abilities to control, participate in, and take responsibility for their own programmes.

Over 90 per cent of the resources needed for a successful literacy programme are to be found in every community in PNG. Using training techniques developed from within the discourse of Integral Human Development (Stringer and Faraclas, 1987) all literacy materials can be written and printed by community members themselves in their own language about the topics that relate to their own needs and aspirations. The discourse runs that there is no need for computers or foreign Experts; the people themselves are the world's best experts concerning their own language and their own problems and hopes in life. In contrast, the Technicists have developed and are currently developing computer generated 'shell books' with a sequence of pictures in them that are designed to 'help the people write their own stories'. The Integral Human Development trainers are showing villagers and settlement dwellers that they can create their own materials, without being forced to conform to a 'shell' picture sequence that may have been prepared by a foreign 'development' agency, such as the World Bank, a foreign mission, some of whom are controlled by fundamentalists with a 'New Right' agenda, or a foreign company looking for new markets or cheap labour.

How to do Literacy Work?

One of the more cruel ironies in this scenario concerns the technical efficacy of Technicist literacy programmes. It would, of course, be expected that at the least some substantial technical strides in their reading and writing would be made by people tutored under a Technicist regime. But the inability of Technicist discourse to theorize the political, social, economic, and spiritual features of PNG society render all aspects of their work, including their carefully designed techniques for teaching the mechanics of reading and writing, ineffectual because of their substantive and methodological inappropriateness to the PNG context. In fact, the Technicists have adopted over the period of the last few years a set of methodologies for literacy teaching (in particular, the Multistrategy Method, see Stringer and Faraclas, 1987) which was originally developed and popularized by instructors working from within an Integral Human Development framework. A similar conversion has yet to be made in the area of training, however, and it is here that the approach retains its debilitating features.

Training as Praxis: Juxtaposing Technicist and Integral Human Development

Consistent with some traditional Western educational models, Technicist discourse as it has been applied to literacy in PNG has as one of its key features the cutting up and dividing of training courses into separate pieces: this course for teaching adults, that one for teaching children, this course for materials production, that one for planning, and so on. This relentlessly analytic conceptual strategy has had the effect of preventing Melanesians from taking control over their own programmes. The logic works in such a way that people cannot take control of a literacy programme until they have learned all of the different skills involved in starting and maintaining that programme. In their courses, the Technicists also conform to the Western practice of dividing participants into different groups and giving each group separate training: one course for materials producers, one course for trainers, one course for supervisors, one course for co-ordinators, and so on. This, again, is how Melanesians have been prevented from moving ahead in their literacy work and developing innovative combinations of theories and approaches.

Foreign Technicist Experts have been able to convince many Melanesians that literacy is a very complicated set of practices, and, in the logic of neo-colonialism, that a successful programme must thus depend on extensive help from expatriates. In the Integral Human Development Courses, participants are shown that even the most difficult and mystified tasks, such as writing a new alphabet for a language, designing primers, training teachers, and writing and printing books, are not nearly as difficult as they have been made to seem. The Integral Human Development programmes include attention to techniques by which alphabets and primers for previously unwritten languages can be designed within a matter of days. In four weeks, course participants are given the chance to write, design and print most of the literacy materials that they will need for the following year. By the end of the courses, the participants have realized that, in fact, literacy in Melanesia will only be possible if expatriate Experts are used as little as possible, and only if these Experts are forbidden to make literacy seem to be something that any community in Melanesia could not achieve without expatriate help or expatriate equipment.

In a country with 869 languages and more dialects of these languages, and where the majority of the people are not literate in any language, the discourse of literacy must first cope explicitly with such socio-cultural questions as: does everyone have the constitutional right to become literate first in their own language? Since an explicit affirmative answer has been given to this question in public documents, regardless of the continuing practice, it will be necessary to produce materials and to train teachers for all 869 languages. This state of affairs need not be defined as a problem, but rather as a resource. It is, for example, less expensive and complicated to produce books and to train teachers locally for 869 languages than it is to produce books and train teachers centrally for any one, two, or three of the national languages. In order to do this, however, two priority areas for training have been established: (1) flexible and explicit methods which can be used to train 'pushouts' to become literacy and awareness workers in a short time, and (2) facilities for the local writing and production of materials on silkscreen printers.

The Technicists continue to develop and refine complex monolingually-centred methods for teaching literacy and training teachers. These 'literacy curricula' are complicated and rigid because the Experts who write them have theorized literacy skill in these terms and have in addition little knowledge of Melanesian ways of training and education. In the Integral Human Development

Courses, skills and contexts are explicitly topicalized for learning. Students learn not only the routines but also the reasons for each step of every procedure. The stated goal is to make 'the teacher the master of the book, rather than making the book the master of the teacher'. In the Integral Human Development Courses, the work of materials production is not separated from the work of teacher training. The Western fractionation of literacy work into literacy industry is a covert aspect of the relationship of education to economics — the structures that yield the commoditization rather than the communilization of skills and knowledge.

Conclusion

It is clear that our position is that literacy for Integral Human Development is best construed as a right whose fulfilment has become more not less necessary, especially in a time of 'debt crisis'. Universal literacy in local languages geared to the political, economic, social, and spiritual needs and aspirations of every community is by no means an unreasonably high expectation for Papua New Guineans. There is no technical or economic reason why the mandate to this effect contained in the Constitution and in the stated Philosophy of Education could not have been carried out long ago.

Literacy programmes can be grounded from their commencements in the needs and aspirations of the community. The more opportunities that are provided for community control, responsibility and participation, the more successful a programme is likely to be in any context, but most dramatically in a context such as PNG. However, government must play an active role, commensurate with its legal and political obligations. Demystified, simple, straightforward, and culturally appropriate teaching techniques, combined with local materials production make the training of teachers and the production of materials in 869 languages possible. The main obstacles to literacy and awareness for a community managed and centred literacy in PNG today are the neocolonialist ideological, social, economic, and political tendencies that are becoming increasingly dominant in PNG life, as much through their silent naturalization as through any explicit, publicly debated process, and the Technicist approach to literacy and other educational activities that has allowed itself, either wittingly or unwittingly, to become the underpinning of these tendencies. The growing power of the neocolonial system coupled with the IMF/WB assault on Papua New Guineans' economic base, social services, and standards of living, together catapult literacy into the front defensive line in PNG, and make persistent public critique of the contents and methods of literacy more necessary than ever in this age of 'debt crisis'.

References

CONSTITUTION OF THE SOVEREIGN STATE OF PAPUA NEW GUINEA (1975) Port Moresby, 15th August.

DEPARTMENT OF EDUCATION AND DEPARTMENT OF THE PRIME MINISTER (1989) *Literacy and Information Programme*, Waigani, Resource Management System.

DEPARTMENT OF EDUCATION (1989) *National Language and Literacy Policy*, Secretarial Directive, Waigani.

MATANE, SIR P. (1986) *A Philosophy of Education for Papua New Guinea*, Ministerial Committee Report, Waigani, Ministry of Education.
NARAKOBI, B. (1980) *The Melanesian Way*, Suva, City Typesetters.
STRINGER, M. and FARACLAS, N. (1987) *Working Together for Literacy*, Wewak, Christian Books Melanesia.

Chapter 6

Literacy and Primary Education in India

Krishna Kumar

If education offered little else except lasting literacy to all who spent a few years at school, quite a few states in the world would be happy enough. These would include the states of countries both rich and poor ('Open File', 1987). True, schools are proving ineffective in imparting literary skills in many countries of the First as well as the Third World, but the problem is far more grim in the latter. How many more illiterates India will have, and what percentage of the world's illiterates will belong to India at the turn of the twenty-first century have become staple statistical crescendos of conference speeches. Evidently, India's performance in the pursuit of mass literacy is the central theme of the dismal system of education. The expansion of the education system, accomplished at a very substantial cost, has not had any striking impact on literacy.

The search for explanations has typically been made in the context of the economic conditions prevailing in rural India. The explanation of the failure of the primary schools to retain children is often couched in terms of the poverty of parents. Studies leaning on the 'culture of poverty' concept continue to hold sway, and they tell us that poor parents 'withdraw' their children from school mainly *because* they are too poor to afford to keep children at school rather than at work. Rarely does anyone wonder if primary school pedagogy could have something to do with the school's failure to retain children long enough to make them literate. This is the direction the present paper suggests in search of an explanation for the dismal performance of Indian primary education. It argues that the entrenched pedagogy of reading may be at the heart of the problem of early elimination from school. After examining the problems that conventional methods of teaching in the primary grades pose in the present-day socio-economic context, the paper moves on to considering the linkages between modern pedagogies of literacy and industrial development. It concludes by arguing that mass literacy — of a type that enables people to read in meaningful ways — is a political necessity and can only be achieved by a radical reconstruction of primary education.

Early Elimination

India's education system does not cover all children of the primary school age (i.e., six to eleven years). Indeed, precisely what proportion of children it covers is a matter of some controversy. School enrolment figures for Grades I to V, compiled by the Department of Education, convey the impression that nearly 90 per cent of six- to eleven-year-olds are enrolled in primary schools. This impression has been questioned, most recently and sharply by Aggarwal (1988, pp. 69–109) on the basis of the census figures. Going by the responses collected under the 1981 census, Aggarwal concludes that only 47 per cent of primary school age children are actually in schools, either formal or non-formal. Out of the rest, perhaps quite a few are enrolled but they are not attending school. The discrepancy between census data and enrolment data is very great indeed. The government's pressure on teachers to enrol every child in the community can account for some part of the discrepancy. Another part can be accounted for by referring to the high rate of elimination (official term 'dropping-out') from school. Indeed, the two explanations complement each other. Teachers enrol children under orders from above, but fail to keep them at school. This is what the well-studied phenomenon of 'dropping-out' is all about. Earlier planners in India, most predominantly the late J.P. Naik, referred to it as the wastage rate, for they argued that the resources spent on a child who leaves school before completing a stage were wasted. Naik had worked out the wastage rate to be about 60 per cent between Grades I and V, i.e., out of 100 children enrolled in Grade I only 40 reach Grade V (Naik, 1975).

There is no reason to think that this rate has declined. Apparently, collection of age and grade-wise enrolment data was discontinued in the early seventies (*Journal of Educational Planning and Administration*, 1988). This may be why the statistical appendix to the document called 'Challenge of Education', which outlined the perspective for the 1986 education policy, was content to carry a table (compiled in 1983) showing grade-wise enrolment rates up to the 1970–78 batch of elementary school-going population.[1] According to this table, the national average of elimination between Grades I and V was 64 per cent. In other words, out of the 100 children who enrolled in 1970–71 in Grade I, only thirty-six remained until Grade V. Of the sixty-six who left, thirty-nine had already done so within the first year, resulting in 61 per cent enrolment in Grade II (compared to Grade I). These rates of elimination seem to have remained quite stable, which implies that the general processes of socio-economic development and change have not had much impact in this matter.

Widespread and stable though the phenomenon of early elimination has been, it continues to be rather poorly understood. The general belief is that economic pressures on children and parents of 'backward' socio-economic backgrounds are responsible for the high incidence of premature school leaving. This belief gains support from the fact that child labour is widespread in India. Children's usefulness as cheap and readily available labour is widely cited in social and demographic research to explain why school enrolment does not remain stable over the elementary years. No less than 500 studies have been listed in a recent annotated bibliography on the so-called 'drop-out' rate. (Patil, 1984) With few exceptions, these studies conclude that poverty drives parents to withdraw their children from school and the assumptions underlying the majority of these studies are clear enough. The major assumption is that early elimination is caused by poverty and backwardness. The argument is simple: since almost all children who leave school early are poor, this kind of behaviour ought to be related to poverty.

No study has yet explained why the child's labour changes dramatically between Grade I and II where the elimination rate is highest. As the enrolment data given earlier indicate, thirty-nine out of the sixty-six children (per 100) who stop attending school between Grades I and V do so within Grade I. In other words, nearly 61 per cent of the 'drop-out' children belong to the youngest age group attending school. Most likely, these children are five to seven years old. Now if these children are leaving school due to the economic necessity of their families, there ought to be a sudden jump in the children's labour value between Grades I and II, roughly age six to seven. Surely we need a medical explanation for this sudden jump. Why would, otherwise, a parent send their child to Grade I but withdraw him/her from Grade II? The question takes the bottom out of the theory that early elimination has a satisfactory economic explanation in our conditions in the late twentieth century. It also hits at the research convention of asking poor parents why they 'withdraw' their children from school. The basis of such interviewing lies in the 'culture of poverty' theory which continues to influence social research in India.

It is time we turned our attention to the child's perspective on this problem. One of the questions we would ask if we took the child's perspective is: 'Does the primary school provide what a grade one child is looking for?'. The paramount motivation in Grade I children is to make sense of the world around them. Poor health, malnutrition, and oppressive control of the child's routine can weaken this drive but they cannot wipe it out. The child of six, irrespective of existential conditions, is curious about the world, and wants to manipulate it, research it, and understand it. One of the primary means of doing these things is language, and grade one children are already familiar with its marvellous capacities. They have already used it to establish relationships, to internalize these relationships, and then to apply the internalization to explore a wider world (Vygotsky, 1962). Along with movement, touch, vision, hearing, and smell, children of six are familiar with the exciting possibilities of language. They know from social lore that the school is where they will learn two powerful new skills, namely reading and writing, and much else.

We can hardly capture the associations of growth, power, and knowledge that the child of five or so years makes with the school before entering it. If we are able to hold even a small fraction of these associations in our view, we would know how frustrated the child must become after he or she has spent a few days at an average Indian primary school. He or she would find out that the school is not the place where he or she can make sense of the world. Skills that any child would use to solve new problems have no place in the Grade I class. Indeed, 'making sense' and 'solving problems' are not on the agenda at all. What is on the agenda, to begin with, is to learn the shapes of letters that form the syllabary, and to know the names by which they are called. The child is required to master the syllabary by sounding out the names of all the letters and practising writing them out correctly over and over again. When the syllabary has been mastered in this manner, the child is called upon to recognize the different letters forming a word given in the primer, and to pronounce the word. The words they are asked to confront at this stage are part of a long convention of pedagogy, and have nothing to do with children's perception or curiosity.

Moreover, the school has hardly anything that the child is free to touch, manipulate and examine. The Fourth All India Educational Survey showed that over 50 per cent of primary schools in India did not have a concrete structure, playground, or even drinking water facility, 40 per cent were without black-boards, and 70 per cent had no library of any kind. The school is a colourless, alienated, stuffy little place from the point of view of a six-year-old. Any excuse would be good enough to stop going there.

Literacy and Meaning

This reconstruction leads us to hypothesize that the pedagogy of language, particularly reading, may be at the heart of the problem of early elimination. The manner in which Indian primary schools attempt to impart the capacity to read could well hold in it an explanation that has not yet been heard. Listening to this explanation does not mean that we negate the validity of other explanations, such as the ones related to poverty and child labour. There can be no doubt about the impact of destitution and hunger in the family on school attendance. The point is to prepare a model consisting of all the salient features of the phenomenon. The few researchers who have paid some attention to pedagogical conditions of primary schools have treated them as a peripheral aspect of the overall picture. It may be worthwhile to look at pedagogy more carefully, particularly the peda-gogy of reading and writing. These are the two foundation skills on which the edifice of the school's system of teaching and certifying rests. Also, competence in reading and writing determines the child's ability to benefit from the infor-mation storage systems that are characteristic of a literate society. The school system as we know it today is a key agency serving literacy-based information storage systems essential for modern social organization. If the school fails to impart lasting literacy to a great proportion of its clients, it is not only failing in its duty to provide effective literacy to all, irrespective of class/caste, gender, and ethnicity, but must also be seen as a case of serious institutional dysfunction in the overall social system. We have reason to accept that such personal and institutional dysfunctioning has occurred in India. Early elimination rates are one indication of this. It is self-evident that the majority of children who enrol for primary education abandon it without acquiring lasting literacy. Of the children who continue to study, a great many do not acquire the ability to comprehend what they read. The dismal performance of Indian students in the IEA tests (Thorndike, 1972) was only a proof of what every secondary school and college teacher knows from daily experience.

In the sphere of reading, the common practices applied in our primary schools sharply contrast with what current knowledge about the reading process suggests. The general state of the teaching of reading in Grade I is close to what contemporary reading researchers would identify as the 'traditional' approach. In brief, this approach is characterized by the treatment of script as a complex pack-age of information to be learned for its own sake. Children must learn the names of different letters, and they must develop the ability to recognize them separately and as part of a word. Only after this familiarity with letters becomes reliable is the child allowed to apply it in a sentence representing a meaningful statement. This takes time, for the process involves a considerable amount of mechanical work which offers no immediate pay-off or satisfaction. Reading is treated in this approach as an end product which the child must wait for, suspending the desire to find meaning in written material, especially to find meaning with which he or she can relate.

Current research on the reading process tells us that the desire to relate and to find meaning are at the heart of reading (Moon, 1984, pp. 20–7; Olson, Torrance and Hildyard, 1985; Glaser, 1988, pp. 21–44). Reading the word, is indeed then, as Freire and Macedo argued, also a process of reading the world (Freire and Macedo, 1987). It is now understood that reading and writing skills represent later stages on the continuum on which symbolic interaction through talk, play, and drawing appear earlier. The continuum encapsulates the human child's desire to be involved in communication. We cannot isolate the tasks involved in reading from this continuum without seriously altering the nature of these tasks. If we teach children to recognize letters as an isolated task, we influence the nature and the role of this task in the overall process of reading. Children breaking down words into letters, and sentences into words are a common sight in Indian primary schools. Those who so do internally may far outnumber the ones who do so verbally, and this category could well be applied to many adult members of the literate population. For a child who has learnt to read letter by letter or word by word, there is no choice except to recode the text into a sound system which then has to be decoded via the phonological, syntactic, and semantic components (Ingram, *et al.*, 1977). It is an arduous and necessarily wasteful process which overloads the child's short-term memory and the capacity to pay attention to meaning.

There is of course a chance that children taught to read by the traditional methods may also become competent readers. The presence of a loving and encouraging teacher can imbue any process, however mechanical, with a sense of worth. This is especially true if the teacher has all the time in the world to work with the child. This condition may well have pertained during the eras when only a few people were required to possess literacy skills. Availability of leisure, freedom from competition, and the small number of pupils for a teacher were the other complementary conditions that made the traditional approaches of imparting reading skills reasonably successful. These conditions were characteristic of a society whose culture sanctioned an elite to monopolize the means of using literacy and the means to store accumulated knowledge, particularly knowledge about the society's past. In such a society, teachers could well afford to expand the process of learning to be literate in every possible mechanical detail. In turning the phonology and the graphology of the language into a full-blown curriculum, they did not have to worry about imparting a sense of meaning at every stage. In the cultural milieu referred to, a sense of meaning need not have been a part of the daily learning experience, for meaning was generated elsewhere, for example, in the association between educational opportunity and high social status.

An altogether different set of circumstances exists today, under which the persistence of traditional methods of reading and writing presents a case of cultural anachronism. Industrial development and the socio-political institutions that are conducive to industrialization demand mass education, especially, mass literacy. Industrialization breaks down the personal meanings and sources of self-respect that an oral culture might offer to its members. Particularly under capitalism, industrial development forces all members of society to generate meanings by individual effort, and be prepared to surrender self-respect if the meanings thus generated do not help one survive in the market economy. Some societies have succeeded in softening this power of industrial development to a certain extent, by projecting national identity and ideology as reservoirs to which individuals can turn for deriving a sense of worth. But many societies have neglected the task of assisting the individual child to generate a sense of personal meaning through education. This is the reason why versions of childcentred education have been accepted as essential not just in the bourgeois United States but also in the socialist Soviet Union. The significance of these methods lies in the capacities they have for sustaining mass motivation for learning and for making sense of situations. The methods were born out of the needs created by industrialization, and they continue to serve industrial development, both by imparting universal and effective literacy, and by sustaining the individual's desire to live and to make sense of conditions brought about by the advancement of industrialization.

Debunking of Literacy

The assumption that literacy — of the kind we have been discussing — is essential for industrial development has received considerable criticism over recent years. Indeed, it has become fashionable to question the assumption. Many Western scholars have eulogized oral cultures and their wisdom has led some to question the relevance of universal literacy for Third World societies. A pronounced example of this tendency can be found in Street (1984), who argues that there are many different types of literacy, and that the sense in which we have talked about literacy (i.e., as the ability to relate to a text in an interpretative or meaningful manner) refers to just one type of literacy. This type, it is argued, is situated in the ethos of Western societies. It follows that literacy of this type need not be suitable for, and may contrast with the requirements of, non-Western societies. Although the argument was originally mounted to challenge the dichotomy certain researchers had identified between 'oral' and 'literate' societies, it is being used for the more general purpose of debunking the idea of linking literacy with industrial development. The former, limited purpose of the argument has validity, but the latter use to which it is being put can only be described as a new, and seemingly radical variety of Western paternalism. Earlier, the pathos of the Western scholar used to flow from the realization that the Third World inhabitants were illiterate; the pathos has now graduated to the perception that the Third World should be permitted its own kind of literacy which is more conducive to its cultural traditions.

Debunking the linkage between literacy and industrial development is sometimes attempted in a different form, by referring to the history of industrialized societies (Winchester, 1985). If they could industrially develop without mass literacy, the argument goes, why must today's Third World societies treat literacy as a pre-condition for development? According to this argument, large-scale literacy is an outcome, rather than a precursor, of industrial and economic growth. Those who propose this argument do not recognize the difference between the economic and political circumstances under which industrialization is taking place now in the Third World and those that prevailed in Europe in the eighteenth and nineteenth centuries. The basic difference has to do with the emergence of an

international economic order which does not permit the independent development of Third World societies. These societies are not free to evolve their own
norms and values. They are obliged to respond to the norms set by the wealthy
and powerful countries of the industrialized world. The gap in the economic
capacities of the two kinds of countries is so vast that any attempt by the poorer
countries to pursue the norms set by the rich ends up becoming a tiring exercise of
coping with the impossible. It implies serious distortions in the values pursued
in polity, planning, and implementation. The distortions leave Third World
countries with little chance and capacity to pursue welfare aims such as universal
literacy and health in the manner in which the Western societies were able to
pursue these aims. The distortions are further exacerbated by the dependence of
the poor on the rich countries for monetary, technological, and intellectual
resources. The distortions are so deep that they get internalized by the polity of
the poorer country. It is against this complex background that we need to assess
the role of literacy in countries like India today, not with reference to the history
of industrialization in Europe and North America.

Norm Differential

Let us examine why the rich countries are able to exercise a great deal of influence
on the norms that guide development policies in the poorer countries. The reason
lies primarily in the colonial legacy which encircles North-South relations
in many cases. Colonial rule provided Northern societies with a sustained
opportunity to decimate the independent norm-building capacities of Southern societies. Today's situation is a direct product of the colonial heritage of
North-South bonds. The heritage determines, for instance, why the Indian state
observes international norms only in matters which are directly monitored by
North-based bodies of norm-maintenance. In other matters, it feels free not to
observe any particular norms. It is expected, for instance, that as a participant in
global aviation, India will fulfil certain standards of aircraft maintenance. In this
matter India's performance is open to being monitored by North-based bodies of
norm-maintenance, and also by India's small population of aviation consumers.
Maintenance of the advanced technology used in military equipment and nuclear
reactors presents a similar case. It is expected that India ought to behave like a
modernized country in these matters, whatever her economic status and capacity.
The universalistic logic of science is applied to indicate that safety is a prime
human value everywhere.

Indeed, science and technology are the prime symbolic agencies which
permit incessant progress in weapon design and trade to take place without much
opposition by the ordinary public in either the North or the South. No doubt, the
mystification of science is partly responsible for the fact that ordinary people do
not notice or criticize the misuse of science for power maintenance (Bazin, 1986,
pp. 98–109). In the case of technology, the introduction of new tools of comfort
or entertainment often provides legitimacy to the investment of funds in weapon
research and development. The 'invention' of nearly all modern tools of middle-
class convenience and joy can be traced to military needs of the industrialized
nation states. Advanced technologies of information processing and communication, which are said to represent the 'moving interface between learning and

working' are no exception (King, 1986, Kumar, 1987). The demand to maintain them at high levels of efficiency and at the frontiers of innovative capacity is as much an outcome of military compulsions as was their birth. Their educational use serves as a peace market important for the state subsidy it brings to corporate interests. This peace market extends to the starved educational systems of the Third World. Countries like India and Pakistan are persuaded by North-based international bodies to equip their schools and colleges with informatics and video equipment in the same way as these countries are asked by weapon-selling Northern states to maintain their weapon-using capacities at internationally acceptable levels. No such norms are applied when the issue is child health, nutrition, or education. As far as the global human community or its rich families residing in the North are concerned, India is free to keep her children malnourished and ill-educated. The styles of international communication permit no norm-setting discourse in these areas. The most that is permitted is the discourse of lament on the fate of India's malnourished millions.

A subtler variety of influence on the priorities and values of countries like India is exercised by the propagation of affluent life-styles through globally circulated TV programmes, cinema, advertisements, comicstrips and popular literature. Symbols of the 'good' life projected in these materials are rooted in the economies of the rich countries. The role these symbols play in a poor country like India is that of constructing illusions. Neither the economy, nor the social order, nor the natural environment has the capacity to withstand the high levels of consumption implied by these symbols. The greater demand for the objects of consumption, the deeper the penetration it invites from Northern corporate capital and states. Both the political and social orders must suffer as a result of this penetration. The suffering takes the form of a vulnerable, manipulable polity and a permanently volatile social ethos. The natural environment suffers irreparable damage as piece after large piece of land is denuded, mined, and rendered unfit for habitation. Development thus evokes nasty images such as Bailadila and the Narmada basin.[2]

This is the specific context in which the role of literacy needs to be assessed in the Third World today. We have discussed earlier how the ability to read can equip an individual to make sense of situations. We can now place this cognitive function of reading in the context of Third World political economy. In countries like India, the ability to read has its social function as an intellectual and political resource. We assign this role to literacy on the basis of the understanding that the ability to decipher texts and to relate to them represents a cognitive empowerment. Good literary practices offer a chance of sustained reflection which, if it is widespread, can make individuals less susceptible to political manipulation than non-literates. This political role is similar to the one Freire had proposed for literacy but which his approach did often not render sustainable in practice. His model of literacy offered an alternative to the older model which defined the need for literacy in terms of the 'functional' advantages that it could provide to individuals. Such 'functional' advantages were supposed to accumulate in the shape of greater efficiency and productivity in the economy and society. The poor performance of the UNESCO sponsored programme of literacy in the sixties underlined the limitations of the 'functional' model. In Freire's ideological model, the spread of literacy-related skills was seen as a means and an opportunity of equipping the oppressed masses with a resource. It was expected that this resource would enable the masses to struggle against the structures which enable dominant classes in society to oppress them.

This operational part of Freire's model of literacy inspired many programmes of adult education in the seventies. The story of how this model was coopted and misused has been documented elsewhere (Kumar, 1989). Here it should be sufficient to say that if misapplications of Freire's model outnumbered sincere applications, this was at least partly due to the model's dependence on the presence of favourable circumstances. In India, the possibility of Freire's model being applied have proved narrow, and this seems true of many other countries whose material and political circumstances are similar to India's. At least as far as literacy is concerned, adult education in India and in several other Third World countries has reached a plateau in its search of a viable theory to work with. In India at least, the hope that literacy teaching among adults will raise their organizational and intellectual energy appears as much of an illusion now as does the larger idea that adult education will substantially enhance mass literacy in the course of time.

An alternative approach must be sought and the strengthening of primary education has arguably not been taken sufficiently seriously. In the 'developing' world, primary education has been customarily regarded as a cheaper sector in comparison to secondary and higher education. This view of primary education is reflected in the inter-sectoral gap that exists in educational financing of the richer and the poorer countries of the world. Whereas in higher education, the richer countries make five times greater *per capita* investment than the poorer countries, in primary education the richer countries spend thirty times more per child than the poorer countries (World Bank, 1980).

In India, another manifestation of the view that primary education can do with lower-order resources is the declining share of primary education in the educational budget since the fifties. As compared with 1950–51 when primary education accounted for 40 per cent of the expenditure incurred on education as a whole, in 1979–80 it accounted for only 24 per cent. 'Plan' allocation for primary education similarly declined from 56 per cent in the First Plan to 29 per cent in the Seventh Plan (Tilak, 1989). This decline becomes particularly meaningful if we place it against the continual increase of India's child population and the increase in the number of primary schools. In comparison to the 150,000 primary schools that India had at the time of independence, it had about 500,000 at the beginning of the present decade. The implication is clear — that educational policy did emphasize expansion of primary education but allocated fewer resources to it. The consequences of this ambivalent approach are self-evident. If we focus on literacy as the one area in which expansion of primary education could have been expected to show its performance, a sad fact is apparent. While primary education expanded 3.3 times during the four decades following independence, literacy percentage just about doubled, and that with dilution in the norms of recording literacy-related skills in census surveys.[3]

If primary education is to be regarded in future as the key agency for achieving mass literacy, then the perception of primary education as a cheaper sector will have to change. Early schooling of a kind that offers children an absorbing environment and a real chance to become literate implies an expensive model. Such a model will mean extensive equipping of primary classrooms with materials. The creation of appropriate spaces for learning and play equipment will be the first requirements, followed by ongoing supply of basic equipment.[4] At the moment, manufacturing of primary level learning resources is part of a rather poorly developed small-scale industry. Certain sectors of the industry, such as the manufacturing of indigenous toys, are under great stress. In other sectors, such as the manufacturing of modern play devices, and children's books, there is both lack of direction and absence of norms. Regeneration of primary education cannot materialize without the investment of very substantial monetary and organizational resources in the manufacturing of pedagogical materials. What gives this condition an added significance is the prevalence of the 'textbook culture' which I have discussed elsewhere (Kumar, 1988). The thin and repetitive nature of classroom activity in a textbook-dominated culture is further exacerbated by the material poverty of the primary school. The dominance of prescribed textbooks can be expected to abate if the manufacturing and supply of pedagogical resources, especially of children's literature, improves.

The equipping of primary schools for curricular enrichment will also require modernization of teacher training and change in the career conditions of primary level teachers. At present, the primary teacher is both the most powerless, and the poorest paid, professional functionary of the education system. Teacher training for the primary level has extremely meagre academic content or rigour to it, and opportunities for the exercise of judgment and imagination in matters like curriculum and material preparation are non-existent. Literacy-related skills are a particularly weak area of teacher training. Recent work in reading, and the theorizing it has made possible on the relationship between reading and cognitive development, are not known in teacher training institutions in India. What makes this situation worse is the old belief that teachers need only skills, not theory. A major implication of recent research in reading is that it can become a meaningful activity if the classroom ethos is supportive of individual interpretations and intelligent guessing. Building a classroom ethos along these lines requires that the teacher understands the theory underlying a recommended classroom activity.

Changes in classroom conditions along the lines indicated here are incompatible with the perception of primary education as a cheap sector. How will this perception permit an alternative model to gain acceptance? The question forces us to remember that perceptions of education are rooted in the political economy of a society and therefore cannot be altered in isolation.

The case of primary education is, however, different in this matter from that of adult education to which we referred earlier. Even in a society with deeply entrenched inequalities, radical steps to improve primary education can be taken without inviting social conflict. Acharya has indicated the possibility of discontent arising among the richer farmers if effective primary education obstructs the supply of cheap child labour (Acharya, 1984, pp. 56–9). This 'risk' does not justify the state's unpreparedness for making fresh investments in primary education unless the state is merely an instrument of the richer strata of society.

We have argued that the perceptions underlying state policies in Third World countries are affected by international norm-building. Along with internal factors, the demands transmitted by North-dominated global institutions (including financial institutions) and by the North's own life-styles and media shape the priorities followed by the Southern nation states. This is where a critical analysis of 'development' programmes of the richer countries becomes relevant. The UNICEF report on the state of the world's children for 1989 makes a valid attempt in this direction and presents the case of primary education as a 'real development objective' (UNICEF, 1989, p. 54). It says that 'if high literacy rates are to be maintained, then there is ultimately no substitute for universal formal education' (UNICEF, 1989, p. 54). The costs are relatively high and the opportunities for reducing them are few. The report questions the ethics that the rich countries of the North have followed in the last decade and which have led to further depletion to the meagre resources available to Southern states for pursuing programmes like primary education, which are fundamental to literacy development.

Notes

1 This Appendix was apparently withdrawn soon after publication.
2 Bailadila is a region of Bastar district in Madhya Pradesh, known for the denuding of forest, and the disruption to social and cultural life caused by large scale mining. Narmada is a major river in central India, and site of a World Bank development project involving the construction of several dams. These dams are feared to cause massive ecological damage, as well as disruption to the lives of millions of rural dwellers.
3 Whereas earlier literacy was measured in terms of the ability to read a simple passage, the current practice equates literacy with the ability to write one's name.
4 A modest start at equipping primary schools with basic pedagogical necessities has been made under 'Operation Blackboard' in recent years, a part of the 1986 education policy. But it has been saddled with difficulties arising mainly from the rigid bureaucratic norms governing financial expenditures on school supplies.

References

ACHARYA, P. (1984) 'Roots of Bengal's illiteracy', *Future*, pp. 11–12.
AGGARWAL, Y. (1988) 'Towards education for all children: Intent and reality', *Journal of Educational Planning and Administration*, 22, pp. 1–2.
BAZIN, M. (1986) 'The technological mystique and and Third World options', *Monthly Review*, 38, p. 3.
FREIRE, P. and MACEDO, D. (1987) *Literacy. Reading the Word and the World*, South Hadley, MA, Bergin and Garvey.
GLASER, R. (1988) 'Cognitive science and education', *International Journal of Social Science*, 25, p. 115.
INGRAM, D.C. *et al.* (1977) *Cultural Components of Reading*, Singapore, Singapore University Press
KING, E.J. (1986) *International Yearbook of Education*.
KUMAR, K. (1987) *Economic and Political Weekly*, 25, p. 7.
KUMAR, K. (1988) 'Origins of India's Textbook Culture', *Comparative Education Review*, 32, p. 4.
KUMAR, K. (1989) *The Social Character of Learning*, New Delhi, Sage.
MOON, C. (1984) 'Recent developments in the teaching of reading', *English in Education*, **18**, 1, pp. 20–7.
NAIK, B.R. (1975) *Elementary Education in India. A Promise to Keep*, New Delhi, Allied.
OLSON, D.R., TORRANCE, N. and HILDYARD, A. (1985) (Eds) *Literacy, Language and Education*, Cambridge, Cambridge University Press.
'OPEN FILE' (1987) *Prospects*, **17**, 2, Paris, UNESCO.

PATIL, B.R. (1984) *Problems of School Drop-Outs in India. An Annotated Bibliography*, New Delhi, Council for Social Development.

STREET, B. (1984) *Literacy in Theory and Practice*, Cambridge, Cambridge University Press.

THORNDIKE, R.L. (1972) *Reading Comprehension in Fifteen Countries*, Stockholm, Almquist and Wiksell.

TILAK, J.B.G. (1989) 'Political Economy of Education in India', unpublished mimeo.

UNICEF (1989) *The State of the World's Children*, Oxford, Oxford University Press.

VYGOTSKY, V. (1962) *Thought and Language*, Cambridge, MA, MIT Press.

WINCHESTER, A. (1985) 'Atlantans, Centaurans and the litron bomb: Some personal and social implications of literacy', in OLSON, D. *et al.* (Eds) *Literature, Language and Learning*, Cambridge, Cambridge University Press.

WORLD BANK (1980) *Education: A Sector Policy Paper*, World Bank, Washington, DC.

Chapter 7

Adult Literacy in Nicaragua 1979–90

Colin Lankshear

Introduction

This chapter focuses on literacy in Nicaragua during the years of revolution, which 'officially' ended with the elections of 25 February 1990 when the United National Opposition alliance defeated the FSLN[1] and Violeta Chamorro became President. The Nicaraguan Revolution affords a rich and distinctive setting within which to explore literacy. The word-in-print encapsulates much of the character of the revolution, symbolically and materially. It comprised both a site of struggle and a medium for struggle during this period, and gave symbolic and literal expression to the achievements and frustrations, goals and contradictions, aspirations and tensions that collectively *were* the Nicaraguan Revolution.

In 1981 Nicaragua was awarded the coveted Nadezhda Kruspskaya prize from UNESCO in recognition of the 1980 National Literacy Crusade (CNA). Research indicates the importance of literacy within wider revolutionary achievements — for example, in health. Recent studies indicate that the infant mortality rate in children of illiterate mothers in 1983 was ninety-one per 1,000 live births, whereas in children of mothers who had become literate in the CNA the rate was seventy-three per 1,000 (Centro Latinoamericano, 1988, pp. 26–27). One study estimates that even in a population as small as Nicaragua's (3 million), the first adult literacy initiative of the revolution contributed directly to saving over 700 infants per year.

The-word-in-print also accounts for much of the *distinctiveness* of the Nicaraguan Revolution. Guilio Girardi notes the high priority attributed to culture as a dimension of revolutionary development and expression in Nicaragua. While song, dance, craft, film, narrative, theatre, photography, murals and other visual arts were developed to previously unknown levels in affirming 'a new (Nicaraguan) person and a new society', pride of cultural place fell to literary forms: popular journalism; historical, political, and sociological essays; the novel; and, above all, poetry. 'Nicaragua has made poetry the privileged expression of cultural creativity — the legacy of Ruben Dario' (Instituto Historico Centroamericano, 1988, p. 16).

The complex and contradictory significance of literacy and print within the revolution is neatly illustrated by Carlos Vilas. He describes how, as the 1990 election campaign intensified, pro-Sandinista newspapers adopted tactics which negated a revolutionary vision for literacy and doubtless antagonized many voters who first learned to read as a consequence of the FSLN's political commitment to literacy as a human right. Vilas cites the manner in which *La Barricada* (the official FSLN daily) and *El Nuevo Diario* portrayed Violeta Chamorro during her presidential campaign (at this time *Barricada* was edited by one of Doña Violeta's sons, Carlos Fernando. A brother-in-law, Xavier, edited *El Nuevo Diario*):[2]

> . . . Carlos Fernando published letters written by his sister Claudia, an official of the Sandinista government, in which she criticized her mother's association with the Contras and former officers of the National Guard . . . reminding her that these were the ones involved in [assassinating her husband]. *El Nuevo Diario* . . . ran a series of denigrating cartoons in which Doña Violeta appeared dressed in a long priest-like gown with the initials 'GN' (for National Guard), laden with grenades and ammunition belts, and wearing an ugly, evil expression. (Vilas 1990, p. 13)

Vilas comments that such a smear campaign must have provoked reactions of solidarity with Violeta Chamorro among those who saw this as yet another case of a Nicaraguan mother being mistreated by her children. Certainly, such (mis)use of print contradicts the spirit of Nicaragua's justly celebrated National Literacy Crusade and subsequent initiatives aimed at enhancing the recognition and status of women. Indeed, the FSLN's original manifesto had pledged that the revolution would 'establish conditions in which the dignity of women will be raised' (Borge 1982, pp. 19–20).

Considerable steps were taken by women in Nicaragua during both the insurrection and the revolution to actualize their rights to equality and dignity. The obstacles, however, were always many and powerful and, as we will see, remained to the end.

Literacy also provides an index of the declining fortunes of the revolution in its later years, and increasing levels of frustration and disenchantment among (especially) workers and peasants. Ministry of Education officials estimated that by the end of 1988 adult illiteracy had reached 30 per cent in the Managua region, where illiteracy rates had traditionally been the lowest for the entire country (Vilas, 1990). This reflected the marked decline in participation in the Popular Basic Education programme for adults (EPB) evident nationally from 1985 (Lankshear and Lawler, 1987, pp. 200–1) and was part of a wider trend. A poll taken in Managua in October 1989 showed that two-thirds of citizens were no longer participating in activities such as environmental hygiene, vaccinations, or community gardens (Vilas, 1990, p. 13).

Yet such activity had previously comprised the very 'stuff' of the revolution. What had happened to bring about this decline in revolutionary participation and, ultimately, the fall of the Sandinista government?

Post-election analyses identify the Contra war and US trade embargo as major factors. These created 'the extremely precarious state of the Nicaraguan economy', severely eroding early gains of the revolution and undermining FSLN support as programmes lapsed or fell well beneath levels of aspiration. The Contra war, of course, also exacted a huge emotional, psychic, and physical cost as the price of defending national integrity (Vilas, 1990, p. 12; Summerhill and Toser, 1990, pp. 678–9).

Hospitals, health centres, and schools went hopelessly short of essential supplies as national defence sapped up to half Nicaragua's internal budget. Besides such externally imposed factors, however, the most sophisticated analyses also point to trends within the government's policies and practice which undermined its popularity. Vilas shows how from 1986 the FSLN's programme of structural adjustment to the economic crisis resembled 'everyone else's — it favoured the rich and hurt the poor' (Vilas, 1990, p. 12). Government policies reversed the 'logic of the majority' option which largely defined the revolution in its earlier years. To help stimulate production and maintain a united front against the US and the Contra, the government offered economic concessions to large farmers and entrepreneurs while holding back worker and peasant demands. Under these policies income and living conditions among peasants and urban workers, the natural support base for the revolution, declined rapidly. Levels of nutrition and health fell alarmingly, and incidence of disease increased, notably among the young.

The period from 1985, when the Reagan Administration's policies of overt aggression began to hit hardest, contrasts markedly with the earlier phase. From 1979 to 1984, commitment to the emancipation and dignity of traditionally marginal groups was almost uniformly proclaimed and enacted. Popular involvement was promoted by creating programmes and new political, cultural, and economic structures aimed at national development in accordance with 'the logic of the majority'. Participation in mass organizations and mobilizations (for health, literacy, housing, etc.) was widespread and enthusiastic. There was ample evidence of progress toward a more just and democratic ideal of development — at the level of individuals, groups, and the nation as a whole.

Within the course originally charted by the revolution, literacy was officially recognized as an integral element of the Sandinista project. An approach to reading and writing was envisaged by political and educational leaders that would promote critical awareness of historical processes, particularly those which had created an underdeveloped and grossly unequal society and still maintained oppressive structures and relationships. As the same time, literacy initiatives — as well as wider uses of print in revolutionary cultural and literary expression — were aimed at challenging and motivating ordinary Nicaraguans to become agents of history, actively involved in building a new social order based on the values of human dignity, social and economic justice, personal and national emancipation, and progressive development.

A Background to Literacy in the Revolution

In 1969, eight years after its formation as a revolutionary front committed to overthrowing the Somoza dynasty and achieving national liberation, the FSLN published a manifesto of policies to be pursued upon victory. The *Historic Programme of the FSLN* included an agenda for 'revolution in culture and education', pledging to 'establish the bases for development of national culture and the people's education'. The first step would be to 'push forward a massive campaign to immediately wipe out "illiteracy"' (Borge, 1982).

This commitment was reiterated in 1978, as part of an FSLN programme intended to unify and consolidate opposition to the Somoza regime: 'The *Frente Sandinista* will dedicate itself from the very start to fighting against illiteracy so that all Nicaraguans may learn how to read and write' (Documents, 1979, p. 108).

It is important to grasp the rationale for this priority. The legacy of the Somoza era is legion.[3] Given Nicaragua's small population and bounteous natural environment, the political realities of daily life in 1979 were shocking. Infant mortality, mainly from preventible diseases, reached one in three in the poorest areas and averaged 120/1,000 nationally. Living conditions, such as widespread lack of sanitation and running water and a high proportion of dirt floors, militated against sound health — especially, but not only, in rural areas. Such factors reflected a grossly unequal distribution of resources, compounded by economic recessions during the 1970s which coincided with even greater concentration of wealth in the hands of fewer people — notably, the Somoza family (Booth, 1982; Weissberg, 1982).

A very small elite shared in the lop-sided distribution and control of resources. While fewer than 200 families (1.8 per cent of landowners) owned almost half of all farmland — including the best — 58 per cent (small holders) occupied just 3.4 per cent of the land between them. (Weissberg, 1982, pp. 8–10). In 1977 the *per capita* income for the poorer half of Nicaraguans was US$226, while for the top 5 per cent it was US$5,500. Estimates in 1978 indicated that over half of all rural dwellers were existing on less than US$40 per year. Nicaraguans had the lowest life expectancy in Central America and the highest rate of alcoholism. Somoza's government spent less of its budget on health and education than any other in the region (Booth, 1982, p. 85). In addition to being economically marginalized, the mass of people were politically powerless. Elections were notoriously corrupt. Organized efforts concerned with promoting the interests of the poor were systematically and violently repressed by Somoza's National Guard. Attitudes of futility and resignation were widespread (Green Valley Films).

Not surprisingly, when Somoza was finally overthrown less than 5 per cent of the rural population had completed primary school. More than 50 per cent of Nicaraguans above 10 years of age were illiterate. Illiteracy reached 90 per cent in rural areas, where it rarely fell below 60 per cent. Just 18 per cent of those eligible actually had access to secondary education (Barndt, 1985, p. 317).

While many specific details of oppression and degradation evident in Nicaragua at the time of the insurrection — including mass illiteracy — were directly attributable to Somocista policies and practices, we must recognize that *Somocismo*[4] was itself an outgrowth and extension of colonial and neocolonial relations and structures of extreme inequality. Hispanic Nicaragua was conceived, born, and 'nurtured' in structures of domination and exploitation. Its underdevelopment was socially created and maintained throughout 450 years of modern history (Lankshear and Lawler, 1987, p. 183).

Since the wretched conditions experienced by so many Nicaraguans had their roots deep in history and the social structure, genuine change called for *structural* transformation. Real and lasting improvement could not come from superficial change, such as by replacing Somoza's dictatorship with some other government similarly representative of minority interests. Accordingly, the FSLN's *Historic Programme* was precisely an agenda for structural change. It was a programme for *revolution*, designed to 'turn social structures over' (Walker 1985, pp. 2–11). The proposal for a mass literacy campaign and subsequent adult education initiatives must be understood in the light of this political analysis and vision. The FSLN had a comprehensive view of what change would involve in material and ideological terms. The longstanding tradition of foreign control and economic exploitation would have to yield to a dignified and patriotic foreign policy. Economic, commerical, and technical relationships with other countries would have to cohere with Nicaragua's *own* national development and economic growth.

Internally, political and economic structures were required which would permit the full participation of the entire people — at national and local levels alike. Agrarian reform, a labour code, and expropriation and redistribution of *Somocista* property were seen as key components of economic restructuring, together with policies tackling unemployment and guaranteeing freedom of organization to the worker-union movement. Major structural and policy changes were proposed to address concerns relating to ethnicity, gender, culture, health, housing and social security.

Social transformation and national development on such a scale cannot be *donated* to a people. It must be won. It must be answerable to the needs of previously marginalized groups, and develop with their increasing capacity for informed and constructive social action. The practice of a truly empowering literacy — as progenitor *and* outcome of social change — has a crucial role within this process.

The key to this role can be understood in terms articulated by Freire and broadly reflected in FSLN thinking (Freire, 1972, 1976). If oppressed people are to make a new history they need to understand the old: how it was made; how they were excluded from making it; how and why they were dominated and exploited within it; how it can be remade differently; how they can (and must) be involved in remaking history. They must transcend their naive consciousness of the world as a 'natural' immutable reality to which they must simply adapt and, instead, approach the world as being an historical creation always capable of being changed by people just like them (Freire, 1972, 1976). Such understanding is acquired *only* within a praxis of engaging the world — acting on the world to transform it, in the light of their enhanced historical awareness; challenging relations and practices of oppression and underdevelopment, and seeking to replace them with alternatives offering the promise of freedom, justice and development. Literacy can be made into an integral part of this process of historical awakening and commitment.

At the same time literacy has also a more directly *functional* significance for pursuit of development and democracy. Reading and writing can be acquired in ways and in forms that play an important role in improving the level and efficiency of production, help open people to technological change, and assist in meeting demands for administrative and organizational efficiency and progress.

The insights are evident in the policies and programmes centered on literacy that were set in train almost immediately after Somoza's dictatorship was defeated in mid July 1979.

Literacy, Liberation, and National Development: Adult Literacy from 1979

On 2 August 1979 it was announced that a National Literacy Crusade (the CNA) would proceed. A literacy census was conducted in October and November. The

CNA itself began on 23 March 1980, following months of frenetic planning and organization.

The census recorded names, ages, occupations, education levels, which people were interested in learning, where and when it would be convenient to hold classes, who would be willing to teach, where and when. The census revealed some 722,000 illiterate Nicaraguans over the age of 10 — a little more than half the total covered.

The illiteracy figures were an index of poverty and reflected inequalities by urban-rural location. Illiteracy averaged 30 per cent in urban areas — and was especially concentrated in the poorest *barrios* of unemployed and underemployed and in the shanty fringes inhabited by desperately poor *campesinos* (peasants) who had drifted to cities from the countryside — and 75 per cent in rural areas. During the CNA it emerged that some 9 per cent of the population suffered severe learning difficulties which prevented them from studying. This also reflected poverty: 'Poor health was the principal cause. Extensive malnutrition [handicapped] many Nicaraguans, impairing sight and hearing, limiting memory, and often causing early senility' (Miller, 1985).

An especially high level of illiteracy, 75 per cent, was reported for the Atlantic Coast region which occupies half of Nicaragua's land area and is home to its ethnic minority populations. While it is a safe inference that illiteracy was disproportionately high among Amerindian groups — Miskitu, Sumu and Rama — I can find no reliable published figures for illiteracy by ethnic groups. Indeed, even the population estimates for groups like the Miskitu and Sumu vary enormously (Bourgois, 1981, p. 23). Arnove (1986, p. 42) claims that 'illiteracy was relatively low among the English-speaking inhabitants' (Creoles), since many are 'fundamentalist Protestants placing great emphasis on reading the Bible'. Neither are figures readily available for illiteracy by gender, although some estimates indicate that at least 60 per cent of illiterate adults were women (Lawler and Lankshear, 1986, p. 248). Arnove identifies women as 'by far the most educationally neglected group in the country', and Ruchwarger identifies 'the vast majority of the country's illiterate population' as women (Arnove, 1986, p. 33; Ruchwarger, 1987, p. 198). In the event, women accounted for half of all CNA learners.

The Official View of the CNA

The Ministry of Education gave two basic reasons for undertaking the literacy campaign:

1. It is a demand of justice, a moral obligation of the Revolution for our people.
2. With illiteracy it is not possible to prepare all citizens to take up responsibly the massive work demanded by the task of national reconstruction.

The Ministry identified four broad objectives for the CNA:

1. To eradicate the social phenomenon of illiteracy in Nicaragua.
2. To promote a process of critical understanding, on a national level, so

that the previously marginalized mass of people could be drawn freely and effectively into the process of democratizing the country, playing an active part in national reconstruction and development.

3. To contribute to national unity, by integrating the countryside with the city, the worker with the student, the Atlantic Coast with the rest of Nicaragua, etc.

4. To lay a foundation, after illiteracy was eliminated, for continuing with the education of adults through the specially created Vice Ministry of Adult Education.

It was hoped that beyond these formal objectives the CNA would: (i) strengthen the mass organizations (Serra, 1985; Ruchwarger, 1987) which were to form the basis of the new democracy; (ii) deepen the awareness of those Nicaraguan youth who, as literacy teachers, lived with peasant communities throughout the crusade, sharing fully their way of life; and (iii) provide an opportunity to collect examples of natural history and cultural expressions from the most remote parts of the land (Nicaraguan Ministry, 1980a, p. 30).

In short, promoting reading, writing, and literacy skills was seen from the outset as tied to wider social and educational values: specifically,

> to encourage an integration and understanding among Nicaraguans of different classes and backgrounds; to increase political awareness and critical analysis of underdevelopment; to nurture attitudes and skills related to creativity, production, co-operation, discipline, and analytical thinking; to forge a sense of national consensus and of political responsibility; to strengthen channels of economic and political participation; to record oral histories and recover popular forms of culture; and to conduct research in health and agriculture for future development planning. (Cardenal and Miller, 1981, p. 6)

This same conception of literacy infused the Popular Basic Education programme for adults (EPB) which followed the CNA.

The CNA in Practice

Since several excellent detailed accounts of the CNA are available (Hirshon, 1983; Arnove, 1986; Miller, 1985), I will simply identify here three principles that seem most important in the practical pursuit of an activating politicizing literacy in Nicaragua:

1. A serious attempt was made to draw out and confront commonly held beliefs that contributed to oppressed people effectively accepting and consenting to their own domination, such as: 'we are powerless', 'we are nothing', 'we are ignorant', 'there is nothing we can do to improve our circumstances', 'things can't be changed, we have to accept the world as it is'. Literacy lessons were designed to encourage a more critical and analytical understanding of local, national, and international realities consistent with taking on active roles in the pursuit of just and democratic social change.

2. The task of becoming literate was tied as closely as possible to *acting* on the words and themes around which literacy lessons were built. Learners were encouraged to transcend beliefs they may have had about their inability to create a better history, within a literacy programme which was directly linked to practical projects that actually improved the quality of life. Furthermore, organizations for popular participation were being created and consolidated, with teachers and learners alike being challenged to join them by the lesson themes and discussions. As projects unfolded and were completed, participants actually *experienced* historical and cultural agency within the act of coming to see the possibility and importance of becoming literate historical agents.

3. As with the CNA, the EPB programme which followed aimed to maintain a close link between educational content and realities of daily life. It also — largely from necessity — stressed a pedagogy which drew upon and enhanced the sense of historical agency and commitment to active involvement fostered within the CNA.

The content of the CNA primer, *The Dawn of the People* (Nicaraguan Ministry, 1980b), was overtly and unapologetically 'ideological'. Each lesson was organized thematically around a photograph of a life situation and a topic sentence related to the photograph. These uniformly presented strong ideological challenges to learners, openly confronting the practices and hegemony of the past (Miller, 1985, pp. 36–7). Lessons began with a period of discussion focused on the photograph and the topic sentence. Learners were encouraged to relate their own experience, interpretations, and hopes to the situation shown in the photograph; and to translate their ideas and experiences into possible roles they could play within the revolution. The approach was intended to involve learners in an active way from the outset; to offer teachers a chance to promote the learners' critical analysis of their own circumstances and (previous) perception of these circumstances; and to help build within learners a real commitment to the goals, values, and programmes that were to be the revolution.

The literacy teachers were provided with some background information and a basic orientation for each dialogue theme. This was contained in the *Handbook of Directions for Literacy Teachers* (Nicaraguan Ministry, 1980a). Photographs and themes focused on such issues as agricultural production and land reform.

Given that a large proportion of the learners in the CNA were peasants and workers, this theme provided an excellent opportunity to explain the FSLN's analysis of rural life and exploitation under Somoza, and reveal the strategies whereby the revolutionary agenda would correct former injustices. This was designed to help integrate rural people into the revolution, engaging their active support and involvement.

Accordingly, background information provided for the literacy teachers explains Nicaragua's dependence upon agricultural activity, and that, under Somoza, a small group of powerful men appropriated the land and its produce, condemning rural workers and peasants to poverty, insecurity, and distress. With this information and suggested questions for opening up discussion, teachers were to initiate a dialogue intended to stimulate participants to think in new ways about their past and present, and to envisage a new future. In many cases, of course, the dialogue failed to deliver on its potential — hardly surprising, given the youth and inexperience of the vast number of literacy teachers (Miller, 1985, pp. 220–1). The logic and intent of the approach are, however, unmistakable.

The intimate connection of words to action was crucial. As each lesson unfolded, syllables in key words from topic sentences yielded other evocative words. In the English language version of the CNA,[5] for example, the word 'exploited' led to such words as 'choice', 'voice', 'join', 'boil', and 'toilet'. These words offered direct access to an entire matrix of revolutionary ideas, values, and practices and, indeed, other mass campaigns — such as the health campaign. Democratic participation depends on people having an equal *voice, joining* unions and other mass organizations through which they articulate and pursue their *choice*. Lesson 19 ended with the sentence: 'Building toilets means better health'. During the literacy campaign teachers and learners, old and young, men and women, wealthy and poor, worked together building toilets in communities where inadequate sanitation presented a health hazard.

Given this conscious linking of words and action a youth newspaper, *El Brigadista*, could subsequently report major progress on health, cultural and agricultural fronts (Angus, 1981, p. 14). In this simple yet profound way, the 'building blocks' of learning to read and write simultaneously became invitations to actually enter into building a new history. The spirit and logic of the CNA drew heavily on Paulo Freire's insights as to how the 'dead weight of history' bears down on those whose 'voices have been silenced', blinding them to the possibility and relative ease of acting collectively to build a better life.

The Impact of the CNA

In terms of its aims to eradicate illiteracy, integrate the city with the countryside and workers with students, and to lay a basis for ongoing adult education, the CNA can be seen as largely successful. I will comment on these aspects before considering the crusade in relation to the longstanding marginality of women and ethnic minorities in Nicaragua.

Some 406,000 learners passed the examination at the end of the five-month Spanish language campaign. (I will note the campaign in the various ethnic minority languages later.) Relative to the elementary levels of reading and writing defined by the exam (and recognized by UNESCO as equivalent measures of a basic literacy), the illiteracy rate fell to 13 per cent.

With regard to forging links across age, class, and urban-rural divides, the CNA did perhaps as much as might be done. More than 50,000 high school and university students left the cities to spend five months as literacy teachers living with *campesino* families and communities. Numerous accounts tell of the profound effect this experience had on young urban *brigadistas*. Many admitted they had known nothing of rural existence previously, and were distressed to discover and experience the conditions endured by the rural poor (Angus, 1981; Hirshon, 1983; Miller, 1985). The experience did much to build informed compassion and commitment on the part of *brigadistas*, large numbers of whom became active in a range of mass organizations upon returning home after the campaign.

To evaluate the CNA in terms of providing a basis for ongoing adult education we must turn to the EPB. For readers interested in more detail than is possible here, Robert Arnove and I have each described EPB up to its zenith in

1984 (Arnove, 1986; Lankshear and Lawler, 1987) and a comprehensive account is available in Spanish (Torres, 1985).

The EPB was conceived as a 'special elementary school' for adults. In part it was to provide an opportunity for adults who had not become literate via the CNA to do so if they wished. It offered a basic literacy course prior to the first level of study. Mainly, however, EPB was intended to go beyond the learning attained in the CNA and provide an appropriate general education for adults roughly equivalent to an elementary education. Between 1981 and 1984 a new level of study was added to the programme each semester until all six levels were in place. EPB covered language, maths, natural science, and social science (including history and geography). The grades were supposed to equate roughly with elementary school grades in terms of the sorts of skills to be acquired, the level of cognitive demand, and so on. But since it catered mainly for working adults and was intended to relate as closely as possible to their daily reality, the curriculum content stressed themes and examples dealing with production, administration, participation in mass organizations, and the like. There was also a strong ideological emphasis on the need to defend and further enhance the gains of the revolution through active involvement in the newly formed structures and social programmes (e.g., health, housing, vaccination, water supply and sanitation). Texts and workbooks were produced at low cost and distributed free by the Ministry of Education.

Pedagogically, EPB was intended to follow a sequence of observe, interpret, analyze and act — although this is more evident in the language and natural science courses, for example, than in mathematics. The lesson on 'Food and Health' from the first level language course illustrates the general character of EPB.

A codification shows 'basic grains' — circled by a range of fruits and vegetables. The discussion questions ask: 'what foods do we see in the picture?'; 'why do rice, beans, and corn appear in the centre?'; and 'which of these foods do we eat?' The analysis and component of the lesson comprises a brief text, 'Let's Improve our Diet'. The text discusses malnutrition as a legacy of exploitation and oppression. It describes the government's concern to improve the diet of working people and steps being taken to that end. In addition, however, the people themselves must make some changes — eat a more balanced diet by supplementing basic grains with fruit, fish, vegetables, etc.

The interpretation exercise asks learners to make lists of foods with which they are familiar as a group; to discuss the relationship between health and nutrition; and to write a brief statement — based on group discussion — of what is meant by saying 'food is to the body what petrol is to the vehicle'.

Finally, the section 'Let's Transform Reality' asks learners to write individually all they can think of that they could do to cultivate fruits or green vegetables that improve the diet.

Arnove found groups using sociodrama, role playing, small group discussion, and building class montages of newspaper and magazine clippings to illustrate and explore social issues. The media also contributed.

Once a week, the FSLN newspaper, *Barricada*, publishes a page that contains a theme discussed in simple language and printed in large type so that it can be used as part of ongoing adult education activities. Twice daily (5:30–6:00), the program *Puño en Alto* [Fist Raised High — the Sandinista salute] is broadcast over all radio stations providing suggestions for instructional activities and featuring the accomplishments of CEPs [see text below] from different regions of the country. (Arnove, 1986, p. 50)

It is in the establishment and consolidation of EPB between 1981 and 1984 that the motivating and empowering effect of the literacy acquired in the CNA is best evidenced. For the EPB was seen from the outset as an educational programme that in many cases — in the countryside, especially — would have to operate without recognizable teachers.

The CNA had been a mass mobilization. Students, teachers, and other professionals had comprised a large part of the teaching force. Schools had been closed for the duration of the CNA to provide literacy instructors. A very high proportion of these people would be lost to the EPB when they returned, necessarily, to their normal civilian life. If there were to be an ongoing education programme for adults, those who had themselves recently become literate in the CNA would have to assume a major responsibility for creating, maintaining, and co-ordinating the 'popular education collectives' (CEPs): the teacher-learning units of the EPB.

During the CNA, learning had gone on in small groups, for example, a cluster of neighbours attached to a teacher. As the CNA neared its end, a policy to create an ongoing adult education programme was announced. Literacy teachers invited their most able or most willing learner to become a CEP co-ordinator, having responsibility for leading the group's learning activities. Of every ten or so co-ordinators one would serve as a promoter, having responsibility for 'teaching' as well as for promoting interest and involvement in the CEP within the neighbourhood.

Naturally, many who took up the call initially doubted their ability to do the job. In the event, tens of thousands proved equal to the task, proving to themselves that previously illiterate people *could* assume the historical task of continuing their own learning and facilitating that of others, with sympathetic support from government. There were many problems, and frequent frustrations as individuals and groups ran up against the limits of their capabilities. Yet by this approach, born of necessity, teaching and learning were demystified in important ways, and considerable learning *did* occur (Torres, 1985, 1986; Lankshear and Lawler, 1987). Moreover, the experience communicated by one 'popular teacher' spoke for many when he said:

Imagine that as night falls you turn into a popular teacher. I speak of someone like myself, who had never studied and had only been through the 'school of life'. Now, imagine thousands like me giving classes throughout the country at this very moment [Classes ran 5 evenings a week, for 2 hours each]. They give us a little economic help, but the important thing is that the knowledge of one is also for others. And you tell me, with how much money in the world can you pay for that? (Torres, 1986, p. 17)

At its peak, EPB attracted almost 200,000 learners in a single semester (from a total population of barely 3 million), who set aside time after each working day to co-teach and co-learn with their peers. (Co-ordinators and promoters had to devote rather more time, especially on weekends, to be prepared for their roles.) Three years after the CNA had ended the programme could still attract 165,000 to the first semester, despite the many problems and short-comings facing EPB by that time (Torres, 1985, 1986; Ford, 1986, p. 16).

This commitment can be explained in part by the fact that for many Nicaraguans the learning and enhanced literacy skills acquired via EPB did indeed map onto some important daily needs, and were experienced as essential elements of personal, community, and national development.

Adult Literacy and Gender

From the time the Spanish arrived a quite extreme form of patriarchy developed in Nicaragua. Its more widely recognized features are commonly incorporated in the concept of *machismo*. At one level, as a hegemonic celebration of male privilege and supremacy, *machismo* is revealed in open acceptance of double standards favouring males, or in symbolic acts like the order of service at meals. At a more overtly extreme level, the attitude that women are at the service of male ease and gratification underwrites some repugnant practices of female servility and degradation and, not infrequently, extreme acts of brutality and cruelty.

Nicaraguan culture situated women, regardless of their social class location, in extreme subordination to their husbands, to the point of denying them legal rights in respect of their children. The Law of Paternal Dominion defined the man as sole head of the family, with absolute rights over children. At marriage a woman passed from the house of her father to that of her husband in the manner of property. A host of double standards and inequalities followed from such a social construction of gender relations. In matrimonial law, for instance, 'adultery' was interpreted as applying only to wives. A husband's infidelity was not adultery but 'concubinage'. Similarly, a mistress could inherit from her lover, but a wife could not inherit from hers. If a man left home leaving his wife to raise his children, he could legally return at any time, claim the children as property, and remove them from their mother's home.

Poor women bore an additional yoke of oppression. A woman of wealth could expect a patronized existence dedicated to administering the home, domestic economy, and the children's education and, perhaps, working for church or charity. Poor women, however, were forced to seek work wherever it was available — in addition to domestic tasks — and on whatever terms. Their work typically afforded no independence, security or dignity. Undereducated city women relied on domestic work, selling in markets, or prostitution. *Campesino* women depended on scarce seasonal work on large holdings. Wherever they worked women were paid less than men, and where they worked in the same place as their husbands they often endured the husband collecting their pay.

The 1979 FSLN Programme pledged policies 'to abolish the odious discrimination that women have been subjected to compared to men [and] to establish economic, political, and cultural equality between woman and man' (Borge, 1982). Revolutionary leaders and cadres of each sex widely recognized that women experienced a special oppression of their own, and that pursuing the ideal of equality and dignity would be an immense task. Throughout the revolution years regular assessments were made of what had been achieved and what remained to be done. An example from December 1987 is typical.

A new constitution had been signed into law in January 1987, following months of mass public participation in debating issues, proposed clauses, etc. One key article in the constitution, states: 'Family relations rest on respect, solidarity, and absolute equality of rights and responsibilities between the man and woman. Parents must work together to maintain the home and provide for the integral development of their children, with equal rights and responsibilities'. *Envio's* analyst commented as follows:

> The chapter [of the Constitution] as a whole sets the tone for a new vision of the Nicaraguan family, one which will hopefully be translated into reality step by step. Clearly, there is always a gap between law and reality, and the situation for Nicaraguan women lags far behind the ideal expressed in the Constitution. Laws still date back to the 1904 civil code. ... Though laws cannot change reality overnight they are essential in bringing about the first steps towards transformation of that reality. In addition, they serve as an important instrument of education ... [a necessary process given] a deep reserve of *machista* (sexist) sentiments, even among male revolutionaries who recognize the need to change their attitude. (Instituto, 1987, p. 31)

Further examples round the picture out. The women's mass organization, AMNLAE (Ruchwarger, 1987), formed its Women's Legal Office in 1983 to help women gain access to the legal process — recognizing that laws on their own are never enough. In 1985 the Office publicly criticized the failure of existing legal arrangements and drafted a proposal for constitutional change. Its director explained the urgent need for constitutional attention to the rights of women within the household.

> We are confronted with some painful realities. Women mercilessly beaten; pregnant women forced to stoop and remove their husband's shoes; women denied a divorce because they cannot prove they are abused; women who, after living for years with a man, suddenly find themselves without a roof over their heads because he has decided to end the relationship. (*Barricada Internacional*, 1985, p. 5)

In taking such cases to court, the Legal Office often received hostile rulings, because 'interpretations of the law, and often the laws themselves, are still class oriented and sexist' (*Barricada Internacional*, 1985, p. 5). Sexism also operated within the agricultural sector, despite the key role that women play in the rural economy.

Within the crucial arena of employment, while it is true that the Labour Code instituted equal pay for equal work it is evident that for most women work is not equal. Ruchwarger notes the dramatic increase from 1979 in the proportion of the economically active population who were women. 1983 figures estimated that 35 per cent of the economically active population (i.e., paid workforce) were women. This was almost twice the average for Latin America. In Nicaragua's cities the rate was 40 per cent. The overwhelming majority, however, were in services (especially domestic work) or commerce (market vendors). Domestic work is especially exploitative (Ruchwarger, 1987, pp. 198–9). Only 4 per cent of Managua's employed women are professionals and 1 per cent of those on the Atlantic Coast. Women comprise just 14 per cent of Managua's industrial labour force, are still 'concentrated in the lowest levels of the Ministry of Labour's national salary scale and though they are the majority of workers in certain occupations such as textiles, men still occupy the bulk of the supervisory positions' (Instituto, 1987, p. 20).

We are warned, then, against making bold or romanticized claims on behalf of revolutionary efforts to tackle *machismo* and establish gender equality. Yet, it is true that significant steps have been taken to address material and ideological dimensions of women's oppression. Despite extreme economic constraints, day care facilities have grown and by 1985 over 80,000 children received day care. Other oft-cited gains include official prohibition of using women's bodies in advertising, creation of production co-operatives to create new jobs and leadership roles for women, a notable proportion of leadership positions within the Sandinista government held by women (32 per cent), legal provision for three months paid maternity leave, etc. Against enormous odds 195,687 women became literate in the CNA, compared to 210,429 men (Ruchwarger, 1987, p. 199). Against this background we can trace some aspects of the significance of literacy initiatives in addressing gender equality.

The CNA presented a major context in which to unveil, politicize, and begin to address in social practice barriers to liberation in general and women's liberation in particular. Two aspects are especially important:

1. Literacy learning offered an opportunity for Nicaraguans *en masse*, across class, ethnicity, and gender, to problematize gender oppression as a key historical dimension of structured domination. Lessons posed the reality of women's oppression, and the necessary concern of revolutionary practice to address it, to *all* participants.
2. The CNA became a mass exercise in women's participation. Women comprised 60 per cent of the teaching force, half the learners, and almost half the graduates. Prior to the actual start of the campaign AMNLAE had organized and sponsored fundraising events, actively promoted the CNA, and organized literacy classes in the cities — arranging for women to teach in their neighbourhoods, encouraging illiterate adults to enrol as learners, and organizing childcare to enable women to take part.

Lesson 19 in the CNA primer illustrates the concern to problematize patriarchy and women's oppression. Its theme was 'Nicaraguan women have traditionally been exploited. The revolution now makes their liberation possible'. Discussion proceeded from a photograph showing an assembly of women, arms in the air and fists clenched. Focusing questions included: 'why in our society are women considered inferior to men?'; 'what factors help the process of liberation within the Revolution?'; 'can you give some concrete examples of tasks undertaken by the mass organizations to bolster the liberation of women?'; 'why is *machismo* a counter-revolutionary attitude?'

The formal (reading and writing) part of the lesson was based on sentences like: 'We exported more than we imported', 'women participated actively during the war', 'they wanted to defend their rights', which were intended to identify the promotion of gender equality *within* the overall revolutionary project (Instituto, 1987, p. 19). Nicaragua was poor because it was locked into economic deficit in unequal exchange/trade relations with stronger powers. Nicaraguans would have to tackle this by increasing productivity, accepting austerity, and foregoing imports. The other sentences turn to women specifically, addressing consciousness of women's capabilities and legitimate interests. Women were to be seen and to see themselves as effective historical agents with rights of their own to be observed. The theme of women's participation links to that of economic life, shifting the emphasis from Nicaraguans generally having a role in boosting the economy to women *in particular* having this role — and the capacity to perform it, just as they had proved themselves in the war.

While these sentences were being discussed and made into the building blocks of learning to read and write — using Freire's technique — women were joining AMNLAE in increasing numbers, and AMNLAE was encouraging women into the workforce and into other forms of organized participation. Thus the process of becoming aware of revolutionary values and practices relating to women was tied closely to active experience of and participation in these same values and practices within daily life.

The very experience of the CNA challenged traditional conceptions of women's role and the options available to them. Many teachers were young middle-class women (students) who, contrary to the initial fears of their parents, survived the rigours of the CNA in remote and extremely poor communities, where disease and injury were ever present risks, and attacks by Contra groups an added danger. The CNA gave young women a chance 'to test their skills and live independently from their families'. In so doing, many 'gained a new sense of identity and confidence and decided upon new career directions in rural development, careers that had traditionally been closed to women' (Miller, 1985, p. 200). For many the future could not be the same again — a fact for parents to come to terms with, which they often did.

> Returning from the CNA I had certain conflicts with my family; they wanted me to remain a little girl, an object. In the crusade we women felt liberated, we all worked, we helped out in everything and we were not under the thumb of our parents. We survived for five months alone and that gives you the experience to know how to run your own life. (Miller, 1985, p. 203)

Working-class women in the cities and countryside who became literate in the CNA and EPB also began to see themselves differently and take on new roles and tasks accordingly. Some volunteered to co-ordinate learning groups in the EPB. Others assumed roles in unions, defence committees, AMNLAE, and work co-operatives. Thus one young *campesina*, Alva Rosa, 'is not only a health *brigadista*, but also a popular education co-ordinator. Last year she taught two *campesinos* to read, and this year she's matriculated more' (Hirshon, 1983, p. 249). Literacy directly increased the economic options for some poor women, enabling them to take up work in health, administration, teaching, and other areas opened up by government policies. Elsewhere, women benefited from the impetus given to AMNLAE and other mass organizations by the practical, intellectual, and ideological fruits of the CNA. The benefits, however, are qualified.

AMNLAE, for example, played a major role during 1985–6 in stimulating national debate among women on constitutional demands. Women from all walks of life

> participated massively in the meetings on the political constitution, expressing with clarity and precision . . . our demands for free choice in bearing children, respect for our physical and psychological well being, access to positions of leadership based solely on merit, [improved] access to land and land titles, the right to full employment, the protection of maternity, and equality within the couple. (Vargos, 1986, p. 9)

Despite this achievement, a leading Nicaraguan poet, militant, and feminist, Gioconda Belli, questions the extent of the success claimed here and points to a crucial issue. This concerns the inevitable limits of progress towards full equality and emancipation for women within a context of inadequate ideological formation. It raises the further issue of the extent to which women might actually be *exploited* within the process of pursuing wider revolutionary goals, whereby women's concern to play a positive part and not present obstacles to 'the Revolution' may actually result in their interests being submerged. According to Belli, while AMNLAE *has* encouraged women to enter the workforce, enhance productivity, assume active roles in defence, health, education, it has been much less successful in promoting an ideological climate in which women's *real* problems can be addressed effectively. Belli claims that as women become more involved in the revolution and increase their involvement as active agents of change, 'they have to face a complex social and family situation' in which 'women find themselves alone in resolving their problems'. This calls for a strong women's organization which can provide a clear, forceful ideological lead (Belli, in Vargos, 1986).

Belli found AMNLAE unequal to the task. It had to wrestle ideologically with the obstacles facing women's equality and emancipation; going beyond the step of integrating women into the workforce, to play a persuasive intellectual role in pushing society as a whole to embrace a concern for women's problems as ones affecting *all* members of the society. So, in the CNA, EPB, health campaigns, and other revolutionary projects

> AMNLAE actively took on the role of organizer, but was unable to complement it by bringing women's problems to the forefront of society; what was missing was the ideological orientation required for an undertaking of this scope, which involves changing both patterns of thought and action, rather than only seeking material gains. (Belli, in Vargos, 1986)

Belli's critique speaks to the difficulties noted earlier in respect of the legal process and women's full membership and participation in organizations like UNAG and structures like rural agricultural co-operatives. It also suggests that even if the revolution had not been stalled at the ballot box, the principles and goals formalized constitutionally would still have faced a long historical struggle for their actualization.

This forces a realistic appraisal of advances made by women during the brief ten years of the Nicaraguan Revolution, and the impact of literacy initiatives on traditional structures and ideologies of patriarchy. What can be said, however, and what is surely important, is that the revolutionary process in general, the vision and practice of literacy within that process, and the historical role increasingly assumed by women in particular, were 'on the right track'. Involvement in the CNA and EPB exposed women directly — in principle and, increasingly, in practice — to new ideological positions and provided further access to them via print, as well as to the lived practice of historical agency. Institutions and processes — like AMNLAE, its legal office, a constitution and a democratic constitutional process, mass public debate and fora involving leaders and public — with genuine progressive possibilities for the pursuit of women's equality, dignity and independence, had been established. In such a context literacy can assume potent liberatory power. In part, this is reflected in AMNLAE's own efforts to publish material offering literate women access to new transformatory ideas. Thus from 1983 AMNLAE published articles on sexual education, including detailed information on contraception, in its monthly magazine *Somos*. While it was true that 'few women [thought] of birth control in terms of women's rights to control their own bodies' (Ruchwarger, 1987, p. 187) — scarcely surprising in such a profoundly Catholic and patriarchal society — the fact is that critiques like Belli's also were available in the popular media, opening the way for further advance.

Adult Literacy and Ethnicity

From November 1981 Miskitu Indian leaders and many of their people joined Contra forces to fight the Sandinista Government, resulting in the forced relocation of Miskitu communities, massive disruption to Atlantic Coast life, and a tragic cost of life, goodwill and infrastructure. The Miskitu leadership within the representative body of Nicaragua's Amerindians — Misurasata[6] — waged war around claims to land and other conditions of sovereignty seen as alienated by government policies, claiming a general lack of sensitivity and commitment to the rights and claims of ethnic minorities by the Sandinistas.

In 1984 the government admitted earlier errors and about-faced its position regarding the demands of minorities, initiating a process to implement autonomy for the Atlantic Coast within the overall revolutionary project. Autonomy was legislated constititionally in 1987. Key principles included the following:

- The rights to the full expression of their ethnic identity must be guaranteed to all groups . . . in equal measure to Indians who first occupied the lands and to those who came later as ethnically identifiable groups and developed culturally within a shared historical experience different from the other side of the country.
- The rights guaranteed are not inherently 'special', but are those historically taken for granted by the dominant culture and denied to all others; if they are given special attention now, it is in compensation for that long denial.
- Ethnic identity is not limited to cultural expressions such as language, traditional religions and customs, but encompasses the political, economic and social spheres as well. In particular, it is acknowledged that a culture

cannot preserve itself and grow without an economic base (Instituto, 1989, 41).

This position was embraced by the Atlantic Coast people, bringing an end to local hostilities. It sought to retain the original Sandinista commitment to addressing gross material inequalities and establishing a base for just economic development, whilst satisfying the quest of minority groups for cultural integrity. Within autonomy, the government would retain control over international relations, national defence, juridical norms, and national economic planning. It would preserve government intent to prevent in the long term a situation like that 'where an impoverished Mississippi can coexist alongside a prosperous California'. To this end, Nicaragua's strategic economic resources had been nationalized and their exploitation would continue to be controlled by 'a state committed to the development of its poorest sectors, not to the capital accumulation of its richest' (Instituto, 1989, p. 42).

Language and literacy policies were essential ingredients in the pursuit of autonomy, development, and justice within the revolution. In 1980 Misurasata had demanded a literacy campaign in Miskitu, Sumu, and Creole to augment the Spanish language CNA, which had taken place on the Atlantic Coast as well as in the west. This had proceeded, together with a dramatic extension of primary schooling, prior to Misurasata linking with the Contra in war.

To grasp the ethnicity issues involved and the significance of literacy and minority language programmes, it is necessary to sketch the demography and history of the coast. In 1979, with some 300,000 inhabitants, the Atlantic Coast comprised 10 per cent of Nicaragua's population. It was home to six ethnic groups. As elsewhere, Spanish speaking *mestizos* predominated, accounting for 65 per cent of the people. In addition there were 70,000 Miskitu, 26,000 Creoles, up to 7,000 Sumu, 1,500 Garifonas or black Caribs, and 700 Rama. Many of these groups were bilingual, but each had its 'mother tongue'. Only 23 living Rama speakers and a few Garifona speakers remained. Like the Creoles, most Rama and Garifona spoke Creole English. In all, minority groups comprised 5 per cent of Nicaragua's population.

Historically, the Atlantic Coast developed along completely different lines from the Pacific Coast. The traditional mistrust of 'things from Managua' was strong when the revolution arrived. *Envio* provides the best short historical backdrop:

Between the mid seventeenth century and 1894 the region was indirectly ruled by the British, through their local allies, the Miskitu Indians, while the Pacific side was directly settled by the Spanish, who assimilated, exterminated, or exported to work in the Peruvian goldmines the Indian people originally living there. The period bracketed by the 'reincorporation' of the coast in 1894 and the overthrow of Somoza in 1979 saw the British-backed Miskitu monarchy displaced from power by a Creole elite, themselves almost immediately subordinated by racist administrators from Managua; the ravaging of the coast's resources [especially gold, timber and fruit] by North American companies; the consolidation of the Moravian Church — first by US missionaries and much later by native pastors and administrators — as the social, and often political,

> backbone, of community and urban life; and the Somoza government's awakening economic interest in the coast in the 1960s . . . The latter half of 1979 brought to the coast, full blown, a wide-reaching revolution in which [its] population had taken little or no part. (Instituto, 1988, pp. 31–2)

One of the most important features of the 1894 'reincorporation' by Zelaya's government was that Spanish became the required language of instruction in Atlantic Coast schools. While Moravian schools remained open and strove to ensure retention of English as an academic subject, the language requirement, combined with a dearth of schools in the region as a whole, contributed to extreme educational and social marginality of Amerindian groups and, by 1978, had also put the survival of Creole English in jeopardy.

The situation in 1979 was complex and had its ironies. Amerindian groups (excepting Rama) retained their language, but literacy levels were extremely low. In the south, where Creoles concentrated, there were more schools and higher literacy levels. But, as Holm observed in the 1970s,

> it must be asked how much longer . . . Creole will continue to be learned by the children of Creoles in Bluefields . . . Everyone in Bluefields agrees that Creole children speak better Spanish than their parents; in school they learn not only to read and think in Spanish but also to play games. In Bluefields I noticed that groups of children playing and shouting in Spanish sometimes included no *Ladinos*. (Holm, in Hurtubise, 1990, p. 18)

To the problem of cultural erosion must be added those of racism and extreme poverty endured by undereducated ethnic minorities. According to Bourgois, the revolution confronted a reality in which, unlike *mestizo* workers and peasants, ethnic minorities suffered ethnic oppression in addition to class exploitation.

> The Miskitu, Sumu, and Rama were at the bottom of the local class-ethnic hierarchy, performing the least desirable, and most poorly paid jobs. In the goldmines . . . for example, the Miskitu and Sumu were usually relegated to the most dangerous, strenuous jobs . . . where they suffered from the highest rates of silicosis. (Bourgois, 1985, p. 36)

The poor *mestizos*, many of whom were landless labourers who had migrated from the west, came above the Amerindians and below the Creoles. Like many Miskitu they worked in poorly paid agricultural jobs, were often unemployed, and had a high illiteracy rate. The better educated Creoles dominated skilled jobs and found white collar work in disproportionate numbers. A stratum of upper-class Pacific born *mestizos* in administrative and politically appointed positions had the highest status among locals, surpassed in the hierarchy only by North American and European whites who owned or ran the mining and timber export companies. To this picture must be added a deeply entrenched racial prejudice, whereby *mestizos* and Creoles regarded the inferiority of Indian groups 'as a matter of common sense', and working-class/peasant *mestizos* looked down on the Creoles for their colour (Bourgois, 1985, p. 36).

The revolutionary agenda for education on the Atlantic Coast admitted multiple aims, all of which had implications for language and literacy. Full integration into the life of the nation presupposed literacy. As Spanish was the national language there were obvious advantages to having oral and literate fluency in Spanish. However, to equalize educational opportunities and wider social chances contingent upon education, it was also seen as necessary to open up education via mother tongues as far as possible. Collectively, these aims ultimately led to a bilingual and bicultural education policy.

The government's first steps, prior to the internal war from 1981, were to act on Misurasata's demand for a second stage to the CNA in Creole, Miskitu and Sumu, and to pass a bilingual education law promising Miskitu-Spanish and English-Spanish schooling in Miskitu and Creole communities. The ethnic languages CNA was launched on 31 August 1980 and resulted in 12,500 people, from Miskitu, Sumu, Rama, Garifona, and Creole communities, becoming literate.

This was accompanied by an ongoing adult education programme which drew 6,000 students, and a dramatic extension to primary schooling. In the north of the Atlantic Coast the number of teachers increased from 333 to 719, and students from 7,610 to 24,783, between 1979 and 1983. Despite the increases, a mere 22 per cent of eligible students were in primary school and drop-out rates were high. Secondary schooling was almost negligible, with just six secondary schools in total. In the southern part of the coast primary teachers increased from 156 to 410, thirty-six new primary schools had been built and fifty more started. Workshops to improve the instructional level of teachers were held regularly. By the end of 1983, however, the aggression had forced thirty-eight of the 100 schools in the zone to close.

The major subsequent development was the introduction of bilingual education from 1983, in a context of emerging peace. Hurtubise identifies three legislative moves which together provide the legal basis of bilingual, bicultural education: Decree 571, the revolutionary Constitution, and the Autonomy law (Hurtubise, 1990).

Decree 571 (1983) expresses commitment to promoting the educative, political, and economic development of Nicaragua, paying special attention to previously neglected areas. The Atlantic Coast peoples were to be integrated into the rest of the country, emphasizing their rights as Nicaraguan citizens. This entailed introducing 'a bicultural and bilingual education . . . responsive to the needs of integrating the ethnic minorities, taking into consideration ethnic identity and the historical realities of the region', and using 'mother tongue as a teaching technique as a fundamental factor in the development of identity and as a determining factor in the process of integration and for the consolidation of national unity.' The Decree authorized 'the teaching of preschool and the first four grades of primary school in the English and Miskito languages in the schools of areas occupied by indigenes and Creoles. At the same time, teaching of the Spanish language must be introduced in a gradual form' (Hurtubise, 1990, pp. 21–2). The Constitution guaranteed ethnic minorities the rights 'to preserve and develop their cultural identity within the national unity'; to 'freely express and preserve their languages, art and culture, having access to education in their mother tongue at levels determined in accord with national plans and programs'; and the right 'to live and develop under norms of social organisation that correspond to their traditions, histories and cultures' (Hurtubise, 1990, p. 23). These principles were further endorsed in the Autonomy law.

The most detailed description and evaluation of the bilingual programme available to date is Josef Hurtubise's study of the English-Spanish component in the south of the Atlantic Coast. Hurtubise chronicles the considerable efforts taken to conceive a viable programme, develop methods and materials, and implement bilingual education against the mighty odds faced by every educational initiative in Nicaragua. The latter include a very scarce supply of trained teachers, chronic shortfalls in funding and resources, lack of experience in preparing teachers, methods, and materials for bilingual schooling, and the legacies of a costly and disruptive war. In addition, however, he notes problems peculiar to the English bilingual programme which had yielded less satisfactory results after four years than had been hoped for. Of particular note here is the government's choice to use Standard English rather than Creole as the language variant, and the absence in Nicaragua of a familiar alternative to the FAS (Phonetic Analytic Synthetic) system of literacy instruction. FAS works remarkably well with regular languages like Spanish and Portuguese, as demonstrated by Freire and the Cuban and Nicaragua literacy campaigns. But it is far less effective when used with irregular languages like English.

Local officials specified five long-term goals for the English bilingual programme. It was hoped that bilingual education would:

1. reduce the primary school drop out rate;
2. raise general academic achievement on the coast;
3. increase the numbers of students completing the basic cycle so that more could go on to higher specialized courses;
4. increase the productivity of the rural population;
5. enrich the cultural identity of ethnic minorities, enabling them to participate more effectively in Nicaragua's cultural and technical development.

In 1983 31 per cent of pupils on the coast dropped out in first grade. Despite an enrolment of 7,500 in the first two grades, just 464 students completed sixth grade in the south of the Atlantic Coast. Language was the main factor blamed for dropping out. In a complex linguistic setting, 'children who were not first language Spanish speakers were suffering directly as a result of language difficulties . . . and further . . . as a result of an incomplete grasp of Spanish [by] teachers'. It was a case of children learning 'to speak one language without learning how to read and write in it' and learning 'to read and white in another without learning well how to speak it' (Hurtubise, 1990, pp. 28–9).

Bilingual education was introduced gradually, beginning with a four year trial. Selected schools took a cohort of students through the first four grades in Standard English. This would provide a data base and an opportunity to identify and tackle problems, assess materials and methods, and evaluate teacher training in new strategies. Progress and problems were tabled and addressed in workshops. Each year more classes and more schools were introduced. The aim was that by the end of four years all primary schools with English speaking students would have their first grade classes integrated into bilingual education.

The academic base [involved] instruction in all curriculum subjects in English with the introduction of Spanish as a second language in the Second, Third and Fourth grades, at which point it was the intention of . . . central government to have Bilingual classes streamed back into the Spanish speaking school system. (Hurtubise, 1990, p. 37)

A workshop held in May 1987, in the fourth year of the programme, revealed the following results from an informal selection of cases.

3rd grade   9/122 students read 'adequately'
             17/122 students read 'slowly'
             96/122 students were not reading
             22 per cent reading; 78 per cent not reading
4th grade   10/26 students read 'adequately'
             16/26 read 'badly'
             38 per cent reading; 62 per cent reading badly

The four schools with bilingual and bicultural classes at third and fourth grades reported pass rates as follows.

Table 7.1:   Third and Fourth Grade Pass Rates: Bautisto, Tabernaculo, San Marcos and Luisa Velasquez

	English	Math	Spanish
Bautisto	29/58–50%	37/54–68%	34/54–63%
Tabernaculo	4/26–15%	16/26–62%	7/26–27%
San Marcos	19/29–66%	24/29–83%	14/29–34%
Luisa Velasquez	13/22–59%	16/22–73%	15/22–68%

Tabernaculo, San Marcos and Luisa Velasquez reported pass rates in Social Studies of 47 per cent, 34 per cent and 68 per cent respectively. All schools, however, reported 100 per cent pass rates in Physical Education and Arts and Crafts, where no performance in Standard English is required. Schools aim at achieving 100 per cent pass rates, hence the results actually achieved were highly disappointing.

The teaching and assessment situation was complex. While instruction was *supposed* to occur in Standard English across the curriculum teachers were in fact forced to resort to Creole, because their own Standard English was book-learned and rudimentary. All written assessment, however, *did* take place in Standard. Measured performance in subjects requiring written responses consequently reflected difficulties with English, where students who could sight read were often 'reading' with minimal meaning and comprehension. In effect, Standard English was effectively being taught as a foreign language rather than as a heritage language and the medium of instruction.

Hurtubise concludes that after four years the students had largely failed to acquire satisfactory skills in reading and writing English. 'They did not become confident users of Standard English nor did they gain even basic literacy skills in their mother tongue, as was achieved in the Miskito and Sumu programmes' (Hurtubise, 1990, p. 71). He sees the primary reason for the poor results of the English programme being the government's choice of Standard rather than Creole English — a choice clearly based on perceptions of the greater economic and technical value of Standard English, although there were very likely 'elitist' factors operating as well.

Interestingly, the programme brought a dramatic increase in retention rates among Creole students. 1985 figures indicated 94 per cent of students staying at school, a figure maintained through 1988. This, however, seemed to indicate 'more a parental approval of the aspiration to Standard mastery than any increased ease experienced by students' (Hurtubise, 1990, p. 52). All the same, Hurtubise reports improved performance in Spanish and Mathematics.

Any final assessment is difficult. Such educational change takes time. Moreover, we are speaking of a context in which of the 334 teachers in the zone, three were university graduates, eighty-one had graduated from primary teacher training, and the rest were 'empirical' teachers, young people moving directly from secondary school into classroom teaching. The difficulties in training teachers and developing satisfactory instructional methods and materials were immense. Part of the problem undoubtedly stemmed from the relative unease of *all* personnel involved in developing the bilingual programme with Standard English. Text materials were extremely stilted and generally inadequate in technical terms for instructional purposes. The Creole tradition is rich in poetry and prose, and good instructional materials are more easily produced from such a basis. Hurtubise recommended using Creole as the instructional language, adopting standardized spellings, developing personal content rather than imposing content through largely alien texts, and teaching English along with Spanish as a foreign language. Against this, we must weigh the vastly improved retention rates and resultant improvement in the general level of educational achievement in the population. Ironically, for all the social and educational debate that went on, it was nature which spoke loudest in the short run. In October 1988, Hurricane Joan ripped through the Atlantic Coast, causing vast destruction and ensuring that the most urgent education efforts for some time would be confined to rebuilding schools and replacing lost materials.

In the end, by the time it was voted from power, the government *had* won overwhelming support and enthusiasm for the principle of Atlantic Coast autonomy within the revolution. As an indication of goodwill and serious intent, the bilingual/bicultural education approach contributed much to this acceptance. As with the case of women, material and ideological conditions conducive to progressive historical advance had been established, and the significance of language and literacy initiatives within these was considerable.

Postscript

There are many important issues relating to literacy in the Nicaraguan Revolution that cannot be addressed here. Most have not yet been explored in any depth. Throughout the revolution years there was considerable debate about classroom texts, which bore a distinct FSLN imprint. Arnove offers the best account available to date in English, but there is a need for more detailed work. *Envio* provides brief sketches of some of the aspects involved (Instituto, 1983, 1984) and it is evident that text production over the years definitely reflected a softening of Sandinismo ideology. The UNO alliance stated its intention to revise all texts, and moved to make major educational change immediately after taking power by changing most high level *funcionarios* in the Ministry of Education — indicating that 'reform' of texts and curricula would surely follow.

The print media itself comprised a site of protracted and bitter struggle, focusing mainly around the overtly anti-Sandinista stance increasingly taken by *La Prensa*. This stance resulted in the brief suspension of the daily following editorial support for the US$100 million 'aid' package voted to the Contra by the Reagan Administration in April 1986. *Envio* again provides the best source here.

In the final analysis we are left with the question of what literacy initiatives meant for the lives of traditionally marginalized Nicaraguans during this period. For many the impact was minimal and temporary — especially once economic conditions and reactive policies eroded, and in many cases ended, initiatives bringing the kinds of improvements that give *meaning* to becoming literate and persevering with education (Lankshear and Lawler, 1987, 200–2). For others, however, becoming literate was integral to the experience of personal and collective empowerment and tangible material progress. A brief case study provides an appropriate basis for closure.

Among the earliest policies of the revolutionary government were initiatives encouraging co-operative production wherever appropriate (Ruchwarger, 1987). Generous incentives and techno-administrative support were made available. With encouragement to form and join co-operatives came a new opportunity for previously underemployed Nicaraguans to secure steady work and experience shared control over the work process. This development also imposed administrative demands on co-operative members, such as deciding how best to purchase raw materials, how much to charge for their product, how best to market and distribute it, etc. Many who formed or joined co-operatives had only recently become literate through the CNA.

The San José Co-operative in Monte Fresco — mid-way between Managua and the Pacific Coast — is a quite typical case. This is a light industrial manufacturing enterprise set in a traditionally agricultural community where work was always scarce, irregular, and poorly paid, and where men were commonly forced to live away from home to get work in the city. Founded in 1984, by 1989 the co-operative had grown to contain fifteen full members.

From a narrow initial production base, San José has diversified to make a range of products which feature in city supermarkets as well as in Managua's Oriental and Huembes markets. All involve intensive labour, although plant is becoming more sophisticated. Products are fairly simple, some being more lucrative than others. This level of activity, however, seriously strains the members' administrative and accounting capacities. Isabel, the Treasurer, put it well.

> My task as Treasurer is to have control of all the finances, materials, what we buy and sell, what we bring in; to know how much is in the bank, how much has been spent. I have to see which cheques go out and which come in; what the money was spent on. Sometimes I am supposed to make a statement of finances, and I can't because I understand only a little about numbers. Accountancy is based on numbers and one needs to multiply and divide, and I'm lacking in that. Sometimes when I can't do it I ask them to change me for another person, but they tell me I have to be there . . . There's no one else to do it.

Some limited assistance was available from a man who, however, worked full time for a co-operative in another region and was away for long periods. At these times, said Isabel,

> I can't keep up to date and be sure if he's up to date. When I was asked how much money was in the bank I didn't know — because he was away at the time and only he knew the figures then.

Isabel first learned to read and write in the CNA and continued in the EPB, completing Level 3. At that point the EPB classes folded in Monte Fresco. Her excitement at finding she could learn as an adult and her frustration when the classes came to an end were clear.

> Before the CNA I couldn't sign my name. I didn't even know what letter my name began with. I had to be led by the hand when I began, but the more I learned the more I could do on my own. When I couldn't write a sentence I worried, but when I started to be able to do it alone I was pleased . . . When I finished *Dawn of the People* I could read, and in the second level all seemed easy to me. Slowly I lost the fear. When I saw I could do it on my own I was thrilled.

Unfortunately, the EPB classes ceased at the very point where its curriculum could have assumed real value for her role as treasurer. She had learned to do basic mathematical operations in Levels 1–3. But

> in the 4th level they have much more . . . You learn accounting. it's in the textbook, but as I didn't finish I couldn't learn it . . . I'd like to be able to go on learning and finish the 6th level.

Even so, there were other opportunities to acquire administrative and accounting skills which built on what Isabel could already do. In February 1989 the Support Office of the Organization for Small Industry (Pequeña Industria)[7] offered the first in a series of week-long seminars on business administration and accountancy to members of co-operatives like San José. Isabel attended, and while she struggled rather more with the content and procedures than other participants who had completed EPB, she learned.

The seminar was built around a twenty-page 'text', *Concepts of Accountancy*, produced by the Pequeña Industria. Its central theme — that the bases of good business administration are accurate records and the orderly handling of accounts — was clearly accompanied by abundant everyday examples in accessible language. A simple system of accounts was introduced. Participants were taught how to complete a statement of profits or losses, and why this is important. They were then taken through the process of producing a general balance for a small business.

The text was supplemented with example sheets and problem sheets for group discussion and solution. Imagination games were a popular heuristic tool.

Much of the work was done in small groups, and participants were drawn as far into the *teaching* process as possible: for example, by having them work through their method and answer for the rest of the class, writing their procedure on the board or on paper displays, and by answering questions or responding to corrections posed by the class. A new point was never introduced until the previous one had been exhausted and the instructors were satisfied that everyone understood it as well as they were ₜoing to. In a key section the theme of the 'co-operative's doctor' was taken up. This was a trouble-shooting exercise. The 'doctor' diagnoses problems in the operation of a small business — by checking records to locate losses and the likely source of these — and, having located causes of problems, prescribes a cure.

Isabel commended the seminar in respect of its content, pitch, and pedagogy: virtues reflecting the pedagogical efforts undertaken in adult education since the planning stage of the CNA. The teachers, she said, taught well, using language she could understand. In group work, other participants would explain to her things she found difficult to understand: how income and expenditure work, how the balance sheet is done, how to discover if you are making a profit or loss on individual items and overall. This was revealing.

> I realized that here in San José we sometimes do things that are making a loss, and we carry on anyway. I learned to do the accounts and the balance, to keep the bankbook, how to see the expenditure and income figures. This was important because I didn't understand it before, yet it's my job. I've started to check our bank account. I was able to do it. One day I sat down to do what I'd learned in the seminar and I did it well.

She looked forward to the remaining seminars in the series, after which, 'the seminar instructors told us, we would know how to manage a co-operative well'.[8]

In such cases, we observe the potential of policies which address literacy in conjunction with wider structural change and programmes for just and democratic development. Whether or not adult education initiatives and the kind of support available to emergent producers through agencies like the Pequeña Industria survive the change of government in Nicaragua remains to be seen. What is certain, however, is that the adult literacy and education initiatives of the Sandinista Government were distinctive, and distinctively successful within the constraints experienced. They represent a notable moment in the dialectics of knowledge, culture and power, providing a telling counterpoint to the timid and conservative approaches generally taken to adult education elsewhere. Moreover, they will continue to present a signal challenge to adult literacy policies and practices worldwide in the years ahead.

Acknowledgment

I am indebted to my life-friends on the San José co-operative and throughout the Monte Fresco neighbourhood for making apparent to me just how important the important things in life are. They are a continuing source of inspiration, and their struggles are not in vain.

Notes

1 The Sandinista National Liberation Front. Originally an insurrectionary front, the FSLN became the political party of government after November 1984 and enjoyed the effective voice in the revolutionary government of 1979–84.
2 For an account of the Chamorro family in the Nicaraguan media see *Instituto Historico Centroamericano*, 1986, pp. 28–43.
3 The period from January 1937 to July 1979.
4 *Somocista* means 'of the Somozas and their governments.' *Somocismo* denotes the model of governing of the Somoza dynasty, and the general ideology that 'legitimated' it.
5 Because several non-Spanish linguistic communities exist on the Atlantic Coast, the CNA contained English, Sumu, and Miskitu variants as well as the Spanish programme.
6 A abbreviation for Miskitus, Sumus, Ramas and Sandinistas Working Together. See Center for Research and Documentation of the Atlantic Coast (CIDCA, 1984, p. 17).
7 An agency formed by the government specifically to assist small scale industrial producers.
8 The interviews with Isabel were conducted by the author on the San José co-operative during January and February 1989.

References

ANGUS, E. (1981) 'The Awakening of a People: Nicaragua's Literacy Campaign', *Two Thirds*, 2, 3.
ARNOVE, R. (1986) *Education and Revolution in Nicaragua*, New York, Praeger Press.
BARNDT, D. (1985) 'Popular Education', in WALKER, T. (Ed.) *Nicaragua: The First Five Years*, New York, Praeger Press.
BOOTH, J. (1982) *The End and the Beginning: The Nicaraguan Revolution*, Boulder, Westview Press.
BORGE, T. *et al.* (1982) *Sandinistas Speak*, New York, Pathfinder.
BOURGOIS, P. (1981) 'Class, ethnicity and the state among the Miskitu Amerindians of Northeastern Nicaragua', *Latin American Perspectives*, 29.
BOURGOIS, P. (1985) 'Nicaragua's ethnic minorities in the revolution', *Monthly Review*, 37, January.
CARDENAL, F. and MILLER, V. (1981) 'Nicaragua 1980: The battle of the ABCs', *Harvard Educational Review*, 51, p. 3.
CENTER FOR RESEARCH AND DOCUMENTATION OF THE ATLANTIC COAST (CIDCA) (1984) *Trabil Nani, Managua*, CIDCA.
CENTRO LATINOAMERICANO DE DEMOGRAFIA (1988) *La Mortalidad en la niñez en Centroamerica, Panama y Belice*, San José, CELADE.
'DOCUMENTS: WHY THE FSLN STRUGGLES IN UNITY WITH THE PEOPLE' (1979) *Latin American Perspectives*, 20, VI, Winter.
FORD, P. (1986) 'Nicaragua: total literacy deferred', *Development Forum*, April.
FREIRE, P. (1972) *Pedagogy of the Oppressed*, Harmondsworth, Penguin.
FREIRE, P. (1976) *Education: The Practice of Freedom*, London, Writers and Readers.
GREEN VALLEY FILMS, *The Dawn of the People*, 28 minutes, Burlington, Vermont.
HIRSHON, S. (1983) *And Also Teach Them to Read*, Westport, Lawrence Hill and Co.
HOLM, J. (1990) 'The Creole English of Nicaragua's Miskitu Coast', unpublished PhD dissertation, University of London, cited in HURTUBISE, J. (1990) 'Bilingual Education in Nicaragua: Teaching Standard English to Creole

Speakers', Unpublished Diploma of Education dissertation, University of Auckland.

HURTUBISE, J. (1990) 'Bilingual Education in Nicaragua: Teaching Standard English to Creole Speakers', Unpublished Diploma of Education dissertation, University of Auckland.

INSTITUTO HISTORICO CENTROAMERICANO (1983) 'The new education in the new Nicaragua: An open debate', *Envio*, 2, April.

INSTITUTO HISTORICO CENTROAMERICANO (1984) 'A new challenge: A people's education in the midst of poverty', *Envio*, 3, June.

INSTITUTO HISTORICO CENTROAMERICANO (1986) 'La Prensa: Post mortem on a suicide', *Envio*, 5, August.

INSTITUTO HISTORICO CENTROAMERICANO (1987) 'Becoming Visible: Women in Nicaragua', *Envio*, 6, December.

INSTITUTO HISTORICO CENTROAMERICANO (1988) 'Women, Poetry, New Nicaraguan Culture', *Envio*, 7, May.

INSTITUTO HISTORICO CENTROAMERICANO, (1989) 'From separation to autonomy — Ten years on the Atlantic Coast', *Envio*, 8, April.

LANKSHEAR, C. and LAWLER, M. (1987) *Literacy, Schooling and Revolution*, London, Falmer Press.

LAWLER, M. and LANKSHEAR, C. (1986) 'Adelante Mujer, con tu Participacion', *Landfall*, 158.

MILLER, V. (1985) *Between Struggle and Hope: The Nicaraguan Literacy Crusade*, Boulder, Westview Press.

MINISTRY OF EDUCATION (1980a) *Cuaderno de Educacion Sandinista: orientaciones para el alfabetisador*, Managua, Nicaraguan Ministry of Education.

MINISTRY OF EDUCATION (1980b) *El Amanecer del Pueblo*, Managua, Nicaraguan Ministry of Education.

'PENDING THE WOMEN'S ISSUE' (1986) *Barricada Internacional*, Managua, 8 May.

RUCHWARGER, G. (1987) *People in Power: Forging a Grassroots Democracy in Nicaragua*, South Hadley, Bergin and Garvey.

SERRA, L. (1985) 'The Sandinista mass organizations', in WALKER, T. (Ed.) *Nicaragua: The First Five Years*, New York, Praeger Press.

SUMMERHILL, D. and TOSER, L. (1990) 'Nicaragua: The psychological impact of "low intensity" warfare', *The Lancet*, 15 September.

TORRES, R-M. (1985) *Nicaragua: revolucion popular, educacion popular*, Managua, CRIES-INIES.

TORRES, R-M. (1986) *Los CEP: educacion popular y democracia participativa en Nicaragua*, Managua, CRIES.

VARGOS, M. (1986) 'Women in Revolution', *Barricada Internacional*, Managua, 9 October.

VILAS, C. (1990) 'What went wrong', *NACLA Report on the Americas*, XXIV, 1, June.

WALKER, T. (Ed.) (1985) *Nicaragua: The First Five Years*, New York, Praeger Press.

WEISSBERG, A. (1982) *Nicaragua: An introduction to the Sandinista Revolution*, New York, Pathfinder.

'WOMEN PROPOSE CONCRETE CHANGES' (1985) *Barricada International*, Managua, 3 October.

Chapter 8

Literacy and the Dynamics of Language Planning: The Case of Singapore

Anna Kwan-Terry and John Kwan-Terry

The year 1990 was not only the International Year of Literacy but also the year when Singapore celebrated the twenty-fifth anniversary of its independence as a nation. It is appropriate at this point to ask what literacy policies Singapore has adopted since independence and what effects have been brought about in Singapore today by these policies. In order to arrive at an understanding of the present Singapore situation, it is useful to begin with a brief look at the language and education history of this island-state, as questions of literacy in the country are inextricably tied up with its education and language policies.

Historical Background

The island of Singapore first came under British control in 1819. The settlement then had a population of about eighty Malays and forty Chinese, but it grew rapidly with immigrants from China, India and the Malay Archipelago. In the early years, the British administration decided that it would sponsor primary education in Malay, it being the language of the indigenous people. It also sponsored education in English to some extent, mainly for the practical purpose of training people to serve the local British administration. Thus in the early years of Singapore, literacy in Malay and English was the first to be developed, although only on a small scale. The teaching of the other local languages, Chinese and the Indian languages, on the other hand, was left mainly to schools set up by individuals or various communal or religious organizations (Gopinathan, 1974, pp. 2–3; Doraisamy, 1969, pp. 13–4; Soon, 1988, pp. 3–4).

By 1871, the population of Singapore had grown to 97,111, of which 56.2 per cent were Chinese, 11.1 per cent Indian, 26.9 per cent Malay and the rest of European and other stock. The Chinese character of the settlement became even more pronounced over the next fifty years, with the Chinese community accounting for three-quarters of the population. Between 1867 and the Second World War, there was substantial expansion in education using English as the medium of instruction, as more primary and some secondary schools were set up, mainly to serve the needs of the colonial administration and the British commercial enterprises. However, only very select pupils were given places in such English schools. There were also set up during this period many Chinese schools which came into existence, not through the initiative of the government, but through donations and efforts by the Chinese themselves. The colonial government continued to sponsor education in Malay, although only at the primary school level, while education in the Indian languages remained very much undeveloped. During this period, as the only avenue to secondary and higher education was through English, those who received their education in the local or ethnic languages were at a great social and economic disadvantage. The government's preferential treatment of schools in the different language streams created a chasm, in particular, between the Chinese-educated, which formed the majority, and the English-educated, which formed an elite minority, and this chasm was to be a source of political tension in the post-war years (Yong, 1968, p. 283).

After the war, a Ten-Year Programme was introduced by which primary education was made available in English, Malay, Chinese and Tamil in government-sponsored schools. However, the Malay and Tamil schools remained very much undeveloped, and this provoked criticism from the Malay community. Because of the Malay origin of Singapore itself, the location of Singapore among Malay-speaking neighbours, and Singapore's political affiliation to the Federation of Malaya, the Malay community were particularly aware of their right to their own language. The Indian community, on the other hand, showed relative lack of interest in preserving or promoting Tamil. No doubt its small size, the consequent lack of either economic or political power, together with the fact that not all Indians have Tamil as their own language, accounted for the fact that 'there were ten times more Indian children in English schools as in Indian schools' (Doraisamy, 1969, p. 121). As for education in Chinese, this continued to develop, up to the secondary level, although the government could hardly claim credit for it, as it was again the Chinese themselves who persevered with providing education in their own language. The interest of the government was to provide education in English, probably in order to ensure loyalty towards the British government, as there was much discontent among students in the Chinese schools (Mason, 1959, p. 25). The unequal distribution of financial resources for education in the different language streams is reflected in the figures for 1957 where 64 per cent of the total educational expenditure was used on English schools, 24.1 per cent on Chinese schools, 4.2 per cent on Malay schools and 0.3 per cent on Tamil schools (Gopinathan, 1974, p. 30). The attention given to English schools, in comparison with the lack of attention given to the Chinese, Malay and Tamil schools, brought about much dissatisfaction, especially among the Chinese. The problem was compounded by the lack of employment opportunities and career prospects for students from the Chinese schools. This remained the situation until the mid-1950s.

Towards Independence

Incipient discontent finally erupted into the Chinese student unrest of 1955 which in turn led to the setting up of a specially appointed All-Party Committee to look into the problems of the Chinese schools. This Committee included nine members, one of whom was the current Prime Minister, Lee Kuan Yew (Gopinathan, 1974, p. 19). The All-Party Report subsequently produced proved to be a very important document in Singapore education and literacy history and laid the foundation of language and education policies in Singapore today. Central to the report is the contention that it 'could not consider Chinese education by itself but had to delve into general policy on education and the trends of such education before and after the war' (Doraisamy, 1969, p. 50) and the philosophy that all the local, ethnic languages and cultures have an important role in contributing towards the development of a Singaporean national culture and ideology. With reference to the Chinese language and culture, and by implication other local, ethnic languages and cultures, the report declares:

> Chinese education will have to play its part, as also Chinese culture, with which it is inextricably mixed in the formation of a nation marching rapidly towards self-government and independence not by jettisoning its cultural ideals and values, but by tolerance and ready acceptance of the contributions of the other races and by sinking communal differences and jealousies, playing a significant if not predominant part in shaping a common ideology and embracing political entity and common outlook, which are inseparable features for national existence. (*Report of the All-Party Committee*, 1956, p. 4)

This motto of equal treatment for the major races and their languages to avoid racial conflicts and to foster nation-building was to be a cornerstone in the building of Singapore as a nation.

One recommendation of the All-Party Report was that of equal treatment for schools in the four language streams and the introduction of bilingual education in the primary schools and trilingual education in the secondary schools. The bilingual policy meant that a second language would be made available in all schools: English in the Chinese-, Malay- and Indian-medium schools and one of the local, ethnic languages — Chinese, Tamil or Malay — in the English-medium schools. In addition, Malay was to be made available for at least two years in the secondary schools. Thus from the start, English was given priority, no doubt because of its status as the language of science, technology and international commerce. Prominence was also given to the Malay language partly because of its regional value, and partly because Singapore was hoping to merge with the Federation of Malaya eventually. These recommendations were subsequently adopted and put into practice.

In 1963, Singapore merged with the Federation of Malaya. The union did not work, and in 1965, Singapore separated to become an independent nation.

Singapore Since Independence

With independence, Malay was proclaimed the national language and together with English, Chinese, Tamil, one of the four official languages. This is in keeping with the government's motto of multiculturalism and multilingualism that Lee Kuan Yew affirmed at the time:

I would like to believe that the two years we spent in Malaysia are years which will not be easily forgotten, years in which the people of migrant stock here — who are a majority — learnt of the terrors and the follies and the bitterness which is generated when one group tries to assert its dominance over the other on the basis of one race, one language, one religion. It is because I am fortified by this that my colleagues and I were determined, as from the moment of separation, that this lesson will never be forgotten. So it is that into the Constitution of the Republic of Singapore will be built-in safeguards, in so far as the human mind can devise, means whereby the conglomeration of numbers, of likeness — as a result of affinities of race or language or culture — shall never work to the detriment of those who, by the accident of history, find themselves in minority groups in Singapore . . . We have a vested interest in multi-racialism. (Josey, 1968, pp. 435–6)

As can be seen from what follows, Singapore's vested interest in multiracialism and multiculturalism has played a central role in shaping the country's language policy which in turn has determined its literacy policy.

Demographic Characteristics and the General Language Situation

The demographic and language situation in Singapore is complex and bears directly on any issue of literacy. The population of Singapore today, which stands at 2.6 million, is made up of about 77 per cent Chinese, 15 per cent Malay, 6 per cent Indian, and 2 per cent other races (Kuo and Jernudd, 1988). The language used in the home by people of different ethnic origins is not necessarily the user's ethnic language and much depends on the educational background of the speaker. Among the Chinese and Indians, for example, there is a proportion who have had English-medium education and who would use English in the home. The picture is further complicated by the fact that among the Chinese, a variety of local 'dialects' are used, depending to some extent, although not always so, on the dialect origin of the speaker. The most commonly used dialects are Hokkien, Teochew and Cantonese. In the 1960s, Mandarin Chinese was more a school language, used in inter-group communication among the Chinese to some extent, but not commonly used in the home domain. Among the Indians, there are again a variety of Indian languages used, Tamil being one of the more widely spoken, followed by Hindi, Gujarati, Malayalam and Punjabi among others. The Malays are the most homogeneous in that the Malay language is without rival the main language of communication in the home. In the early days of independence, it was also the language for inter-ethnic communication at the lower levels of society, although this position has been gradually eroded over the years and taken over by English. As the national language, it is also used on ceremonial occasions, but its use in society at large is rather limited. English, on the other hand, plays a dominant role and has become the main working language in a wide range of situations from the market-place, counters in government departments to the floor of Parliament, the Courts, industry and commerce (Llamzon, 1977, p. 36; Tay, 1979, p. 93; Kuo, 1980, p. 52; Kwan-Terry, 1989, pp. 5–6).

Expansion of Education in English

After independence, Singapore continued to support and practise equal treatment for education in the four language streams, although English retained its central position as the required language in all schools. The social-economic situation too, for many years both before and since independence, has put English at a great advantage over the other languages. It has become not only the language of prestige and upward social mobility, but also the *de facto* working language which enables a person proficient in it to command a higher income relative to the other official languages. Tables 8.1 and 8.2 below reflect the differences in the earning potentials of persons with different language backgrounds in 1966 and 1980:

Table 8.1:   Average Monthly Income of Full-time Employees without Job Training (1966)

Age	10–19	20–29	30–39	40–49	50–59
Education					
Completed Secondary Chinese-Medium (Males)	141.67	200.31	347.35	438.81	403.52
Completed Secondary English-Medium (Males)	177.28	352.00	631.61	774.78	674.9
Completed Secondary Chinese-Medium (Females)	153.65	178.73	263.41	357.42	—
Completed Secondary English-Medium (Females)	184.84	251.67	404.30	486.92	—

Source: Unpublished Worksheets Sample Household Survey, Singapore, 1966 (Gopinathan, 1974, 60).

Table 8.1 shows that in 1966, the English-educated commanded a much higher income than the Chinese-educated, and this was true of all age groups and both sexes. The difference in income ranged from a minimum of about 20.3 per cent to a maximum of 81.8 per cent. Sharon Ahmat, in his book, *Malay Participation in the National Development of Singapore*, points out that 'the fact still remains that Malay school leavers command no economic value' (Ahmat, 1971, p. 9). The Census of Population of 1980 shows similar differences in income between people literate in the different official languages. Table 8.2 shows that the highest income group in 1980, those earning $3,000 and above a month, was dominated by people literate in only English. These made up 66.1 per cent (10,324), with those literate in both English and Chinese constituting another 20.5 per cent (3,200). Those who were literate in only Chinese formed only 2 per cent (307) of this high income group while those who were literate only in Malay or Tamil were not represented at all (see Table 8.2). With the great economic advantage that literacy in English gave, it was no wonder that education in the English stream became

Table 8.2: Employees Aged 10 Years and over by Income, Languages of Literacy and Sex (1980)

Monthly Income ($)	Literate												Not Literate		
	Tamil only			English and Chinese only			Other 2 or More Official Languages			Non-official Languages					
	Persons	Males	Females	Persons	Males	Females	Persons	Males	Females	Persons	Males	Females	Persons	Males	Females
Total	10,606	8,216	2,390	188,303	104,526	83,777	141,456	94,800	46,656	4,941	2,526	2,415	61,478	30,590	30,887
Below 200	1,062	805	257	12,488	9,907	2,581	9,932	7,155	2,777	579	101	478	10,264	3,024	7,240
200–299	3,632	2,113	1,519	29,227	10,712	18,515	34,741	16,779	17,962	2,148	629	1,519	24,095	7,854	16,241
300–399	3,446	2,918	528	32,271	12,956	19,315	31,868	20,407	11,461	850	488	362	15,089	9,222	5,867
400–499	1,373	1,318	55	24,175	11,919	12,256	19,300	14,208	5,092	402	392	10	5,771	4,785	986
500–599	624	619	5	18,918	10,299	8,619	12,050	9,449	2,601	206	206	—	3,351	3,079	272
600–799	327	312	15	23,320	14,254	9,066	12,186	9,771	2,415	111	111	—	2,124	2,033	91
800–999	55	50	5	13,871	8,684	5,187	7,089	5,419	1,670	30	20	10	292	262	30
1,000–1,199	15	15	—	10,133	6,958	3,175	4,066	3,140	926	50	40	10	166	136	30
1,200–1,499	5	5	—	6,798	4,780	2,018	3,038	2,319	719	20	20	—	35	35	—
1,500–1,999	10	10	—	7,945	6,048	1,897	3,024	2,440	584	116	116	—	30	25	5
2,000–2,499	—	—	—	3,653	3,135	518	1,434	1,268	166	50	45	5	10	10	—
2,500–2,999	—	—	—	1,615	1,414	201	715	619	96	96	86	10	5	5	—
3,000 and over	—	—	—	3,200	2,974	226	1,585	1,530	55	191	191	—	—	—	—
Not stated	55	50	5	689	488	201	428	297	131	91	81	10	247	121	126
Mean income ($)	328	347	265	686	812	530	540	602	416	550	856	240	303	360	247

Source: Khoo, (1981a) pp. 42–3.

increasingly popular at the expense of the other language streams, as Table 8.3 shows:

Table 8.3: Percentage of Primary One Registration by Language Stream (1960–76)

Registration Year	English	Chinese	Language Streams Malay	Tamil	Per cent	Total
1960	51.81	39.32	8.64	0.23	100	52,560
1961	55.37	36.45	7.89	0.29	100	55,234
1962	60.27	31.01	8.43	0.29	100	57,878
1963	62.07	29.30	8.41	0.22	100	59,084
1964	63.05	27.90	8.84	0.21	100	61,015
1965	62.28	28.59	8.94	0.19	100	61,931
1966	60.24	32.80	6.76	0.20	100	59,128
1967	61.28	33.19	5.36	0.17	100	56,736
1968	63.09	33.06	3.66	0.19	100	55,526
1969	66.42	30.92	2.51	0.15	100	56,152
1970	69.30	28.98	1.60	0.12	100	54,730
1971	71.42	27.44	1.06	0.08	100	52,284
1972	74.89	24.26	0.79	0.06	100	51,747
1973	77.88	21.46	0.61	0.05	100	47,599
1974	78.51	21.03	0.43	0.03	100	44,918
1975	82.52	17.16	0.32	—	100	42,409
1976	86.06	13.75	0.19	—	100	43,730

Source: Prime Minister's speech to Parliament, 23 February 1977; reported in *The Straits Times*, February 26 1977 (Kuo, 1985, p. 346).

Enrolment in English-medium schools had increased steadily from 51.81 per cent in 1960 to 86.06 per cent in 1976, whereas that in Chinese-medium schools had declined from 39.32 per cent to 13.75 per cent, in Malay-medium schools from 8.64 per cent to 0.19 per cent and in Tamil-medium schools from 0.23 per cent to 0.03 per cent in the same years. In a study of ethnic Chinese students at the pre-university level, it was found that 10.3 per cent of the sample of students from Chinese-medium schools indicated that they were 'sorry' they had received their secondary education in Chinese, while only 1.6 per cent of the sample from English-medium schools reacted in this way about their having received their secondary education in English. This difference in reaction was even more marked with university students: 18 per cent of the Year 1 students from Nan-yang University, a Chinese-medium university (subsequently merged with the then University of Singapore in 1980 because of falling enrolment to form the National University of Singapore), regretted having obtained their secondary education in Chinese, whereas only 2 per cent of their counterparts at the University of Singapore, an English-medium university, reacted in this way about their secondary education in English (Murray, 1971, p. 150). The increasing popularity of education in English, or literacy in English, backed by economic and social considerations, was the main force behind the government's decision to gradually convert all schools in Singapore to English-medium schools in the 1970s. By 1970, 91 per cent of the school children entering Primary 1 were in English-medium schools and by 1983, the figure rose to more than 99 per cent. As a result, English-medium schools were renamed as national-stream schools where English was taught as the first language and Chinese, Malay or Indian as the second language (Soon, 1988, pp. 7, 21). Thus the closing down of schools using the ethnic languages and their replacement by English-medium schools was brought about through the choice of the people, propelled by social and economic considerations. The government supported this development, as it helped to bridge the gap between the English-educated and the Chinese-educated and thus ease the tension between the two segments of society, and to bring about greater economic prosperity through the use of the world language.

Compulsory Biliteracy

While the government reacted positively towards the popular demand for education in English, it was at the same time concerned about what the declining enrolment in the ethnic language schools (particularly Chinese-medium schools) would yield in the long term as a result of falling literacy in these languages. Thus in 1966, the learning of two languages, English and one other ethnic language was made compulsory in schools when in the past, it was encouraged but not obligatory. The promotion of biliteracy was seen as vital for the success of Singapore and the rationale for it was put succinctly in a statement by Lee Kuan Yew:

> I am convinced that this effort [bilingualism or more precisely biliteracy] has to be made if we are to survive as a distinctive society, worth the preserving. Or we will become completely deculturalized and lost. . . . If we fail to resolve effectively our problem of languages and preserve what is best in our respective cultural values, we could become an even more enfeebled version of the deculturalized Caribbean calypso-type society . . . Please note that when I speak of bilingualism I do not mean just the facility of speaking two languages. It is more basic that, first, we understand ourselves what we are, where we came from, what life is or should be about and what we want to do. Then the facility of the English Language gives us access to the science and technology of the West. It also provides a convenient common ground on which the Chinese, Indians, Ceylonese, Malays, Eurasians, everybody competes in a neutral medium. And it's not just learning the language (mother tongue). With the language goes the fables and proverbs. It is the learning of a whole value system, a whole philosophy of life that can maintain the fabric of our society intact in spite of exposure to all the current madness around the world. (Lee, 1972)

Lee Kuan Yew made it clear in his speech that it is important to maintain literacy in the local, ethnic languages to ensure the preservation of traditional cultural values in the face of a Singapore exposed to 'all the madness around the world'. This concern was already with the government in the early years of independence, but it was to grow in intensity in recent years with English becoming more and more widely used.

Literacy Rates in the Official Languages

The effect of the compulsory bilingual policy in schools can be seen by comparing the figures in Table 8.4. In 1970, four years after the introduction of

Table 8.4: Percentage Distribution of Literate Persons Aged 10 Years and Over by Language Literate In and Race (1980 and 1970)

Languages Literate In	Total	Chinese	Malays	Indians	Others
1980					
Total Literate	100.0	100.0	100.0	100.0	100.0
One Official Language Only	62.0	68.1	39.8	40.6	69.5
Malay	5.6	0.1	36.3	1.8	1.1
Chinese	36.0	47.6	0.1	—	0.3
English	19.1	20.4	3.3	21.0	68.1
Tamil	1.3	—	0.1	17.8	—
Two or More Official Languages	37.5	31.9	60.0	57.7	17.0
Eng. & Ch.	22.5	29.6	0.2	0.4	2.1
Eng. & Mal.	11.3	1.3	59.3	16.0	14.4
Eng. & Tamil	2.1	—	0.1	29.5	0.1
Other Two or More	1.6	1.0	0.4	11.8	0.4
Non-Official Languages	0.5	—	0.2	1.7	13.5
1970					
Total Literate	100.0	100.0	100.0	100.0	100.0
One Official Language only	80.3	85.9	64.7	58.3	79.9
Malay	8.6	0.1	56.4	2.6	2.0
Chinese	40.5	54.2	0.1	—	0.5
English	29.0	31.6	8.1	28.6	77.3
Tamil	2.2	—	0.1	27.1	0.1
Two or More Official Languages	19.1	14.1	35.0	36.5	16.4
Eng. & Ch.	8.9	11.8	0.1	0.1	9.8
Eng. & Mal.	7.2	1.3	34.7	9.4	14.9
Eng. & Tamil	1.6	—	—	19.1	0.1
Other Two or More	1.4	1.0	0.2	7.9	0.5
Non-official Languages	0.6	—	0.3	5.2	3.7

Source: Khoo, (1981a) p. 3.

the compulsory bilingual policy, persons 10 years and above who were literate only in one official language formed 80.3 per cent of the literate population while persons literate in two or more official languages formed only 19.1 per cent. By 1980, the percentage of persons literate in two or more official languages had increased to 37.5 per cent while that of persons literate only in one official language had fallen to 62.0 per cent. The language that was gaining ground was English. While the percentage of persons literate only in English dropped by 10 per cent, from 29.0 per cent in 1970 to 19.0 per cent in 1980, that of persons literate in English and one other official language rose by 18.4 per cent, from 19.1 per cent in 1970 to 37.5 per cent in 1980. This increased literacy in two languages was true of all three major ethnic groups. Furthermore, if one looks Table 8.5, one can see that there was a growing trend in biliteracy with successively younger people, with the highest biliteracy rate (51.8 per cent) resting with the 10–19

Table 8.5: Percentage Distribution of Literate Persons Aged 10 Years and Over by Language Literate In and Age Group (1980)

Languages Literate In	Total	Age					
		10–19	20–29	30–39	40–49	50–59	60+
Total Literate	100.0	100.0	100.0	100.0	100.0	100.0	100.0
One Official Language Only	62.0	48.0	58.0	70.7	77.2	80.3	86.6
Malay	5.6	3.7	5.1	5.7	8.1	10.6	8.1
Chinese	36.0	25.5	30.9	41.9	51.5	50.1	62.5
English	19.1	18.5	21.5	21.9	14.8	14.1	12.0
Tamil	1.3	0.3	0.5	1.2	2.8	5.5	4.0
Two or More Official Languages	37.5	51.8	41.5	28.6	22.2	18.8	12.7
Eng. & Ch.	22.5	32.3	25.5	16.9	11.7	7.6	5.5
Eng. & Mal.	11.3	15.8	12.2	8.1	6.6	6.8	4.4
Eng. & Tamil	2.1	2.7	2.0	1.6	1.8	2.1	1.3
Other Two or More	1.6	1.0	1.8	2.0	2.1	2.3	1.5
Non-Official Languages	0.5	0.2	0.5	0.7	0.6	0.9	0.7

Source: Khoo, (1981a) p. 4.

year-old group. Biliteracy dropped successively with increasing age until, with the group aged 60 and above, only 12.7 per cent were biliterate. A comparison of the figures from the 1970 Census and the 1980 Census also shows that literacy among women, which was substantially lower than that among men in 1970, was fast catching up. In 1970, the general literacy rate per thousand population for men was 237 higher than that for women. By 1980, the difference had fallen to 153 per thousand (Khoo, 1981a, p. 2), reflecting the growing liberalization of women in Singapore with increasing modernization and industrialization.

Promotion of Biliteracy and the 'Speak Mandarin' Campaign

However, even though literacy in two languages was becoming more common, the government was not completely happy with the situation. The census data measure only a person's ability to read a newspaper with understanding, but what the government was aiming at was literacy of a higher level. It was concerned about both the younger generation's low level of ability in English and their lack of control of their ethnic language in its written form. This concern translated itself into an intensified drive for bilingualism in the late 1970s and 1980s, launched by Lee Kuan Yew in April 1978 in the form of a televised discussion. On the importance of English in Singapore the Prime Minister pointed out that

> The way our economy has developed has made it necessary for those who want to reach executive or professional grades to master English, spoken and written. The earlier in life this is done, the easier and the better the mastery. (Lee, 1978)

The Minister of State for Culture, Major Fong Sip Chee, pointed out in his speech given on the opening of the Malay Language Month in August 1982 that the ethnic language was important for the retention of one's own 'cultural ballast' (Fong, 1982). The renewed drive for biliteracy coincided with the 'Speak Mandarin' Campaign of 1979. One objective of this campaign was to persuade parents to speak Mandarin rather than any other Chinese dialect in the home in order to help their children develop their spoken and written Chinese, since the Chinese taught in school is based on Mandarin. Furthermore, the promotion of Mandarin, and hence the promotion of literacy in Chinese, would help to spread Chinese cultural values. The 'Speak Mandarin' Campaign was supported by the mass media, in particular, the Singapore Broadcasting Corporation. Radio and television programmes in the local Chinese dialects — Cantonese, Hokkien, etc. — which had been very popular in Singapore ceased to be broadcasted; instead such programmes were dubbed into Mandarin. The 'Speak Mandarin' Campaign was apparently very successful as Mandarin was later found to be more commonly used in public and in Chinese families. According to a Ministry of Education study, in 1980, 64.4 per cent of the Primary 1 Chinese students came from homes where a dialect other than Mandarin was used, as against 25.9 per cent speaking Mandarin. In 1987, 68 per cent were speaking Mandarin in the home (Kuo and Jernudd, 1988). Perhaps it is appropriate to point out that it was probably not the 'Speak Mandarin' Campaign itself which achieved such spectacular results; more likely, it was the campaign, in conjunction with the bilingual education policy, and the concern of Chinese parents for their children to perform well in examinations, which together brought about the switch to Mandarin in many homes.

The New Education System

Together with the drive for bilingualism in schools and the 'Speak Mandarin' Campaign, the government started re-examining its education system in an effort to raise the students' command of English and the ethnic language and also to eliminate educational wastage. The re-examination was led by the Deputy Prime Minister and Minister for Education, Dr. Goh Keng Swee. The influential *Goh Report* that resulted from this brought major changes to education in Singapore.

The Goh Report, which was subsequently adopted by the government to become the basis for what has come to be known as the New Education System, recommended the channelling of students into different academic ability groups. Students at Primary Three level, at around the age of nine, are divided into four ability groups: a 'gifted' stream, consisting of a small but highly selected group of students who may take both English and Chinese at first language level; a 'normal' stream, made up of average and above average students who would complete the rest of their primary education in three years, taking English as the first language and their ethnic language as the second language; an 'extended' stream for weaker students who learn the same languages as the 'normal' stream students but who have to take five years to complete the rest of the primary education; and finally, a 'monolingual' stream for the weakest students who are required to develop literacy in only one language, English. This system of streaming reflects firstly, the emphasis placed on English and secondly, the government's keen interest in promoting literacy in the ethnic languages, the learning of which is made compulsory for all children except those deemed incapable of handling two languages and who, as a result, are unlikely to gain admission to higher education in Singapore. Streaming is also introduced at secondary school level to reinforce biliteracy. At the Primary School Leaving Examination, students with scores which place them among the top 10 per cent of the cohort are placed in what is known as the Special Assistance Plan schools where they are expected to take both English and Chinese as a first language at the secondary stage of education. The selection of 'gifted' students continues at this stage and those chosen are similarly encouraged to take both languages at first language level. The rest of the students are divided, in almost equal proportion, into an 'express' stream where students will take four years to finish their O-levels, and a 'normal' stream where those found capable of doing the O-levels will take five years to complete the course. In this way, the government tries to ensure there will still be a proportion of people in Singapore with a first language command of Chinese. To further promote the learning of the ethnic languages, the government also makes it a requirement for students to obtain a pass in their ethnic language before they can be admitted to the local university.

The New Education System, according to Soon, has achieved remarkable results in students' control of English and their ethnic language, if one goes by public examination results (Soon, 1988, pp. 25–6). The picture is probably not as rosy as Soon's statistics suggest, as the improved percentage passes at both the Primary School Leaving Examination and the O-level Examination since the introduction of the New Education System are based on the performance of students in the academically better streams. In examining literacy level, it would be useful to find out to what extent students who take their ethnic language at either the first or second language level make use of their literacy in these languages in their life, and to what extent their knowledge of the language is an academic one which remains within the four walls of the schoolroom. The answer to this is reflected in part in the discussion on language and the mass media.

Language Policy, Home Language and Education Attainment

With the prominence given to English in the education system, reinforced by the economic value of the language, one immediate effect can be seen on language use in the home. In a study conducted in 1982–83, Kwan-Terry concludes that the importance of English in Singapore prompts many parents, who do not normally speak English with their spouse, to use it with their children if they are in a position to do so, in order to expose their children to the language. The positive attitude of the parents towards English could also have contributed to children's readiness to use English with their siblings at home. In cases where the parents are not in a position to use English with their children, some of them would use Mandarin Chinese with their children when normally they use a

Chinese dialect with their spouse. The reason is again that the students want to expose their children to a school language. As for homes where the parents normally use English with their spouse, their concern for their children's ability in Chinese prompts some of them, more so the mother than the father, to introduce Mandarin Chinese in interactions with their children, again to expose them to the language which they have to learn at school and with which they may have problems. Among the siblings, one can also note a similar trend towards using more Mandarin Chinese in place of the dialects (Kwan-Terry, 1989, pp. 17–19, 21, 24–5, 27–8). Thus it can be seen that the bilingual policy in the education system has far reaching effects, influencing language use in the home.

Another effect of streaming and the emphasis on English in Singapore education is that students from English-speaking homes enjoy a substantial advantage over those who do not speak English in the home, firstly because education is conducted in the language they are most at ease with, and secondly because homes where English is the main medium of communication are usually professional homes where the children receive strong support academically. A study done in 1990 (Kwan-Terry, forthcoming) shows that about 65 per cent of the students selected for the 'gifted' stream were from English-speaking homes when children with this language background formed only about 21 per cent of the total sample. Those speaking both Mandarin and English in the home together with those who spoke Mandarin alone in the home formed another 21 per cent while those speaking a Chinese dialect (or a mixture of Mandarin and a Chinese dialect), Malay or Tamil formed only 3.6 per cent of students in the 'gifted' stream.

Language Policy and the Mass Media

The multilingual policy of the Singapore government ensures that due attention is given in the mass media to each of the four official languages. However, what is interesting is not so much the official sponsorship of the different languages in the mass media but the extent to which the public makes use of media communication in these languages. In his speech on the twenty-fifth anniversary of television in Singapore, Lee Kuan Yew points out that on an average day, of the two million Singaporeans aged 15 and above, 33 per cent watch news broadcasts in Mandarin Chinese, 14 per cent in English, and 9 per cent in Malay (*The Straits Times*, 30 April 1988). This suggests that among the Chinese, a larger proportion of the people feel more at ease with Mandarin Chinese than with English. When it comes to entertainment programmes, Mandarin Chinese programmes are by far the more popular. Kuo and Jernudd point out that 'for several years, the top ten most popular TV programmes have been consistently those in Mandarin, and even the tenth most popular Mandarin programme enjoys a viewship 50 per cent higher than the most popular English programme' (Kuo and Jernudd, 1988).

The dominance of Chinese oracy evident in the distribution of TV viewership is, however, not complemented by Chinese literacy as measured by size of newspaper readership as Table 8.6 shows:

Table 8.6: Percentage of Population Aged 15 and Over Who Read Singapore Newspapers by Race (1985 and 1975)

Language of Newspaper	Ethnicity							
	Chinese		Malay		Indian		Total	
1985	(N = 3,533)		(N = 624)		(N = 294)		(N = 4,567)	
1975	(N = 3,888)		(N = 656)		(N = 478)		(N = 5,063)	
	'85	'75	'85	'75	'85	'75	'85	'75
English	40.4	25.4	40.5	23.1	72.4	62.9	43.7	28.7
Chinese	60.1	49.0	n	n	0.8	3.8	46.3	38.3
Malay	0.07	n	80.0	50.5	3.0	11.4	11.8	7.8
Tamil	n	n	n	n	30.0	41.9	2.0	2.9
English and Chinese	16.1	n.a.	n	n.a.	0.8	n.a.	12.5	n.a.

Note: n: Less than 0.1 per cent.   n.a.: Not available

Source: Computed from Survey Research Singapore (1985, Table 42A), Kuo (1978, p. 5) and Ng (1986, p. 7).

Table 8.7: Newspaper Readership by Age (1986)

	Age				
	15–19	20–29	30–39	40+	Total
Language of Newspaper	(N = 700)	(N = 1,409)	(N = 1,075)	(N = 1,383)	(N = 4,567)
English	57.4	54.4	46.3	27.8	43.7
Chinese	48.3	46.4	47.5	45.0	46.3
Malay	15.0	15.0	12.0	9.0	11.8
Tamil	2.0	2.0	1.0	3.0	2.0
Eng. and Chinese	23.1	16.4	11.3	6.3	12.5

Source: Ng (1986, p. 12).

Table 8.6 shows that in 1975, the Chinese newspaper was clearly the most widely read among newspapers in different languages, commanding a readership of 38.3 per cent when the readership for the English newspaper stood at only 28.7 per cent. By 1985, with increased literacy, readership for newspapers in both languages had increased, but much more sharply with the English newspaper, whose readership reached 43.7 per cent, an increase of 15 per cent, while readership for the Chinese newspaper had only increased by 8 per cent. If one looks at the pattern of newspaper readership by age, given in Table 8.7, one can see that among the Chinese, those aged 40 and above were more likely to read the Chinese newspaper (45.0 per cent as against 27.8 per cent who would read the English newspaper). The picture is reversed with the 15–19 year-old group where more people reported reading the English newspaper than the Chinese newspaper: the proportion is 57.4 per cent as against 48.3 per cent. It is also worth noting that the percentage of people who read newspapers in both English and Chinese increased with succeeding younger generations, which no doubt testifies to the effect of the compulsory bilingual education policy. As for readership for the Malay newspaper, Table 8.6 above shows that there was increase from 7.8 per cent in 1975 to 11.8 per cent in 1985, despite a drastic reduction in the number of students in the Malay-medium schools. In 1985, as high as 80 per cent of the ethnic Malays reported reading the Malay newspaper, no doubt because the Malay language is seen as closely associated with Malay cultural heritage and identity. As for the Indians, there was actually a decrease in the percentage of people reading the Tamil newspaper, from 2.9 per cent in 1975 to 2.0 per cent in 1985, reflecting the diminishing role of Tamil in Singapore, partly arising from its lack of economic value, its lack of symbolic cultural and identity value and the greater readiness of the Indians to be merged with people of other races.

It should be interesting to look at a small segment of the Singapore population to see their language affiliation as reflected in their newspaper reading habit. A small scale study conducted in 1986 among students in various faculties at the National University of Singapore shows the following figures:

Table 8.8: Readership of Newspapers among University Students by Race

Language of Newspaper	Chinese (N = 175)	Malay (N = 25)	Indian (N = 20)	Total (N = 220)
English	98.9 per cent	100 per cent	100 per cent	99.0 per cent
Chinese	53.7 per cent	NIL	NIL	42.7 per cent
Malay	NIL	100 per cent	0.5 per cent	11.8 per cent
Tamil	NIL	NIL	NIL	NIL
English and Chinese	52.6 per cent	NIL	NIL	41.8 per cent
English and Malay	NIL	100 per cent	0.5 per cent	11.8 per cent
English and Tamil	NIL	NIL	NIL	NIL

Note: The one Indian who read Malay papers is an Indian Muslim (adapted from Ng, 1986, p. 21)

As can be seen from the above, the English language newspaper was widely read by university students from all three racial groups. Among the Chinese students surveyed, 99.2 per cent who had their education in the English-medium read the English newspaper, as against 46.9 per cent reading the Chinese newspaper (Ng, 1986, p. 24). Among the English-stream students, reading the Chinese newspaper had been a way of preparing for the second language examinations. Many of them therefore claimed that now that they were at the University, the need to read the Chinese newspaper was no longer present (Ng, 1986, p. 25). Those among the English-educated who continued to read the Chinese newspaper did not read it regularly or daily; furthermore, they read it not so much for high-level discourse, like news on international and local political and economic issues, but for the news on the entertainment world and the short stories which are not found in the English newspaper. Only ethnic Chinese university students who received their earlier education in the Chinese-medium would read the Chinese newspaper regularly and would read it for serious matters like international and local news. Among Malay university students, 100 per cent read both the English and the Malay newspaper. For them, the Malay newspaper was a source of news about the Malay community and Islam (Ng, 1986, p. 23). Among Indian university students, none read the Tamil newspaper.

The question of the extent to which the bilingual education policy affects the life of Singaporeans after their formal education is therefore problematical. Among the ethnic Chinese, it has helped to maintain the Chinese language in society, and this has been instrumental in transmitting Chinese cultural values to some extent, although at a somewhat superficial level. As for the Malay language, it is more the Malay commitment to their own culture and religion than the bilingual education policy that has largely helped to maintain the language, and very successfully, among its people. On the other hand, the bilingual policy has failed to maintain Tamil literacy.

Emigration and the Language Imperative

Apart from increasing the use of Chinese among the Chinese, the bilingual education policy with its emphasis on the second, ethnic language, has brought about an effect totally unexpected by the government. This is the emigration of largely English-educated, well qualified families on account of the pressure learning Chinese has put on their children. A letter expressing a mother's anguish in such a situation was published in the papers in September 1989. This letter elicited a volume of supportive responses pointing to the burden felt by children and their parents caused by the problem of having to take Chinese at school (Appendix A). The problem of learning Chinese is caused partly by the difficulty of developing literacy in the language because Chinese is not phonetic, and therefore the recognition and writing of every character has to be laboriously committed to memory, and partly by the very traditional, outdated way in which the language is taught in the schools. The problem is further compounded by the lack of opportunity for children to apply their literacy in the language and the low social status of the language compared to English. The letter demonstrates graphically the dilemma faced by many parents from English-speaking homes, and these are usually professional people with a high standard of education. The seriousness of this problem can be seen in the fact that the government has deemed it necessary to mount a small scale campaign to persuade Singaporeans to stay on in their homeland.

Language Policy and National Ideology

Since the independence of Singapore, the government has taken steps to ensure that Singaporeans have a good command of English, for economic as much as political reasons. The increasing dominance of English, however, has caused much soul-searching, as Singaporeans through the English language become more and more exposed to Western culture and values. In his National Day Speech in August 1988, Prime Minister Lee Kuan Yew pointed to the danger 'that we have got so much of EL1 (English as a first language) — books, newspapers, magazines, television — that we can become a pseudo-Western society' (*The Straits Times*, 31 October 1988). It was partly the concern for the preservation of Asian values that prompted the government to introduce a bilingual education policy in the first place, and to establish streaming that enables the best students to develop a command of Chinese at first language level. To further strengthen the preservation of Asian values, the government in the late 1980s started a campaign to frame what it calls a National Ideology. The objective was clearly set out by the Minister of Trade and Industry and Minister of Defence, Brigadier General Lee Hsien Loong:

In the short term, Westernization has helped our economic growth. It has made us more cosmopolitan, less inscrutable. It has helped us to run a more rationalistic government, and build a more efficient economy.... But in the long term, further Westernization holds many dangers. Singapore has succeeded because we have been different. Although we are in close contact with the Western world, our values and expectations, and our responses to challenges as a people, have so far been different from Westerners.... As a society, we are absorbing ideas from outside faster than we can digest them, and in danger of losing our sense of direction. (*The Straits Times*, 12 January 1989)

The solution lies in building a strong sense of Singapore identity which can be embodied in a National Ideology. The call for a National Ideology has elicited strong responses from the various communities. The Malays above all fear that the new National Ideology would be no more than Confucian ethics imposed on the general population, which would mean that the Chinese would have a greater hold over the nation. This fear is also shared by the Indian community. One Indian Minister, for example, called for a 'Singaporean Singapore' rather than a Singapore made up of distinct ethnic identities. The government is quick to assuage such apprehensiveness. The Singapore that is being built, as Brigadier General Lee explained in his speech, is going to be a mosaic, with each culture enjoying equal status but sharing universal values.

Besides the question of what values to promote, there is the question of through what language such values are to be taught in the schools. Prime Minister Lee Kuan Yew seems anxious to teach the values through the ethnic language, particularly Chinese, no doubt as a way to arrest and reverse falling competence in it. He thus advocates using Chinese as the medium of instruction in primary schools, switching to the English-medium only at the secondary level (*The Straits Times*, 10 March 1989). The belief is that it is only through learning the written language of a culture that the values can be fully imbibed. The Second Prime Minister, Ong Teng Cheong, is in agreement with the Prime Minister and points out that the spoken language, Mandarin in the case of Chinese, is 'insufficient for the appreciation of Chinese culture and traditional values, for which a knowledge of written Chinese (is) necessary' (*The Straits Times*, 31 October 1988). The Minister of Education, Dr. Tony Tan, on the other hand, is worried about the additional stress that will be placed on the school child if the teaching of Chinese is going to be further strengthened (*The Straits Times*, 1 November 1988). The problem of learning written Chinese is fully in the mind of the Minister of Education. There is also a political aspect to the choice of language, as the non-Chinese communities are worried that through emphasizing the ethnic languages, particularly Chinese, the majority race would be strengthened in their power. Hence they call for the use of English in the teaching of the core values.

Conclusion

Looking back at the last twenty-five years of Singapore as an independent nation, it is clear that from the start, the government has had two main objectives in its language/literacy policy. One is the promotion of literacy in English so as to propel the development of Singapore into a modern industrial, commercial centre and to foster the integration of the various races. The other is the development of literacy in the local, ethnic languages so as to shape the world view of its people. In the early years of its independence, the first objective seems to have taken centre-stage, as the government was faced with the urgent task to improve the livelihood of its people by developing the country's economy. English, as the language of science and technology and international commerce, came to the foreground. The government's objective of raising the literacy rate of its people was in large part facilitated by the economic power that English carried with it, so that more and more people chose to send their children to English-medium schools. In this way, the desire of the people worked in unison with the will of the government and almost immediate effects were achieved. With the rising literacy rate in English, the government began to be concerned about the declining literacy rate in the other languages, particularly Chinese. As Chinese is not a phonetic language, the development of literacy in the language is particularly daunting. The problem of learning Chinese has also been enhanced by the fact that literacy in the language is of little practical, economic or prestige value in Singapore, and someone who is literate in English has little need for it. This creates a tremendous problem of motivation among students who study the language mainly to pass examinations but not for its inherent communicative, cultural or social values. The same can be said of Tamil which, partly due to the small size of the community, faces the danger of extinction. The situation is much more positive with Malay which is closely tied to Malay community life and to Islam, the religion of the Malays. Among the three local, ethnic languages, it is the preservation of Chinese and Chinese cultural values, that seems to have caused the gravest concern among those in power. While the government, as the central planning body, sees the importance of retaining and developing traditional cultural values through retaining and developing literacy in the local languages, particularly Chinese, the language of the majority race, the individual on the street who has in recent years seen with his own eyes the economic advantage of literacy in English relative to literacy in the other languages, is likely to be less moved by cultural appeal than material benefits. The link between the cultural values of a people and the economic development of the country is less likely to be recognized on the individual level. The question at this point is to what extent is that 'individual on the street' ready to support the government in its search for cultural roots and values, especially when this search means greater pressure on their children in terms of education, pressure which has already been found by many in this meritocratic society to be almost unbearable, and that has driven some to leave their homeland. In its search for a way to retain cultural roots and values, through developing literacy in the local languages, particularly Chinese, the government may face a task more arduous than the task of developing literacy in English, but perhaps one of the cultural values of the Chinese, the respect for education and authority, would help it towards this goal.

References

AHMAT, S. (1971) 'Singapore Malays, education and national development', in *Malay Participation in the National Development of Singapore*, Singapore, Community Studies Centre.

DORAISAMY, T.R. (Ed.) (1969) *150 Years of Education in Singapore*, Singapore, Teachers' Training College Board.

DOUGLAS, M. (1971) 'Multilanguage Education and Bilingualism: The formation of Social Brokers in Singapore', unpublished PhD Dissertation, Stanford University.

FONG SIP CHEE (1982) 'Every Singaporean can be adequately bilingual', published policy speech, Singapore, Ministry of Culture.

GOH KENG SWEE (1979) *Report on the Ministry of Education 1978*, Singapore, Ministry of Education.

GOPINATHAN, S. (1974) *Towards a National System of Education in Singapore, 1945–1973*, Singapore, Oxford University Press.

JOSEY, A. (1968) *Lee Kuan Yew*, Singapore, Donald Moore.

KHOO CHIAN KIM (1981a) *Census of Population 1980, Singapore, Release No. 3, Literacy and Education*, Singapore, Department of Statistics.

KHOO CHIAN KIM (1981b) *Census of Population 1980, Singapore, Release No. 7, Income and Transport*, Singapore, Department of Statistics.

KUO, E.C.Y. (1978) 'Multilingualism and mass media communication in Singapore', unpublished manuscript.

KUO, E.C.Y. (1980) 'The sociolinguistic situation in Singapore: Unity in diversity', in AFENDRAS, E.A. and KUO, E.C.Y. (Eds) *Language and Society in Singapore*, Singapore, Singapore University Press, pp. 39–62.

KUO, E.C.Y. (1985) 'Language and Social Mobility in Singapore', in WOLFSON, N. and MANES, J. (Eds) *Language of Inequality*, New York, Mouton.

KUO, E.C.Y. and JERNUDD, B. (forthcoming) 'Language management in a multilingual state: the case of planning in Singapore', paper given at the Language Planning Seminar, *National University of Singapore*, September 1988.

KWAN-TERRY, A. (1989) 'Education and the pattern of language use among ethnic Chinese school children in Singapore', *International Journal of the Sociology of Language*, 80, pp. 5–31.

KWAN-TERRY, A. (forthcoming) 'The economics of language in Singapore: Students' use of extra-curricular language lessons', in COULMAS, F. (Ed.) *Asian Pacific Communication, 2: The Economics of Language in the Asian Pacific*.

LEE KUAN YEW (1972) 'Traditional values and national identity', *Mirror*, **8**, 47, pp.

LEE KUAN YEW (1978) Text of a discussion on TV with Mr. Lee Kuan Yew, Prime Minister, Singapore, 6 April 1978, Singapore, Ministry of Culture.

LIND, A.W. (1974) *Nanyang Perspective, Chinese Students in Multilingual Singapore, Asian Studies at Hawaii, No. 13*, Hawaii, University Press of Hawaii.

LLAMZON, T.A. (1977) 'Emerging-patterns in the English language situation in Singapore today', in CREWE, W. (Ed.) *The English Language in Singapore*, Singapore, Eastern Universities Press, pp. 34–45.

MASON, F. (1959) *The Schools of Malaya*, Singapore, Donald Moore for Eastern Universities Press.

MURRAY (1971) *Multilanguage Education and Bilingualism: The Formation of Social Brokers in Singapore*, Ann Arbor, Stanford University Microfilms.

NG CHYE LEN, K. (1986) 'Newspaper: A Case Study in Language Policy and Mass Media in Singapore', academic exercise, National University of Singapore.

REPORT OF THE ALL-PARTY COMMITTEE OF THE SINGAPORE LEGISLATIVE ASSEMBLY ON CHINESE EDUCATION (1956), Singapore, Singapore Government Printing Office.

SURVEY RESEARCH SINGAPORE (1985) *Media General Report*, Singapore, Survey Research Group.

SAW SWEE HOCK (n.d.) *Demographic Trends in Singapore, Census Monograph No. 1: Demographic Trends in Singapore*, Singapore, Department of Statistics.

SOON TECK WONG (1988) *Singapore's New Education System: Education Reform for National Development*, Singapore, Institute of Southeast Asian Studies.

THE STRAITS TIMES, 26 February 1977.

THE STRAITS TIMES, 30 April 1988.

THE STRAITS TIMES, 31 October 1988.

THE STRAITS TIMES, 1 November 1988.

THE STRAITS TIMES, 12 January 1989.

THE STRAITS TIMES, 10 March 1989.

THE STRAITS TIMES, 26 September 1989.

TAY, WAN JOO, M. (1979), 'The uses, users and features of English in Singapore', *RELC Occasional Papers*, Singapore, RELC.

YONG CHIN FATT (1968), 'The Preliminary Study of Chinese Leadership in Singapore, 1900–1941', *Journal of Southeast Asian History*, 9, 2, pp. 258–85.

Chapter 9

'The Troubled Text': History and Language in American University Basic Writing Programs

---

James Collins

Introduction

The recent spate of studies decrying the state of American education testify to continuing doubts about whether America's schools can reliably inculcate the values and skills that are imagined to hold us together as a nation. Universities figure prominently in various recent accounts of the crisis of school and society, whether in conservative argument or left-progressive analyses. For conservatives, elite universities and a reconstituted traditional curriculum, purged of contemporary distractions and faithful to the Great Books of Western Men, must serve as the cultural-intellectual pinnacle of a squalid, though necessary, social pyramid (e.g., Bloom, 1987). For left-progressives, universities are the locus of a gilded defeat, the site and sign of a dissolution of democratic discourses and possibilities, as public issues and political concerns have been fractured and rendered opaque in the 'New Latin', the specialized jargons of academic exchange (e.g., Jacoby, 1987).

I want to engage this general argument about universities and the larger society, first by providing historical readings of the concern with university curriculum, seen as part of a general discourse about language, culture, and politics, then by focusing on a particular aspect of the contemporary university, the Writing Program, and especially its remedial or 'basic writing' component. The historical arguments reveal the enduring social dilemmas embedded in the debate about college curriculum and literacy; the case study illustrates some of the particular institutional arrangements and pedagogical challenges that bedevil writing programs. Taken together, the historical and ethnographic arguments illustrate how literacy is simultaneously knowledge and politics, culture and language.

The Curriculum Crisis and the Turn to Language

At the heart of much of the debate about the state of the American university is a troubling sense of the incoherence of liberal arts curricula. Thus at many universities there are efforts underway to redefine the baccalaureate, whether at

162

elite institutions such as Harvard and the much-publicized Stanford, or large urban universities, such as the research site for the case study, which serve economically and culturally diverse student populations and which are truly multiversities in their vast size and heterogeneous range of 'degree options'. Again, contributors to the debate about curriculum crisis are both conservative and left-radical. Among the conservatives, former education secretary William Bennett calls for us to revamp the humanities, in order to 'reclaim a legacy' (1984); Allan Bloom proposes a reactionary return to the firm rule of high culture, with philosophy as the 'queen of the sciences'; E.D. Hirsch, while putting forth a less elitist program, nevertheless defines the core of a 'cultural literacy', a knowledge base which is essentially static, incontestible, and exclusionary (1988). Among American radicals, there is not a call for return to an elite cultural definition of liberal arts, but rather a concern with the corrosive effects of institutional developments on the general capacity for critical social thinking, especially as located in universities. This argument is found in the 'New illiteracy' Christopher Lasch saw as part of the *Culture of Narcissism* (1979); it is found in Russell Jacoby's analysis of the dynamics of university development and the cooptation of dissenting views in post World War Two America (1987); and it is found in Jerry Herron's suggestive analysis of the displacement of language and work in the current 'crisis' of the humanities (1988).

Despite profoundly different visions of schooling and society, there are congruent points in the conservative and radical critiques. Both identify centrifugal tendencies in knowledge production, especially the accelerating specialization and fragmentation of academic knowledge (a process complexly related to the ongoing integration of universities and governmental, military, and economic interests). Both also point to the consequences of the 1960s. These consequences included massive growth in the scale of post-secondary education, which meant a vast increase in the number and diversity of students attending college. The 1960s also presented universities with challenges from the social mobilizations so emblematic of the time, challenges to the university and its role in society and to established disciplines and their curricula.

Both conservative and left accounts contrast the 1960s with earlier periods. For the conservatives there is a paradise lost of the pre-1960s, when the humanities and the transcendent values of Western Civilization were secure, curricula were well-defined, and universities knew that their mission was to educate. Paradise is favorably compared with the social conflicts of the 1960s and 1970s and the disabling effects of too much democracy. For the radicals there is also an important earlier period. It is not a paradise and not the 1950s and early 1960s, but usually just before World War Two and the post-war transformation of America. It is a period when critical thinking and public discourse were seen to flourish, with significant bases outside of the university system. For left analysts, the conflicts of the 1960s are seen as a sharpening continuation of earlier struggles, but the 1960s and since have shown grim institutional developments. In particular, incorporating radical voices into the academy has muted those voices more than it has changed the university, which, as a massive bureaucratic institution, undermines the conditions for critical public thinking and acting.

In either account, the college curriculum has become problematic, whether from students' demands to include the excluded (e.g., studies of gender, race, and class, in diverse manifestations), calls for increasing vocational relevance, or the hyper-specialization of faculty research orientations. The provisional solution has been to abandon the quest for a coherence in curriculum. The shattered image of a well-rounded gentleman-scholar, object of the conservative's fantasy, has not been replaced with an alternative vision and program, instead highly provisional 'cafeteria menus' of curriculum-by-elective have proliferated. An embattled and shrinking permanent faculty has acquiesced and conspired in administrative solutions: programs of study which keep more and more people studying longer and longer for reasons fewer and fewer can discern, beyond the rapidly devaluing currency of 'jobs'.

The provisional solution has achieved coherence by administrative fiat: this is the curriculum. And that solution has involved a 'turn to language'. As college curricula have been transformed, and the meaning of the baccalaureate has grown more difficult to comprehend, there has been a focus on writing, seen as a basic, prior skill, essential for preparing students for whatever paths they take through the multiversity. Thus in the 1986 US Department of Education pamphlet 'What Works' we find writing, defined in terms of a simplified model of writing process, separated from curricular domains, such as 'History' and 'Social Studies', and treated as an area of basic study. In a 1986 ACE (American Council of Education, 1986) study of curriculum problems in post-secondary education, we find 80 per cent of so-called 'education leaders' defining writing assessment as an essential measure of the work of college teachers. Although there is no agreement about the content of college education, there seems to be consensus about an essential skill, writing.

There are serious problems with conceiving of writing as a basic 'skill' and with the pedagogies that flow from such a conception. We will discuss these problems more fully below, but first let us consider the larger historical trends which motivate this 'turn to language'. These trends extend over several centuries and show that behind the concern with writing lies a specific institutional history of class-divided, gender-biased higher education and, further, that the dominant conceptions and forms of that higher education are themselves a symbolic displacement of political conflicts in the wider society.

Historical Background to the Curriculum Crisis: Why Liberal Education Matters

Let us begin by noting that while writing is proposed as a neutral skill, foundational to all (higher) education, the debate about curriculum raises basic questions of politics and values. For a conservative such as William Bennett, a college education should inculcate essential social values such as individualism, respect for family and community, and veneration of spiritual achievements, as defined in the Western literary-philosophical and religious canons. These are all elements of Bennett's 'moral literacy', which would form the ethical basis for vocational training and for informed political participation. For a radical such as Russell Jacoby, universities and their curricula are negatively defined, for they have failed to provide a public language, a public sphere of discussion and social critique; indeed, rather than providing a space for critical discussion of public issues, they have undermined the conditions of effective dissent from state doctrine.

A cynic might ask, of course, why all the fuss? Why would anyone think that universities, 'degree mills', were in the business of ethical orientations or democratic discourses? I would suggest that many do think so, if not when considering the university as a corporate institution, then when we think about our own teaching and learning and about the values we attach to rational inquiry and public discussion. And universities promote this impression by suggesting that formal education makes us into better people, better able to separate the particular from the general, the private from the public, better informed and hence able to make more conscious decisions about matters personal and political; in short, able to participate in discussions about the social good.

But where do these ideas come from about private and public, about informed, participating citizenry, about some sphere of public debate shaping the expression of a popular will? They are in part native coin, for an indigenous political theory, which we in America associate with such names as Thomas Jefferson and James Madison, draws upon such distinctions and images. That indigenous theory has European antecedents, however. In a recently translated work, Jürgen Habermas (1989) discusses the historical emergence of the ideas, discursive forms, and institutional underpinnings of a domain of public political discussion, a 'public sphere', separate from and contesting state power in the name of common will and universal principles of reason and citizenship.

In Habermas' account this domain of 'public opinion' defined itself during the seventeenth and eighteenth century critiques of the absolutist state (i.e., of the monarchies of England, France, and Germany). It was a discursive sphere, instantiated in coffee-houses and literary salons, where propertied men gathered to read newspapers and argue the ideas and events of the day, and organized through magazine and journal subscription societies, which widened the flow of ideas and opinion. It was also a political sphere, for through such gatherings and networks there emerged an organizational and discursive basis for the parliamentary opposition in England and the Fourth Estate in France. It supported and was constituted by a literate, rational discourse, criticizing state power, and articulating demands for civil rights.

This discursive domain emerged in complex complementarity with a set of social categories which defined the social world in particular ways, including some actors and activities within the political world, while excluding others; a public sphere, it was understood in contrast to the 'private'. Separated from the public domain of politics was the 'domestic', a domain of feminine sensibility, itself also literate, as a novel-reading consciousness began to emerge that articulated the personal and social. The 'public' also stood in contrast to the economic, 'private interest' that was clearly a social force, yet was to be distinguished from ideas of citizenship and equal participation. Finally, the public stood in contrast to the state, that congerie of monarchal sovereignty, feudal privilege, and constitutional provision that comprised the eighteenth century absolutist regime. The public sphere was thus a bourgeois public sphere. Patriarchal and class-based, it consisted of property-owning men and excluded women and the working classes from its literate deliberations.

The dissolution of this public sphere, this limited, historically novel domain of democratic discussion, resulted from various causes. Among those discussed by Habermas are the increasing centralization of the media, which removed the space for non-profitable dissent and discussion, and the rearticulation of the private and public achieved under the modern welfare state, which transformed political subjectivities in essential ways, as citizens became clients of bureaucracies. There were also challenges to its monopoly of political discourse, initially by the mobilizing working classes.

It is this last challenge I would like to focus on, for liberal education emerges as a proposed resolution to the conflict this challenge engendered. The illustrative events and texts are the Hyde Park riots of 1869 and Matthew Arnold's *Culture and Anarchy* (1869 [1971]). The Hyde Park riots were one moment in the long effort by the Chartist labor movement to gain a political voice in British politics. Denied the right to assemble in London's Hyde Park and criticize upcoming legislation that would deny them the vote, men gathered anyway and began to dismantle police barricades, as well as to damage some of the surrounding gardens. The police responded by cracking heads, as they often do in periods of civil disobedience, and the media proclaimed a 'riot'. Let us merely note that a denial of rights — to vote, assemble and speak — lay behind the riot and turn to one influential response.

Matthew Arnold published *Culture and Anarchy* in an effort to specify a civilizing role for a publically-provisioned education that would ameliorate the social conflicts of nineteenth-century Britain. His 'anarchy' had a clear referent: it was the events at Hyde Park, working people's frustration and potential for violence, and, most generally, the contending interests which seemed to be tearing his society apart. His 'culture' stood in opposition to anarchy. It was a body of disinterested knowledge, combining the moral and the natural sciences in a manner Americans would now call 'liberal arts'. It would make those who acquired it a spiritual-intellectual elite, an elite not of land and inherited privilege, but of intellect and acquired dispositions. The essential proposal concerned education, liberal education, and the idea that the educated would somehow transcend the interested, divisive struggles of rulers and their unlettered, subaltern opponents.

Arnold's *Culture and Anarchy* provides a basic definition of and ideological support for 'liberal arts' education. Offering a resolution to a fundamental social contradiction, class division, it has been influential in England and the United States for its vision of education and the university (Eagleton, 1984; Herron, 1988). The discipline of 'English' emerged by the end of the nineteenth century as a centerpiece of the liberal education and meritocratic rule Arnold advocated. The development of English in the late nineteenth century replays the Arnoldian drama — of social disorder and tension resolved by education — but now acquiring a specific disciplinary form within an assumed institutional context of general and university education.

We can see this clearly in the United States during the 1890s, a time of open social conflict. Severe economic and political conflict prevailed: strikes and industrial unrest were pervasive; and the Populist Party threatened the hegemony of Democrat and Republican rule, putting forth a radical, alternative vision of the social order. This was also the time of the formation of professions, and in the ideology and organizational underpinnings of professionalism, the troubled middle class found its place: above the social fray, providing rigorous, disinterested knowledge. One relevant profession emerging at this time was the academic discipline of English.

In 1894 the Committee of Ten, a self-appointed body of prominent educators, businessmen, and professors from elite universities, began fashioning 'School English', a set of prescriptions for the form of English to be promulgated in the primary and secondary schools of America (Wright, 1980). They also defined a vision of the discipline of English in the transforming university. This new discipline was based on a primary distinction between reading and writing, or, as Ohmann (1988) has put it, between leisure and work. Reading was the domain of literature, the consumption of which distinguished a spiritual aristocracy with the leisure to so consume. Literary criticism (reading) emerged as and continues to be the prestige activity of English studies. Writing was work, training in skills deemed useful for a middle class in its future employment. Composition emerged as and continues to be the non-prestige activity, the 'dirty work' of English studies. Thus a dichotomy and hierarchy was established, one that informs and undergirds the current place and predicament of writing programs in universities.

Basic Writing at Urbane U: A Case Study

In the foregoing I have argued that the curriculum controversy resonates with longstanding tensions in general civil society. Liberal education, as ethos and organizational reality, arose in response to crises to civil society, especially those of class division and conflict. But divisions of class and, more recently and more pointedly, those of gender and race, pose basic dilemmas for traditional curriculum and pedagogy. They pose problems of curriculum range, for liberal education was designed to speak to and shape an elite, not to confront the issue of canon and non-canon; they pose problems of pedagogic practice, for liberal education assumes an elite preparation, not a diverse range of preparation and underpreparation. The field of composition and university-based programs of basic writing have emerged as complex responses to these dilemmas in the contemporary university, but like liberal education more generally, they have emerged in specific historical and institutional circumstances which shape and constrain their typical form and their possible alternatives.

In the section which follows, I will present a case study of writing programs at an American public university in a major East Coast city. The study develops an historical analysis of the recent antecedents and general institutional conditions of the writing programs during the last twenty-five years and it then compares two classrooms within the remedial or 'basic' writing program. These classrooms, which were studied in the fall of 1988, illustrate the severe difficulties faced by a curriculum which relies on an unexamined category of 'experience' as basis for a writing curriculum.

The institution being studied is a large urban university, which I will call 'Urbane U'. Urbane currently serves a diverse student body and a large (though not unusual) proportion of its entering freshman classes wind up in special remedial writing courses. Like other institutions of its size and situation, Urbane has had major budget problems and significant labor unrest. The history of the writing program during the past two decades resonates with the labor politics of the institution, politics in which gender figures centrally. Before examining specific classrooms, I will discuss that history, organizing the account around three topics: changes in theories of writing and discourses of remediation; changes in patterns of administrative control and focuses of administrative concern; and changes in the class, race, and gender composition of students and writing teachers.

Formation of the Writing Program from the 1960s to the 1980s

The twenty-year period from the late 1960s to the late 1980s represents several significant shifts in program and broader institutional history, occurring roughly at ten-year intervals. The late 1960s was a period of rapid expansion at Urbane U, as elsewhere in the country. Previously a private institution, Urbane had affiliated with the state system of higher education, bringing monies into its coffers, but also increasing its historic obligation to serve a wide range of students. Within a few years of affiliation, with a faculty aware of the wider range of educational preparation that the new, less elite student body brought to the classroom, a program of language remediation was being developed in writing, reading, and speech (Ad-Hoc Committee on Basic Writing, 1969). By the late 1970s the world had turned upside down, so to speak. The United States had settled into economic restructuring and decline, and Urbane U, facing budgetary problems, had begun to contract. Programs and departments were cut; faculty were given the pink slip. The Writing Program, in its regular and remedial components, had grown considerably, and had come to occupy a central place in an emerging sector of cross-disciplinary 'service' courses. It served, in the words of one administrator, as a place to 'hide faculty' from the cruel attentions of the budgetary process.

By the late 1980s the terrain had again changed. The number of permanent faculty had shrunk by more than 300, or 25 per cent, and enrollments had again increased (American Association of University Professors, 1986), largely because of a refiguring of the meaning of higher education. Schooling now seemed rather like Original Sin, something from which one never escaped; now there was a 'lifetime of learning', a potentially endless process of taking courses and accumulating credentials. The narrative of self-improvement and social mobility addressed itself to yet newer groups of 'non-traditional students': people who had made it into their 30s and 40s without a college degree; mothers returning for an educational retooling before a foray into the marketplace; and the targets of Special Admissions programs, the underprepared who would struggle for and occasionally achieve their diploma. With permanent faculty sharply reduced in number and hard-pressed to satisfy the teaching needs of their own departments, the writing programs had become the domain of 'temporary' teaching labor.

Changes in theories and discourses of writing There were sharp changes in theories and discourse of writing during this period. We may begin by outlining changes in curriculum in the regular writing program, which will serve as contrast to the remedial ('basic') writing program. Regular composition in the 1960s was English 10, a literature and philosophy version of 'Western Civ', in which students were introduced to and wrote with and against the texts of Plato, Herodotus, and Erasmus, as well as Hemingway and Woolf. By the late 1970s, when the program had been removed from direct English department control, a narrowing had occurred, a common teaching text was 'Ten Great English Essays' and writing was inculcated as a literary, typically modernist project. By the late 1980s there had been turn to what are called 'discipline-based rhetorics', and textbooks such as Axelrod and Cooper's (1987) *Reading Critically, Writing Well* presented students with a range of textual types drawn from diverse academic disciplines.

Throughout its development, the basic (remedial) writing program has been defined by an absence and a process. The founding documents of the program identified language deficiencies, whether in writing, reading, or speech (Ad-Hoc Committee, 1969). In writing, students were to learn 'Standard English', plus expression and logical argument. Curriculum was not formally specified, but tended over a ten-year period to follow, in simplified form, the regular composition program. By the mid-1980s the absence was no longer defined in terms of a Standard English, but rather as a lack of 'academic discourse skills' (Program Description, 1986). This is surely a different characterization, and perhaps more precise, but nonetheless it marks a lack. Unfamiliar or unpracticed with the essay formats characteristic of academic writing, basic students must first learn to write narratives, beginning with personal experience and working outwards to a public position.

At the time of research, a model of process writing was used in both regular and basic writing programs. In this approach, writing result from the familiar sequence of brainstorming, drafting, revising, and so forth. The model was more dominant in the basic writing program, as reflected in teacher training, curriculum, and classroom process. There is an irony here, for the basic writing program avoided the authoritarian formats of the regular composition program, for good reasons, but with unintended consequences. The students most defined as structurally 'lacking', as needing special, remedial courses, were given the most 'polite' curriculum, one in which the discursive demands of the institution were soft-pedaled and their experience was given pride of place. We will return to this issue later, after examining specific classroom practice, for the emphasis on experience is a crucial and problematic response to the challenge of underpreparation and diversity.

Changes in patterns of administrative control and concern The changing curricula, in both the regular and basic writing programs, have been embedded in a larger process of shifting control of the programs. Although the writing programs began firmly ensconced in the university English Department, control shifted in the late 1970s from departmental faculty to central college administration. Recall that this was a period of emerging cross-discipline programs, initially serving, among other purposes, to protect permanent faculty from budget cuts, but developing over the next decade as the lower tier of a hierarchy of teaching, in which the 'service' courses of writing, reading, math, and 'Western Civ' were taught by non-permanent and part-time faculty, while permanent faculty taught the advanced undergraduate and graduate courses in their disciplines.

Three areas of interest stand out in the administrative centralization of writing instruction. The first is curriculum, which has been progressively formalized, in both programs, over the past twenty years. This was done because, with the departure of permanent faculty from the labor force in this arena of teaching, the informal mechanisms of corporate solidarity, insuring that the right books are used and the right issues addressed, could no longer be assumed. When dealing with what one administrator called 'casual labor', it was seen as necessary to specify work routine, that is, to render curriculum explicit, specifying books to be used, topics to be covered, and sequence of assignments, and instituting procedures of evaluation that would insure adherence to the program. In short, it was necessary to make the curriculum 'teacher proof'. It is of course no coincidence, and will be discussed more fully below, that the removal of autonomy from the teachers coincided with a change in the gender of teaching, from male to female (see Apple, 1986, for a discussion of this dynamic of gender and control in the history of American public education).

A second area of administrative concern has been testing and placement. A recurring problem, through the 1970s and 1980s was predicting placement through testing. Early in the program, that is, throughout the 1970s, placement involved using an 'objective' multiple-choice instrument, plus an essay. A 'pass out' from basic writing could be achieved if the instructor determined on the basis of a student's first in-class essay that the student was capable of work in the regular composition program. This procedure created an administrative problem because on average 20 per cent of those placed in basic writing 'passed out' in the first week. The problem was dealt with around 1977 by eliminating the 'pass out' option. An essay test was incorporated into the initial placement procedure, henceforth conducted earlier in the summer, and the in-class assessment was eliminated. This solved the placement problem, but also entailed an alienation of evaluation from teachers and students. No longer conducted in small groups, between students and teachers who had at least got to know one another's names, placement evaluation was now conducted in large settings, not unlike 'standardized' testing conditions.

The problem of unpredictability remained, however, changing from that of 'pass out' rates to that of variation in the numbers placed in one or the other program by the initial tests. Between 1978 and 1982 the placement rate into basic writing varied between 35 per cent and 55 per cent of incoming freshmen (Orsten, 1982). Beginning in the 1980s, a new set of placement procedures was therefore instituted. These used a set of holistic ratings, with multiple readings of an essay, and required careful training of raters. By judicious manipulation of placement criteria, program directors were able to insure less of a swing in placement numbers, and intake figures for basic writing stabilized around 35–40 per cent of incoming students for 1982–85 (Sullivan, 1985).

A third area of administrative concern has been labor recruitment. Urbane U is a large institution, and 35–40 per cent of incoming students fill up a lot of classrooms. In the Fall of 1988, for example, there were ninety-six sections of basic writing. This has meant that recruiting teachers has been a recurring problem for program administrators. As the number of full-time faculty rapidly declined, graduate assistants and part-timers, recruited on a year-by-year or term-by-term basis, came to constitute the teaching force. But this is temporary labor, and poorly paid, so shortages frequently occur.

Such labor problems affect testing and placement. In the Fall of 1988, because of shortages in available graduate assistants (due in part to pressures for teaching other entry-level courses), and an unwillingness to hire part-timers (due to anti-union sentiments as well as budgetary concerns), there were not enough people to staff the courses of the regular and basic writing program. A solution was ready to hand, one not particularly high-minded, but nonetheless effective:

Table 9.1: *Family Occupation and Income for Freshman Entering Classes at Urbane U (1967, 1973, and 1977)*

	Occupation	1967	1973	1977
Father				
	Blue Collar	43 per cent	43 per cent	53 per cent
	White Collar	57 per cent	57 per cent	47 per cent
Mother				
	Blue Collar	79 per cent	84 per cent	72 per cent
	White Collar	28 per cent	16 per cent	28 per cent

Sources: 1967: Testing Bureau Research Report #68.1, Urbane University Archives.
1973: Measurement and Research Center Technical Report #73.1, Urbane University Archives.
1977: Figures from Orsten (1982), cited in Sullivan (1985, p. 13).

placement criteria were changed. Above a certain score, students bypassed the writing program altogether. This definitional ploy shrunk the pool of students 'needing' writing instruction. The regular composition program took in students with lower scores than previously, thus freeing up spaces in the basic writing program. The numbers of students per class remained the same for the programs, although the teachers had to deal with the consequences of altered entry criteria.

Let us now look more closely at what motivated the changing discourses about writing and the shifting efforts at administrative control. Behind both were changes in the 'demography' of the pedagogic encounter, that is, changes in the social characteristics of students and teachers.

Changes in the Student Body

If we look at overall changes in the student body during the research period, Urbane seems like other similarly-situated urban universities. There have been notable changes in the socio-economic backgrounds of students and larger changes in the racial and gender composition. The socio-economic profile changed, though not dramatically, between the 1960s and 1980s. There were progressively more students from working-class backgrounds, but the overall mix was much the same in the 1980s as in the 1960s — lower-middle-class and working-class students drawn from the surrounding metropolitan area, a major characteristic being that their generation was the first in their family to attend college. Table 9.1 shows parents' occupation for 1967, 1973, and 1977. As noted above, the general change in occupation is not remarkable. What is not shown in this table is that the number of working mothers increases steadily during this ten year period. In effect, increasing numbers of two-income blue collar families were sending their children to this institution.

A significant social class difference does show up in writing program placement. As we might expect, those from more prosperous backgrounds tend to wind up in regular composition, those from less prosperous background in basic writing. A faculty study of the writing programs (Orsten, 1982) reports that 30 per cent of regular composition students in the early 1980s were from families making more than $20,000 annually, whereas only 20 per cent of basic writing

Table 9.2: Minority Enrollment of Undergraduates at Urbane U, 1967–83

	1967	1973	1983
Race			
White	94.5 per cent	86.0 per cent	76.0 per cent
African American	5.0 per cent	11.0 per cent	19.0 per cent
Other Racial Minority (Asian, Puerto Rican, American Indian)	0.5 per cent	3.0 per cent	4.0 per cent

Sources: 1967: Testing Bureau Research Report #68.1, Urbane University Archives.
1977: Figures from Orsten (1982), cited in Sullivan (1985, p. 13).
1983: Higher Education General Information Survey, XVII, Fall Enrollment and Compliance Report, Urbane University Archives.

Note: Figures for 1967 and 1973 are for freshmen entering classes; figures for 1983 are for entire undergraduate registration.

students were from families with this income. In addition, a much larger proportion of relatively prosperous 'out of town' students were placed in regular composition (78 per cent regular versus 22 per cent basic), while a much larger proportion of struggling, special admission 'continuing education' students were placed in basic writing (76 per cent basic versus 14 per cent regular).

When we look at race, there has been considerable change at Urbane. The university is located in a city with a 'minority' population that is quite close to being the 'majority' population. The relevant minority groups are African Americans, Puerto Ricans, and Asians. The largest group by far is African American; figures for both latter groups were quite small until the late 1970s, though both grew considerably since that time. As shown in Table 9.2, in the mid 1960s Urbane had a 5 per cent minority student population; by the early 1970s a 14 per cent minority population; by the early 1980s a 23 per cent minority representation. This final figure is not proportional to minority population in the city, but is a high figure for four-year universities. It is difficult to get demographic information on race and placement in regular or basic writing. There is indirect information, however, that African Americans are placed more often in basic writing. In the comparative study I conducted in 1988, there was a much higher proportion of African American students, especially males, in the basic writing course compared to the regular writing course. This pattern — that basic writing courses had disproportionate minority membership — was confirmed in conversation with four different basic writing teachers, who were basing their comments on experience with over a dozen basic writing sections.

When we look at gender, there has also been change at Urbane, consonant with the increasing numbers of female students found throughout American universities. In the mid 1960s there were 39 per cent female students; in the early 1970s there were 45 per cent female students; by the early 1980s there were 47 per cent female students. The figures are shown in Table 9.3. When we look at writing placement, however, there is a different picture from that found with class or race. Females are disproportionately placed in regular composition: in 1981 they comprised 49 per cent of regular writing students and 39 per cent of basic writing students (Orsten, 1982).

These patterns of placement should not surprise. Working-class students of all races, and especially minority students, are disproportionately grouped in

Table 9.3: *Gender of Undergraduates at Urbane U, 1967–88*

	1967	1977	1983	1988
Male	61 per cent	55 per cent	53 per cent	50 per cent
Female	39 per cent	45 per cent	47 per cent	50 per cent

Sources: 1967: Testing Bureau Research Report #68.1, Urbane University Archives.
1977: Figures from Orsten (1982), cited in Sullivan (1985, p. 13).
1983: Higher Education General Information Survey, XVII, Fall Enrollment and Compliance Report, Urbane University Archives.
1988: Public Memorandum from the University President to the Campus Community, concerning Campus Diversity, December 1988 (only approximate figures, i.e. 'more than 50 per cent female students').

Note: Figures for 1967 and 1973 are for freshmen entering classes; figures for 1983 are for entire undergraduate registration; figures for 1988 are approximations for entire university.

financially-strapped and otherwise hard-pressed inner-city schools. In such schools, writing instruction, as much other instruction, is often highly routinized and unlikely to prepare students for the demands of post-secondary writing — in particular, for the normative expository format of the depersonalized analytic essay. That female students are placed more often in regular than remedial writing is also unexceptional: it agrees with a linguistic and sociolinguistic literature suggesting that in Western urban contexts women are often more 'linguistically adept' than men and that they are more likely to conform to the authoritative prescriptions of 'Standard language' (Philips, Steele, and Tanz, 1987; Trudgill, 1984).

Changes in the teaching force When we look at changes in the composition of the teaching corps, class and gender stand out as major areas of movement. Although it was not possible to obtain direct information on the socio-economic background of teaching staff during the 1960s through 1980s, there are suggestive general differences in educational background. The full-time faculty at Urbane, who taught in the early years of composition, were drawn from non-local, elite private and state universities. The current teaching force is overwhelmingly composed of graduate students from Urbane or part-timers from other local, non-elite institutions. Concurrent with this general change in the social background (i.e., status of educational credentials) of teaching staff has been a more important change in the class position of teaching, at least teaching in writing programs at universities.

Recall that in the 1960s writing instruction at Urbane, as at many American universities, was the province of a white, male professoriat located in an English Department. The job was solidly middle class: it was well paid, secure, and there was considerable autonomy in the work. That picture has now changed. The job is nominally the same; it is teaching 'writing' in a university. But the conditions of work have undergone a drastic proletarianization, and the job is no longer middle-class. Once well paid, it is now very poorly paid; once secure, it is now temporary; once enjoying considerable autonomy, it is now hierarchicized, with much control removed from the teachers and housed in administrative offices.

This change in the organization of work, a class process, has been gendered,

Table 9.4: *Gender of Teaching Force for English Department and Writing Program (1969, 1979 and 1989)*

		Male	Female
English Faculty 1969			
	Total (N = 91)	71 per cent	29 per cent
	Permanent (N = 61)	80 per cent	20 per cent
	Temporary Full-time (N = 30)	53 per cent	47 per cent
English Faculty 1979			
	Total (N = 77)	72 per cent	28 per cent
	Tenured (N = 51)	84 per cent	16 per cent
	Nontenured (N = 26)	50 per cent	50 per cent
English Faculty 1989			
	Total (N = 61)	68 per cent	32 per cent
	Tenured (N = 57)	70 per cent	30 per cent
	Nontenured (N = 4)	50 per cent	50 per cent

Sources: *English Faculty: Graduate and Undergraduate Bulletins*, (1969, 1979, 1989) Urbane U.

Notes: 'Permanent' = Assistant, Associate, and Full Professors; 'Nonpermanent Full-time' = Instructor (a category found only in 1969); 'Tenured' = Associate and Full Professors; 'Nontenured' = Assistant Professors.

Table 9.5: *Gender of Teaching Force in Regular Composition and Basic Programs (1979 and 1987)*

	Male	Female
Basic and regular composition, 1979	54 per cent	44 per cent
Basic composition, 1987 (N = 100)	35 per cent	65 per cent

Sources: Basic & Regular Composition: Instructors' Schedules, Spring, 1979.
Basic Composition: Instructors' Schedules, Fall, 1987.

for typically in the new organization, men administer and women teach. The nature of these gender changes can be illustrated with some aggregate data. In the late 1960s, English faculty, the group which controlled writing instruction, were predominantly male. By the late 1980s, the faculty was still predominantly male, and it still controlled the writing program through the appointment of Program Directors. The stability of overall gender proportions from 1969–89 obscures a basic trend, however, discernible in the rank and gender tabulations given in Table 9.4. As a cohort of determined female scholars made their way up the faculty hierarchy, from non-permanent 'Instructor' positions in 1969 to 'Associate and Full Professor' positions in 1989, the English Department itself was shrinking, and permanent positions previously occupied by senior men were being eliminated. Concurrent with the decline of full-time faculty staff in the English Department, was the growth of the Writing Program. Its new positions were predominantly and increasingly (compare 1979 and 1987) staffed by women. The increased number of women teaching writing courses has not resulted from recruiting women into permanent faculty positions. Rather, as noted earlier, the use of part-time and graduate student labor has increased, and women predominate in this category. Table 9.5 shows the increasing use of part-time instructors

Table 9.6: Percentage of Part-time Instructors in Basic Writing, Reading, and Speech at Urbane U (1980–84)

	Year	Total	No. Part-time	Per cent Part-time
Fall	1980	169	47	28
Fall	1981	174	61	35
Fall	1982	160	67	42
Fall	1984	182	100	55

Source: AAUP Bulletin #133 (1984) Urbane U Chapter.

in the basic programs overall (basic writing, reading, and speech courses) during the early 1980s. If we compare the post-1979 period in Tables 9.4, 9.5, and 9.6, we see several linked processes: a decline in faculty positions; an increase in the proportion of women teaching in writing programs; and an increase in the proportion of part-time teaching labor.

Interim Summary on Class, Race, and Gender Demographics

The challenge of course is to make something of these various demographic profiles. Each poses its own complexities and unanswered questions, but the overall trends seem clear. The writing program at Urbane has developed as the student body became more diverse in terms of economic background, race, and gender. The program has evolved in tandem with a shrinking of permanent faculty and an increase in the use of non-permanent teaching labor. This process has involved contrary tendencies toward control and fragmentation, and it has been starkly gendered, as women have taken up teaching at Urbane and have borne the brunt of worsening working conditions.

Changes in the demography of pedagogy, in the social composition of students and teachers, often triggers an educational 'crisis': profound uncertainty about the goals and methods of education, institutional alarm and efforts at restorative reaction (see Bourdieu and Passeron, 1977, and Bourdieu, 1988 on such crisis in the French university system; Rose, 1985 on the recurring crises of American higher education). At Urbane as at many other universities during this period, changes in student characteristics provoked an initial discourse of language deficiency, and this discourse quickly settled into a general conception of educational deficiencies needing remediation. The fragmentation (diversification) of an earlier, homogeneous student body was accompanied by the fragmentation (diversification and destabilization) of an earlier, homogeneous teaching force. These processes of fragmentation were met by administrative efforts at centralization and control of testing, curriculum, and work evaluation.

This argument thus far has concerned general trends, but let us now turn to a more interesting and difficult question: how do the general trends influence actual classrooms? How do the class and race of students and the class position and gender of teachers affect the teaching and learning of writing? We can develop this question — which essentially asks how general institutional characteristics affect local circumstances — by turning to particular cases, examining how curriculum and responses to curriculum shaped the course of writing, for specific students and teachers.

A Comparison of 'Basic' Writing Courses

Let us briefly recall the changes in the formation of curriculum. The content and structure of the early 1960s writing course, English 10, had been the responsibility of a committee of English faculty members, who also taught the course; to serve on this committee had been, in the words of one senior English faculty, 'an honor'. The course had been a 'Western Civilization' survey course, with extensive writing focused in response to a fairly traditional canon. By the 1980s both the regular and the basic writing curriculum were decided by the Program Directors, in consultation with a few assistants. As noted earlier, the decision structure had become a gendered hierarchy: men conceived and planned, women taught. The curriculum itself had bifurcated: regular composition explicitly taught a variety of academic essay formats; remedial composition emphasized a process approach to writing.

A Basic Writing Course: The Absent Text

The 'process' was carefully circumscribed, however, by a prescribed sequence of assignments and a hierarchy of evaluation. The formal syllabus of basic writing was structured around four writing assignments: (1) a narrative of a significant incident in the student's life; followed by (2) an essay which dealt with some contradictory aspect of personal experience; following this was (3) a formulation of a personal problem and its solution; and finally (4) a position paper addressing some public issue. Each essay had to be passed by two readers, the course teacher and another teacher; and course dossiers with four passing essays were read by a group of third readers, at the end of each semester. One acknowledged reason for this structure of evaluation was to insure that teachers were adhering to the program.

A striking feature of both the regular and basic writing courses I attended was the students' collective and individual difficulty in understanding what the teacher wanted of them. This is typical of beginning college courses, but in the basic writing course this difficulty was palpable and enduring. It was frequently and repeatedly expressed, in students' questions to the teacher (What do you mean by . . .?) and the teachers' questions to the students (Do you understand . . .?), in the *sub rosa* muttering that accompanied each question, and in conversations that I had with the teacher and various students outside the classroom, over the course of the semester and subsequently.

This difficulty pointed to a lack of shared understanding and textual orientation that I began to think of as the 'absent text'. For the teacher, a novice, the four assignments and the 'Weekly Lesson Plan' proved insufficient for the vagaries of this encounter with relatively unprepared students. For the students, also novices, the assignments and classroom discussion were frequently baffling. What was meant by an 'incident' and how did you know when one was important enough? What was a 'contradiction' and what trickery lay behind the phrasing about 'something being the same and yet different?' These generalities masked very specific assumptions about kinds of writing, which they only discovered when they failed to meet those assumptions. Finally, there was a literal absence of text. The assigned textbooks (Random House, 1987) managed to be both voluminous and simplistic. It focused on 'the activity of writing', and provided only fragments of essays, very few of which were from academic sources. Finding it unhelpful, the students quickly stopped reading it. The teacher, charitably referring to it as 'a good reference book, but not for classroom discussion,' stopped assigning it. So the 'text' consisted of the weekly lesson progression, structured around the four assignments, what material the teacher could find to bring in, and the students' 'experience'.

There are good reasons why basic writing programs such as the one at Urbane avoid overly rigid formats of expository writing. Learning 'canonical' texts does not necessarily lead to critical analytic writing; it may simply lead to an aping of genre forms. In addition, when presented without adequate preparation, in the press and hurry of typical writing courses, rigid formats can just be part of an implicit pedagogy, selecting for those already familiar with these schemes of writing, and mystifying those without prior experience. But there are also problems with a process-oriented curriculum. The students of basic writing generally, and of this class in particular, knew that their personal experience was insufficient for 'college writing'. That experience had been mined through years of journals and personal expression assignments in second-tier writing programs of their high schools, and it had left them placed in 'remedial' writing upon their entrance to college (see Applebee, 1984, for similar data on writing tiers and typical assignments in high schools in the Midwest and California). The teachers of basic writing, themselves beginners, also knew that the students' experience was problematic, that the curriculum which began with narratives of personal incidents and remain oriented thereto left an overly large gap between experience and the analytic essays which ultimately had to be mastered. The instructor of this particular classroom found that the absence of 'text', beyond the sequence of writing assignments, made it very difficult for herself or her students to articulate experience in general ways; she and they found that certain basic facts of the college experience for the students — for example, their race and gender sensitivity, as well as their sense of dislocation and stigmatization — were not 'writable'.

A Counterexample: Texts of Race in a Basic Writing Classroom

Let me develop this point through a comparative example. It concerns the curricular innovations of an African-American graduate student who was teaching basic writing at this institution for the first time. This student, whom I will call Don Brown, was not the teacher whose class I studied, though I had met him during the pre-term teacher training workshops and we had talked on occasion during the semester of classroom research. Later, as I was presenting my initial findings to various formal and informal gatherings at Urbane U, several people suggested that I talk with him because he had taken a creative and apparently successful approach to confronting, rather than avoiding, social difference in the writing classroom.

So I talked with Don Brown, and he told me his teaching story. A beginning graduate student in an institution with a fair number of African-American students, but very, very few African-American teachers, and an institution experiencing several incidents indicative of the 'new campus racism', Mr. Brown decided that race was part of writing. He also felt that learning writing required exposure to good writing, so he did something about that.

He introduced texts along with each writing assignment, and those texts are particularly interesting. For the first assignment to write about a 'significant incident', he had the students read Langston Hughes' 'Salvation', a short five-page story about how Hughes suddenly lost his religious belief one Sunday morning. With this text they could see how a short moment, a brief experience, might have profound implications for the course of a life. For the assignment to write about a 'contradiction' in life, he had them read Frederick Douglass' 4th July 1862 Address 'The Slaveholders' Rebellion' in Upstate New York (Douglass, 1862 [1952]). In that address Douglass did not glorify the Republic but pointed instead to a simple, basic contradiction between a text proclaiming that 'All men are created equal' and the fact of slavery. For the assignment to write about a 'problem and solution', Mr. Brown had his students read Chinua Achebe's *Things Fall Apart*, so that they might have a full textual treatment of the dilemma, not uncommon in modern life, between traditional upbringings and expectations and a world in which those upbringings and expectations are no longer sufficient. For the assignment to write a 'position paper', he had them read numerous items from the student newspaper concerning the controversy of a White Students' Union: documents from the White Student Union advocating its right to exist and defend white interest, as well as numerous attacks on the Union from African-American and anti-racist groups and individuals.

At this point, things nearly 'fell apart' in Mr. Brown's class. The bounds of reasoned dialogue were transgressed, tempers flared, passion and animosity were in abundance. The writing, of course, continued in voluminous amount. From the beginning of the course, there had been an explosion of writing. He had received eight and ten page essays (rather than two to three pages handwritten) on 'a significant incident' and had insisted on and received extensive revisions. Throughout the course there had been much writing, and there was an unusually high pass rate at the end of term.

This is not a simple story, however, in which we learn of curricular innovation, writing being transformed, and teachers and students composing happily ever after. Mr. Brown was killing himself with overwork. Like others in the basic program, he was teaching two courses, attending a teaching seminar, and trying to get on with his own first year of graduate work. In subsequent semesters, he had to lessen the confrontation of text and social difference, to lower expectations and simplify curriculum. His imaginative and successful innovation suggests an exciting way to write 'experience' against texts and historical positions, but it also raises questions about generalizability and viability.

Discussion: The Generalizability and Viability of Classroom Innovations

The issue of generalizability requires us to confront the notion of 'experience' upon which process-writing curriculums ultimately depend. Mr. Brown had chosen particular texts with a particular slant for his students to write with and against. They were African-American writers, male writers, and writers of 'quality' literary prose. His choices were political choices about content with which to engage particular types of writing. They worked well in his classroom, in this university; they might well be inappropriate for other writing classrooms. But the valuable insight his choices illustrate is that writing or composition occurs from social positions.

A major problem with an 'experience-based' approach to writing is that it all too often leaves both students and teachers with no framework for talking about how experience is historically structured, how experiences of gender, class, and race, of personal biography and institutional encounter are expressed, and avoided, in the 'academic discourse' students are expected to learn. To emphasize 'experience' as the foundation of writing is often to focus narrowly on the unhistorical, the immediate and tangible; it is to emphasize the sensible at the expense of the analytical (see also Herron, 1988; Ohmann, 1979; Wells, 1977; Youdelman, 1978). Experience-based process writing always risks representing the source of writing as an unmoored subjectivity with no larger historical or institutional text to write with and against. It risks presenting the source of writing as the isolated individual, that mystifying self-presentation of a privileged bourgeois epoch, now being presented to decidedly unprivileged, non-bourgeois students.

We know that ideas of individuality and equality are basic touchstones of our political culture. Equality, however, is formal, it is equality 'under law', a particular relation between state and citizen. As conceptions of humanness, equality and individuality are important but narrow. Formal (legal) equality can and does exist with extreme substantive inequality, and such inequality of circumstances (between individuals but more particularly between groups and between groups and institutions) cannot be avoided in the critical, self-conscious discourse that is supposedly central to higher education. Individuality is a biohistorical fact and a salient aspect of social existence in societies such as our own. We are, however, not mere individuals. We achieve humanity in groups, with group experiences and differences. Those experiences and differences — of race, language, and gender, of migration, religion, and so forth — are complex, historically situated, and often politically volatile. They should be engaged as part of a process of writing. They demand, however, an articulation, achieved through texts, discussions, and whatever-it-takes, not a flattening out through a false common denominator of 'the personal'.

Mr. Brown's curriculum innovations are thus of partial generalizability, but they provide an important lesson: the need to recognize limits and constraints in all curriculum. Mr. Brown's innovations were also of limited viability, and this points to the need to recognize institutional limits and constraints on pedagogical innovation.

Mr. Brown was a particular teacher and, as noted earlier, his innovations so increased his work load that he was forced to curtail them. In general, and the generalities count, writing programs are underfunded and understaffed. Student teachers and part-timers are paid miserable salaries for very demanding work. Their autonomy in classrooms is limited, in programs in which the curriculum is formalized and evaluation is centralized. These are their conditions of work, and they typically do what more privileged academics do when facing similar situations: they look for shortcuts. They adopt pedagogic routines that leave unchallenged the fragmentation of experience and knowledge found in many (writing) curricula, routines that allow them to satisfy the 'program' while saving time for more rewarding endeavors, such as their own coursework and research. Thus individuals deal with intractable institutional arrangements.

The history of program development at Urbane shows that 'writing' is connected to labor politics at the university. It has not been a simple story of increasing centralized control and degraded working conditions, though that has been part of the plot; rather, it has entailed a complex set of interconnected struggles between actors differently positioned in various institutional fields. Sometimes the struggles are overt; often they are covert, displaced through vocabularies of standards and integrity. They pit faculty and departments against college and university administration; permanent, tenured faculty against part-time faculty; within English itself, they pit younger, research-oriented scholars against older colleagues holding a more traditional conception of teaching and college work.

As far as I can tell, based on conversations and interviews with teachers and administrators, both new arrivals and 'old hands' in the writing programs, the process-writing emphasis was adopted for excellent motives — including a desire not to impose rigid genre formats on students least familiar with them — and with support from a research literature suggesting that process pedagogies were good at tapping and developing students' communicative abilities. These curriculum decisions were neither made nor implemented in an institutional vacuum, however. They were made within a larger dynamic of fragmentation and control.

The upshot has been that differences are downplayed — differences between groups within the faculty; differences between students and traditional curriculum. The problems and potentials of non-traditional and non-elite students are administratively sequestered in 'remedial' writing. The curriculum emphasizes experience, without providing much guidance, for students or teachers, as to how that experience is to be articulated *vis à vis* the complex literacy expectations of a modern multiversity.

A Dialectic of Displacement: Literacy, Social Order, and Social Antagonism

In the preceding case analysis, I have described and argued against a conception and program of writing based on an overly simple and abstract notion of student experience, and I have located the conception and program within a particular institutional context of contradictory tendencies towards the fragmentation and centralization of the pedagogic encounter. Let me now widen the argument to suggest that process writing is of a piece with a broad historical trend in American education to define literacy as a skill and, further, that this skills definition is a displacement, an avoidance of the enduring social conflicts in which literacy — as symbolic practice — is unavoidably implicated. Rather than a basic skill, literacy is an essential aspect of social order and disorder. Just as liberal education emerged from a field of power relations and social struggles, so literacy as we know it emerged from contexts of domination as well as enlightenment and acquired its particular cast from the social arrangements and conflicts of which it was a part.

There is now a large literature analyzing the role of literacy, as technology, practice, and embedded social relation in religious dominions and nationalist movements. Western Europe offers various cases of religious values being promulgated and reinforced through a selective literacy. Thus, for example, in seventeenth century Protestant Sweden there was an active program of public religious education, in which the masses were taught a particular type of reading, so that they might absorb the correct religious beliefs, under the careful tutelage of their spiritual overseers (Gee, 1988; Graff, 1988). It was during this period, and in other parts of Protestant Europe, that we find some of the first large-scale reading tests, formal protocols for evaluating whether the newly print-literate peasantry were receiving the correct, clerically-approved messages from their encounters with texts (Marvin, 1988). These examples are illuminating in two ways. First, they undermine the common Euro-American argument that print-literacy and Protestantism necessarily led to an individual-centered, critical consciousness (see Eisenstein, 1968; Goody, 1977; and Ong, 1982 versus Graff, 1988; Marvin, 1984, 1988; Warner, 1989). Second, they show the shaping, through techniques of authoritative evaluation, of an officially defined literacy. This official literacy is dissociated from the myriad complexities of local practices with texts and linked to a regulated symbolic realm of state religion and, later, to various nationalist projects (Nespor, 1985).

Literacy has often figured centrally in the construction of national consciousness. As Anderson (1983) has argued, such consciousness depends on a complex play of unity and difference: there is an imagined sense of community, in which all members of the proclaimed nation are somehow equals, despite their manifest differences, and thus bound together in a unity of nation, which is itself essentially defined by contrast to other, different nations. The nationalist project has varied greatly within a relatively short historical compass, ranging from the anti-colonial nationalisms of the Americas in the eighteenth and early nineteenth centuries, to the classic progressive and reactionary nationalisms of Europe in the nineteenth and early twentieth centuries, to the post-colonial nationalisms of the mid-twentieth century. But language has frequently played an essential role, providing a symbolic means for defining an inclusive unity within a larger heterogeneity: our nation versus all the others, our language versus foreign tongues. The extrication of language from daily exigencies and its refiguring as an essential, context-free symbol of 'large-scale' association began in modern Euro-American history with the religious promulgation of reading literacy (Marvin, 1988; Nespor, 1985). Nationalism, however, builds upon and extends this simultaneous abstraction and regimentation of language, through educational, bureaucratic, and economic implementation of particular languages, that is, through literacy; literacy in a particular institutional and cultural matrix that Anderson (1983) has called print-capitalism.

However, if literacy plays a central role in large-scale religious and secular political formations, it figures as centrally in the social antagonisms that underlie all such orders. Take the religious literacy discussed above as example. The early Protestant organization of a regulated vernacular literacy began in revolt against a prior Catholic organization of sacred elite literacy, and fundamentalist protestantism in the contemporary United States defines itself by a literalist doctrine of text meaning, which it contrasts with the interpretivist laxities of mainstream protestantism. As noted earlier, nationalism defines itself against others: the 'classic' nationalist movements of the nineteenth century began as subversive agitations, with 'authentic' vernacular literatures posed against the dynastic languages of Hapsburg, Bourbon, and Romanov empires. The most potent of recent nationalist movements in the United States, those of African-Americans, Chicanos, and Native Americans, involve an assertion of languages and literatures as part of projects for cultural-political autonomy (Jordan, 1988; Simonson and Walker, 1988).

Literacy and education often seem to resolve fundamental social antagonisms, but the price of 'resolution' is a particular shaping of literacy in which appropriative definitions and hierarchical institutional arrangements disguise and displace the earlier conflicts. In her masterful overview of the shaping of literacy in Anglo-American cultural traditions, Cook-Gumperz (1986) has described the rise of schooled literacy, an official definition and institutional implementation of a stratified, hierarchical literacy. It replaced and repressed earlier, heterogeneous 'local literacies' based in the popular cultural practices, dissenting religions, and radical political movements that were the discursive wherewithal of English and North American working classes as they emerged in the development of nineteenth-century industrial capitalism. As noted earlier, Ohmann (1988) has analyzed the formation of the profession of English, in which privileged reading came to be valued, and vocational writing devalued. Where Cook-Gumperz describes a shaping of literacy which is also a repression of class, Ohmann describes a hierarchy of literacy which has become, as we saw in the preceding case study, a gendered hierarchy.

What is relevant for our argument at this point is that these institutional appropriations begin in periods of social crisis. Indeed, the recent history of literacy shows a recurrent pattern: a displacement of social crisis onto literacy and its 'skills'. Thus the literacy 'crises' of the late 1970s in the USA and Britain were represented as a perilous decline in basic skills necessary for participation in the economy and, especially, for higher education (Street, 1984). The crisis was announced at a time of severe economic depression and at a time when new groups — women, minorities, large numbers of working-class students — were arriving at the university. In an excellent paper entitled 'The language of exclusion: Writing instruction at the university', Mike Rose (1985) analyzes the discourses and organizational forms employed by traditional inhabitants of the public university as they attempt to come to grips with the new arrivals and what they perceive as a basic deficiency of those arrivals: writing skills. Rose traces the history of defining writing and literacy as 'skills', and he sees in the rise and dominance of a skills model of literacy and typical (elite) American tendency to treat social and political questions — about education, access, and standards — as essentially technical problems. The technical solutions never seem to work, of course, but that does not detract from their usefulness in the general drama of a 'skills' crisis.

Rose also provides a short and illuminating history of the recurrent crises of standards, and that history shows what Rose calls the 'myth of crisis'. In that myth there is a recent, sudden, and precipitous decline in heretofore robust standards, a decline which only intensive, controlled drill in remedial skills can rectify. But, to rework a phrase from Henry Ford, that ahistorical view is bunk. For the crisis, or at least the language of crisis, recurs: studies at Harvard in the 1890s lament the mediocrity and poor preparation of incoming students, drawn from wider strata than the previous elite cadre; commissions at Stanford and the University of Chicago decry, in the 1920s, the inability of students to read or 'write a proper English sentence', as they recruit from new sectors of the middle class;

commissions at UCLA and Berkeley describe, in the 1970s, the new 'illiterates' who darken their doors, as new social groups press for and gain admission to these elite, public-funded institutions. The heart of the matter is the conflict between new populations and traditional pedagogies, and all the implicit assumptions about language, background, and knowledge that such pedagogies contain. For Rose the language of remediation, phrased as basic skill, is a language of exclusion, a definition of the newly-arrived as not-yet-ready.

Conclusion

In the preceding I have presented several embedded historical narratives and a case study. The narratives suggest that the current curriculum crisis has antecedents in profound and enduring political antagonisms and dilemmas, dilemmas and antagonisms which will not be resolved by a liberal solution of multicultural curriculum of literacy. They also suggest that the 'turn to language', as I have characterized the emphasis on literacy-as-skill, shares this troublesome history, these ambiguities and dilemmas, as well as a deteriorating institutional context.

The case study of writing at Urbane U traced a short historical development, examining interconnected changes in discourses about writing, patterns of administrative control, and the social composition of teachers and students. It reveals a basic irony of the 'turn of language': That as writing has achieved organizational prominence in university curriculum, the institutional conditions for teaching and learning to write have seriously eroded. This erosion may be partly understood in the idiom of labor process: the resources devoted to teaching writing have been cut, and control has been progressively removed from teachers. What has also eroded, however, is pedagogical vision. Process writing approaches may help defuse the volatile situation of disempowered teachers facing stigmatized students with a traditional elite curriculum, but such approaches leave students and teachers with few resources for making critical sense of the confrontations — of gender, race, and class, of discipline and specialization within discipline — upon which an institutional literacy is founded.

All has not been domination, control, and retreat, however. My ethnographic encounter with writing programs has shown me that effort, concern, and commitment are pervasive; and simply following the course of a failing and then succeeding remedial writing student is enough to evoke Rose's (1988) phrase about 'the struggles and achievements of America's underprepared'. The teacher in whose class I observed continued to rework her approach, trying to present an explicit curriculum that negotiated the literacy dilemma of enlightenment and domination. Mr. Brown's first writing class showed an impressive refiguring of 'experience', in a text with cultural position and historical depth. But these were uncoordinated efforts by determined individuals that go 'against the grain'. They should be supported, but we must not underestimate the full counterweight of prevailing arrangement and historical tendency that such efforts confront.

In order to show that literacy is simultaneously knowledge, culture, and politics, we must develop analyses of the multiple institutional and interactional contexts that shape actual literacies. I have tried to show in the foregoing that we can investigate both general and concrete historical links between institutional processes and authoritative views of language, culture, and education. Institutions can and should be viewed as structures and constraints, but they also embed contradictions which give them historical dynamism and foretell the dissolution of their given arrangements. Ideologies — whether 'dominant' or 'counter-hegemonic' — are lived in practice, in cultural texts and forms of conscious-ness that are riven with ambiguities and dilemmas. An historical, ethnographic, and discursively-oriented inquiry into social processes, as the preceding attempts to be, must remain aware of the antinomies of thought, language, and social arrangement that pervade those bright promises and dark truths we call 'literacy'.

Acknowledgments

Versions of this paper were presented at a session on 'Literacy and Ideology' of the Boston University Conference on Language Development, October 1989; at a 'Contexts of Literacy' Colloquium, Lehmann College, October 1989; at a joint seminar, Department of Anthropology and School of Education, SUNY-Albany, October, 1989; at an Anthropology Department Seminar, New School for Social Research, December 1989; and at a Fellows Forum, National Academy of Education, Boston, June 1990. I am indebted to members of audiences at these various forums for comments and queries. In addition, I am indebted to Linda Nicholson, Alan Purves, and Brian Street for detailed comments on an earlier written draft. This study is part of a larger research project 'The politics of liter-acy at the urban university' supported by a Spencer Fellowship, National Acad-emy of Education, 1988–89.

References

American Association of University Professors (1986) Bulletin #133, Urbane U.
Anderson, B. (1983) *Imagined Communities*, London, Verso.
Apple, M. (1986) *Teachers and Texts: A Political Economy of Gender and Class Relations in Education*, New York, Routledge and Kegan Paul.
Applebee, A. (1984) *Contexts for Learning to Write: Studies of Secondary School Instruc-tion*, Norwood, NJ, Ablex Publishing Corporation.
Arnold, M. (1869) [1969] *Culture and Anarchy: An Essay in Political and Social Crit-icism*. I. McGregor (Ed.), Indianapolis and New York, Bobbs-Merrill.
Axelrod, X. and Cooper, C. (1987) *Reading Critically, Writing Well*, New York, St. Martins Press.
Bennett, B. (1984) 'To reclaim a legacy', *Chronicle of Higher Education*, **29**, 14, pp. 15–21.
Bloom, A. (1987) *The Closing of the American Mind*, New York, Simon and Schuster.
Bourdieu, P. (1988) *Homo Academicus*, Palo Alto, Stanford University Press.
Bourdieu, P. and Passeron, J-C. (1977) *Reproduction in Education, Culture, and Society*, Beverly Hills, CA, Sage Publications.
Cook-Gumperz, J. (1986) 'Schooling and literacy: An unchanging equation?', in Cook-Gumperz, J. (Ed.) *The Social Construction of Literacy*, Cambridge, Cam-bridge University Press.
Douglass, F. (1862) [1952] *The Life and Writings of Frederick Douglass, Volume III: The Civil War, 1861–1865*, P.S. Foner (Ed.) New York, International Publishers.
Eagleton, T. (1984) *The Functions of Criticism*, London, Verso.

EISENSTEIN, E. (1968) 'Some conjectures about the impact of printing on Western society and thought: A preliminary report', *Journal of Modern History*, 40, pp. 1–57.

GEE, J. (1988) 'The legacies of literacy: From Plato to Freire through Harvey Graff', *Harvard Education Review*, **58**, 2, pp. 195–212.

GOODY, J. (1977) *The Domestication of the Savage Mind*, Cambridge, Cambridge University Press.

GRAFF, H. (1988) *The Labyrinths of Literacy*, London, Falmer Press.

HABERMAS, J. (1989) *The Structural Transformation of the Public Sphere: An Inquiry into a Category of Bourgeois Society*, Trs. BURGER, T. and LAWRENCE, F., Cambridge, MA, MIT Press.

HERRON, J. (1988) *Universities and the Myth of Cultural Decline*, Detroit, Wayne State University Press.

HIRSCH, E.D. (1987) *Cultural Literacy. What Every American Needs to Know*, Boston, Houghton Mifflin.

JACOBY, R. (1987) *The Last Intellectuals*, New York, Basic Books.

JAYNES, G. and WILLIAMS, R. (1989) *A Common Destiny: Blacks and American Society*, Washington, DC, National Academy Press.

JORDAN, J. (1988) 'Nobody mean more to me than you and the future life of Willie Jordan', *Harvard Educational Review*, 58, pp. 363–374.

LASCH, C. (1979) *The Culture of Narcissism*, New York, Warner Books.

MARVIN, C. (1984) 'Constructed and reconstructed discourse: Inscription and talk in the history of literacy', *Communication Research*, 11, pp. 563–94.

MARVIN, C. (1988) 'Attributes of authority: Literacy test and the logic of strategic conduct', *Communications*, 11, pp. 63–82.

NESPOR, J. (1987) 'The construction of school knowledge: A case study', *Journal of Education*, 169, pp. 34–54.

OHMANN, R. (1988) *The Politics of Letters*, Middlesbury, CT, Wesleyan University Press.

ONG, W. (1982) *Orality and Literacy: The Technologizing of the Word*, London, Methuen.

ORSTEN, D. (1982) *Report on Basic Writing Program*, Ms., Urbane U.

PHILIPS, S., STEELE, S. and TANZ, C. (Eds) (1987) *Language and Sex in Comparative Perspective*, Cambridge, Cambridge University Press.

PROGRAM DESCRIPTION (1986) Description of the basic writing program at Urbane U, Ms., Urbane U.

RANDOM HOUSE (1987) *The Random House Guide to Writing*, New York, Random House.

ROSE, M. (1985) 'The language of exclusion: Writing instruction at the university', *College English*, 47, pp. 341–359.

ROSE, M. (1988) *Lives on the Boundary*, New York, Penguin.

SHOR, I. (1980) *Critical Teaching and Everyday Life*, Boston, South End Press.

SIMONSON, R. and WALKER, S. (1988) *The Graywolf Annual Five: Multicultural Literacy*, St. Paul, Graywolf Press.

STREET, B. (1984) *Literacy in Theory and Practice*, Cambridge, Cambridge University Press.

SULLIVAN, F. (1985) 'A sociolinguistic analysis of the distribution of information in university placement-test essays', PhD dissertation, University of Pennsylvania.

TRUDGILL, P. (Ed.) (1984) *Language in the British Isles*, Cambridge, Cambridge University Press.

WARNER, M. (1989) 'The cultural mediation of the print medium', Working paper No. 27, *Center for Psychosocial Studies*, Chicago, IL.

WELLS, S. (1977) 'Classroom heuristics and empiricism', *College English*, 39, pp. 470.

WELLS, S. (1988) 'Gender differences and the cultural arbitrary', unpublished manuscript.

WRIGHT, E. (1980) ' "School English" and public policy', *College English*, 42, pp. 327–342.

YOUDELMAN, J. (1978) 'Limiting students: Remedial writing and the death of open admissions', *College English*, 39, pp. 562–72.

Chapter 10

Workplace Literacy in Australia: Competing Agenda

Peter O'Connor

Introduction

For the past five or six years in Australia the need to redress perceived skills deficiencies among workers, end restrictive work practices and industrial relations, heighten productivity levels, and diminish both the lack of competitiveness of Australian capitalism, and the failure of education, have all been widely accepted. There have been dire warnings of the consequences of allowing Australian business to slip further behind its international competitors, of a failure to orient education and training closely and explicitly to the demands of capitalist rationality and the values of the 'free' market. More often than not this urgent need is expressed in terms of economic imperatives and the 'national interest'. To this extent, Australia mirrors the experience of other advanced industrial states, such as the USA and Great Britain, over much the same time scale (Aronowitz and Giroux, 1986, pp. 200–1).

The argument takes the following form: if Australia is to be internationally competitive and maintain its status and viability as a First World trading nation, if the economy and standard of living are to weather international recession, then Australian business (and particularly manufacturing) needs to be rationalized and restructured, and incorporate the latest technology and work systems, innovation must occur in product and process technology, new managerial techniques need to be introduced, and the skills base of workers needs to be expanded and diversified to meet changes 'flexibly' and to increase productivity. That is, Australians must not only work harder (while also exercising wage and other industrial restraint), they must work 'smarter', and education and training strategies will be central to economic and social success. In the words of the Prime Minister, Australia must strive to become a 'clever Australia'.[1]

The same fears and warnings of this crisis in capital underpinned by a crisis in education are emanating from other industrialized countries. David T. Kearnes, Chairman of the Xerox Corporation, refers to it as the making of a 'national disaster', while Brad M. Butler, former chairman of Proctor and Gamble, fears the creation of a 'Third World within our own country'. (*New York Times*, 25 September 1989, cited in Collins, 1989, p. 26). Politicians of all persuasion, spokespeople for business and even many trade unionists and educationists, have joined the chorus of the need for massive changes in the way that work is performed. The unanimous focus has not been on the failings of local and international capital but individual workers' deficiencies and the failure of education systems to adequately arrest these deficiencies. Thus, the solution to many of the problems is through micro-economic reform grounded in education and training policies. The emergence of this theme can be traced through a number of major government, business and trade union policy documents which have appeared in Australia in recent years.[2]

John Burgess (1989) argues that much of the productivity debate and rhetoric has focused on the issues of trade union power, restrictive work practices and the prerogative of management to manage. That is, that productivity is being pursued and promoted as primarily a worker problem, and as such is misrepresentative of the processes and forces generating productivity growth.

> Behind the public pronouncements on microeconomic reforms in the labour market are hidden judgements concerning the nature of work and employment, and the process of productivity generation. The obvious judgement is the ideological one — that is, the fault for poor economic performance is attributed to labour, or its trade union representatives ... The other judgements involve assumptions about productivity generation — namely that changes in work practices, combined with a diminution of trade union power, will generate a productivity surge. (Burgess, 1989, pp. 23–4)

These views of the changes occurring offer only a selective description and interpretation of the changes taking place, and often imaginative explanations for the causes of those changes. They often overlook or miss the elements of crisis and change shared by most advanced capitalist societies, and the diversity of restructuring efforts being put in place. Consequently, they exaggerate the opportunities and neglect many of the dangers inherent in this approach.

Nevertheless, there has been a flurry of activity surrounding the implementation of these strategies, including the establishment of Industry Training bodies, new industrial legislation, the increasing dependence of award conditions and wages upon demonstrable productivity outcomes, rationalization of coverage through union amalgamations, attacks on 'restrictive' and 'outmoded' work practices, restructuring of major industries, Training Guarantee legislation, Education and Training Foundations funded through diversions of company taxes, as well as a range of major reviews of education.[3] Many have urged the overhaul of education systems, greater emphasis on vocational training, and the need to involve business, and a shift in the balance of costing and responsibility for much of education. A number of writers refer to this shift in emphasis, either positively or critically, as 'post-Fordism' where the new policies, often encouraging skills and initiative of workers, have replaced the traditional 'Fordist' view of labour organization and control at the workplace.[4]

A part of the unfolding changes is the acknowledgment that education has to play a more prominent role in the lives of all citizens, particularly those in the labour force, and that industry has to play a more prominent role in the education of its workforce. Labour market predictions also clearly indicate that those currently in the workforce have to be trained for contemporary as well as for future industry needs. This activity around job skills training and upgrading is slowly occurring, as is the acknowledgment that these terms and activities are applicable to the entire spectrum of jobs, including management, technical and professional staff, white collar and blue collar workers.

Alex Butler (1989) argues that it

is becoming not just desirable but essential to involve people of all ages in a continuing process of education and training. Moreover, many of the very narrow forms of training for specific and highly specialized occupations which have been prevalent to date, especially in the skilled trades area, are rapidly becoming obsolete.

These observations are reinforced by the research of the US scholar Larry Mikulecky and others (1989a), which points to evidence of more jobs being affected by high-technology. Thus the growing demand is for 'broad technicians' rather than 'high technicians'. In order to achieve this, it is argued, workers will require a range of literacy, numeracy, computing, language and communications skills, as the foundation to other skills development and upgrading (Mikulecky, 1989a).

International Literacy Year and Worker Literacy

International Literacy Year provided a useful addendum to the education and industry debate. It also provided a diversionary focus on 'evidence' which vindicated the warnings of educational malaise and economic peril, as well as legitimating the strategies which are being put in place. The media regularly carried claims, 'human interest' accounts, and testimonies of famous public figures who had 'suffered' from illiteracy (perhaps contradicting the intended message). These included actors Tom Cruise and Whoopi Goldberg, the Australian Governor-General Bill Hayden, David Hill (Chairman of Australian Broadcasting Corporation), high profile journalists, trade union officials and politicians, while endless profiles of the plight of contemporary 'illiterates' rounded out the picture.

The findings of a national survey on adult literacy, released in late 1989, were seized upon by the media. The survey, and various reports of it, told us that at least one million adults in Australia have reading and writing difficulties. The survey found that 32 per cent of respondents could not find the gross pay written on a pay slip; 31 per cent could not find a required heading in the Yellow Pages of the phone book; 38 per cent could not calculate their change from $5 for a lunch bill; 57 per cent could not calculate 10 per cent on a bill totalling less than $5; and that at least one in seven workers cannot read or write adequately (Wickert, 1989). Whereas these data are useful in the general promotion of understanding literacy, and provides catchy and ready-to-use statistics for media, government, companies, and advocates of adult literacy, it is only of limited use in the area of workers' literacy.[5]

During much of International Literacy Year there was much discussion of the need for basic skills upgrading in the workplace, as the foundation for, or precursor to the volume of industry training that is to be undertaken. Estimates of costs to industry and society of basic skills deficiencies ranged from the often-quoted $A3.2 billion through to $A8 and $A10 billion, and there was much talk about the benefits which flow to the individual, industry and society as a result of improved basic skills. Most supporting evidence for these claims has been speculative at best. Nonetheless, anecdotes abound regarding difficulties in filling job vacancies, workplace communications problems and workers' inadequate skills, all obstructing industrial, economic and individual development.[6]

The propaganda campaign for International Literacy Year in Australia was organized by media consultants who had responsibility to develop, disseminate and promote propaganda around the main themes. While this obviously assisted in raising the profile of literacy issues, it remains to be seen whether this contributed to a more enlightened or critical understanding of these issues. The main slogans of 'Literacy: The Problem is Bigger Than You Think' and 'Literacy: The First Step' did nothing to promote a positive or sensitive approach. Nonetheless, the Federal Government allocated an additional $4.2 million to literacy provision through its Vocationally Oriented Adult Education and Literacy Program, so arguably the federal government itself at least partly felt compelled by its own propaganda.

A recent Canadian article which assesses general developments in that country offers some chastening predictions which may be relevant in Australia. It states:

> Bureaucrats at all levels are suddenly consulting on 'literacy' to rush policies and perhaps even some funds into the newly found issue ... However, even in the short term, some of what will happen with the new literacy monies is distressing. What is wrong is that many of the programs will repeat the techniques that we already know will fail. Few will have the courage, the time or the curiosity to delve a little deeper and ask what can we do to avoid repeating what we already know does not work. And so, many, if not most, will set up 'new' programs which will not be new, and thus repeat the inadequacies of the past — and ultimately repeat the failures. Most will calculate that the students could not cope with the programs, so they must unfortunately be dumped for better 'investment' returns. (Pearpoint, 1989, pp. 423–4)

If nothing else, this warning is clear about the need for integrity as the basis for new activities, and for the need to examine why the new activities are occurring, rather than simply respond to vague external forces which may not be fully understood. Similarly, we need to remain cautious in adopting 'new' agenda which are not and may never be ours. While there is obviously a need to adjust to changing conditions, it is also necessary to preserve many of the 'old' principles. Pearpoint also uses the concept of 'new frontiers', which I will adopt for present purposes, to describe some of the range of new and potential ventures in workplace basic education.

Furthermore, there has been a renewed interest by the business community in pushing for educational reform, actively defining educational policy, controlling worker education and training and, to a lesser extent, becoming involved in worker literacy. In the absence of organized resistance, business interests have been able, thus far, to dictate the terms of the debate on education (including literacy), particularly by playing to the fears of foreign competition, rising national debt, the growth of an alienated 'underclass', declining wages and living standards for workers.

Attempts have been made to explain the present enthusiasm for economic rationalism as entirely consistent or compatible with broader education principles or to suggest that it is simply a matter of adjusting to the new language in order to communicate effectively. It is important here, however, that we distinguish between being conversant in aspects of this new rhetoric, and adopting the 'practice'. Still others argue that workplace basic education is not really 'new' at all and claim a long historical involvement in the area. Nonetheless, although there has been a plethora of attempts (successful and otherwise) at worker education, and the main education providers such as TAFE (Technical and Further Education) have been at the centre of many of these, this has not been the case with basic skills development or workplace basic education. We must accept that many of the new demands on education have come about precisely because of the limited impact and failures of earlier approaches. To dwell too much on past efforts may indeed distract us from what new responses and opportunities may offer. One drawback of providing uncritical histories of past activities is to overlook the tensions, political forces, conflicts and struggle which were instrumental in winning a range of compromises and concessions.

What is 'new' in the current climate is the unique confluence of factors such as the economic situation which is being managed by an ideology which views the marketplace as the provider and distributor of human services, thus giving a more limited role to government and the public sector; services such as education becoming a commodity within that market; and not surprisingly, a concentration on the training requirements of the workforce as a means of enhancing the productivity of industry. Added to this, or as a consequence, there is a prevailing industrial situation which not only views the education of workers as important, but has been left with training as one of the few negotiable currencies at its disposal in maintaining or winning industrial concessions. What is new is the prominence which vocational training, in particular, has taken in the economic, political, industrial and educational debates. Further, while the main stakeholders in education are not new, their focus, roles, visibility and willingness to contest the area clearly are.

Workplace basic education in Australia is a relatively new area of activity, and has developed in an organized way only since 1984, notwithstanding the work of the Adult Migrant Education Service and its English in the Workplace Program which has operated since 1975. This Program provides English language and communication skills tuition to workers from non-English speaking backgrounds. The main activity in relation to English speaking background workers has occurred in Victoria through the Workplace Basic Education Project of the Council of Adult Education which has operated since 1984. Other more recent developments include the Tasmanian Workplace Basic Education Unit of TAFE established in 1988, the New South Wales Workplace Basic Education Resource Project 1989, and a number of initiatives begun in International Literacy Year.

Responses to this changed and changing environment must also in many ways be new if we are not only to have a place but to have a role which will meet the expansion, and variety, of needs of individuals within that environment. 'New frontiers' exist in the potential to extend basic skills development to encompass a considerably broader 'clientele' and to extend the catchment area for education beyond its present limitations. The potential also exists to provide more directly relevant education, and to provide the environment where workers have much greater control over their education (O'Connor, 1990, 1991). Increasingly the contest is becoming one of ideology and ownership, over who ultimately owns and controls the education and training content and provision.[7]

Despite this warning, the language of the debate is almost exclusively that of the market (in particular, a pristine perception of the 'market' found in Harvard Business Administration studies, and local 'New Right' think tanks), where education is framed in the language of 'cost-benefits', productivity outcomes, stock offerings and economic rationales. Within this conception, education responds in terms of marketing, product development, needs of industry and clients. There has been a dangerously uncritical adoption of the business agenda. Thus, in the education and training debate generally, and in workplace basic education in particular, educationists are being intimidated to the extent that the more substantive educational concerns and principles are losing out to industrial and political interests being asserted through a number of direct as well as subtle mediums. Many of the underlying principles of adult education seem to be getting lost or being hijacked in a range of workplace basic education activities, and supplanted with an extremely narrow and short-sighted vocational functionalism.

Similarly, in the USA, Giroux argues that the language of literacy in the US is almost exclusively linked to right wing discourse that reduces it

> to either a functional perspective tied to narrowly conceived economic interests or to an ideology designed to initiate the poor, the underprivileged, and minorities into the logic of a unitary, dominant cultural tradition. In the first instance, the crisis in literacy is predicated on the need to train more workers for occupational jobs that demand 'functional' reading and writing skills. (Giroux, 1987, p. 3)

He claims that

> At the moment, the neoconservatives have appropriated the concept of excellence and defined it as basic skills, technical training, and classroom discipline . . . In adult literacy programs, the materials and methods used reflect an 'end of ideology' approach that fails to inspire students . . . Few are prepared to speak the traditional language of educational humanism or fight for the idea that a general education is the basis of critical literacy. (Aronowitz and Giroux, 1986, p. 4)

Approaches to literacy as a process grounded in these narrow perspectives are, in Giroux's words, 'as disempowering as they are oppressive'.

This situation raises some fundamental questions regarding the purposes and likely impact and outcomes of this new educational activity. Sheila Collins, writing of the American situation, poses the dilemma in the following series of questions:

Are we seeing an intensified effort — in the midst of the greatest gap between rich and poor ever recorded in the US — to update the old 'frontier myth' of American education: that with the 'right' education the American class and caste system can be permeated? Is business's new concern for education the chance it has long awaited to wrest control from professional educators over socialization of the values and attitudes necessary to maintain labor peace in a period of greater economic instability? Or can worker literacy be an opportunity to develop a more critical, creative and militant workforce? Is worker literacy a new tool for restratifying the workforce to meet the demands of a more mobile regime of capital accumulation? Or can it be the path to genuine upward mobility, self-actualization, and economic democracy for US workers? (Collins, 1989, p. 27)[8]

Lastly, Gribble and Bottomley forcefully summarizes some of the present tensions and the tasks ahead, in recent article titled 'Resisting Hijack and Seduction' when she concludes:

What's needed is a transformation of content and method too, so that our education and training system unleashes rather than represses national intellectual and creative development. Those of us who work in adult literacy and basic education shouldn't expect to be bored or short of things to do in the 1990s. But we should expect to struggle against aggressive efforts to persuade us that a vocationally specific approach is appropriate for adult literacy and basic education in the workplace. If we resist there's hope of success. Surrendering to narrow vocationalism without a fight is unthinkable. (1989, p. 15)

At the moment there is no debate in the workplace basic education sector addressing these issues, and worse, there is active and conscious resistance to subjecting the area to the criticisms, input, and refinements which can be the positive by-products from such a debate. Solutions are being sought almost entirely on an individualized basis with few attempts to collectivize these processes or resources with the intention of building the strongest structures, philosophies and practice which would ultimately benefit all players in the field. Internal bickering, organizational preciousness, and sectarian maligning of other providers or those with whom we simply disagree are poor substitutes for constructive exchanges and informed debate.

To demonstrate the possible scenario which could develop without a disciplined, open and co-ordinated approach, Jack Pearpoint is again blunt but to the point when he describes the predictable battles which will result from this situation:

Since literacy has been a tiny piece of turf with few benefits and enormous liabilities until now, the short term will be characterized by 'turf' battles with the various potential players racing to garner credit with minimum cost. Since bureaucratic guidelines and systems are only just being developed, competing systems will be established that have little to do with teaching reading and writing and an enormous amount to do with finding things that can be 'counted' and audited . . . Consultants will have a field day. A well established pattern will be repeated. Enormous sums will be spent to study and publicize 'good projects', but the support will be substantially less than the study and promotions budget. (Pearpoint, 1989, p. 425)

While many positive developments have occurred to bring educators, unions, employers and government together to address workplace basic education, many more initiatives must be taken to integrate work in this field, and prevent wasteful rivalry and duplication. Some of the loose relationships which are emerging need to be strengthened and formalized to the point where all of these participants are informed of each other's needs and responses, and considerably greater effort must go into creating these relationships where they do not yet exist. Credibility, trust, and mutually acceptable lines of communications need to be forged into a regular working arrangement. When these exist and when the interaction between these is on some sort of equal footing, then some exciting and substantial progress can be expected.

Closer attention also needs to be paid to students of workplace basic education. The temptation is to satisfy employers primarily, then to involve unions and government, and only nominally consider the possible roles for workers in these situations. There are many noble principles, mission statements and policies which refer to meeting students' needs, of providing education where the students are, and some practices which match these. Nonetheless, there are many situations where such expressions ring hollow, or at best take on a very passive form. We must constantly determine the extent of needs and methods of satisfying them, consult the students, involve them in all aspects of programmes, and enable and encourage them to take much greater control of their education. This involves a very clear perspective of the educator's role. Clear choices exist between maintaining a traditional role of 'information giver' or to acknowledge social changes which demand that the role be more one of teaching people how to 'manage' the information they have.

The strengths of workplace basic education include the development of customized courses, materials, and delivery in order to meet flexibly the needs of the particular workers and the workplace;

- provision of skills which enable workers to participate fully in the workplace and society.
- maintenance of a balance of generic and vocational education in achieving these outcomes.
- integration of 'job' skills and more general skills through teaching basic skills in relation to job content.
- provision of greater access to relevant education by conducting programs in the workplace and in paid worktime.
- involvement of all participants in programmes in all planning and decision-making.
- creation of environments suitable for adult learning, including substantial input and control over that learning remaining with the students.
- maintenance of low teacher-student ratios.
- use of a range of delivery methods.

- and use of the identified needs of individual participants as the basis for course content and delivery.

The difficulties in keeping to this basic script come from the pressures of minimal resources and demands to do more for less. They also stem from confusion about whose needs are paramount in this situation, and the compromises involved in attempting to juggle competing needs and delivering services before they are fully prepared.

Workplace basic education does have a modest but significant role to play in many of the contemporary training, educational, economic and industrial developments — regardless of whether or not it ever takes pride of place centre stage. To realize this contribution, workplace basic education should be presented realistically as an avenue for a great many people to enhance their present skills levels, employment and life opportunities. It is not a magic elixir to cure all, but rather is an integral component of a process of presenting people with more vocational and educational choices than they currently enjoy.

To ensure a steady and secure development of workplace basic education there needs to be careful and co-ordinated planning and strategy formulation. There must be extensive promotion of the concepts, objectives and outcomes of workplace basic education; and agreement must exist between education providers, government and industry, regarding the additional resources required to effectively conduct workplace basic education on a scale which will meet the increasing demand and adequately satisfy the spectrum of needs. Decisions will also need to be made regarding who will be responsible for the provision and allocation of those resources. Durable structures must be established to enable the collection, analysis and distribution of reliable data and information which is desperately needed to inform these developments. Considerably greater efforts need to be made to create links between all the major participants at local, regional and statewide levels, reinforced by clear, jointly agreed policies regarding appropriate planning and delivery models, areas of demarcation and responsibility, as well as statements of operating principles, and measures aimed at achieving quality control in the marketplace.

Defining Workplace Basic Education

It is also evident from present activity that there is only a very loose working definition of what constitutes workplace basic education, and consequently widely divergent approaches. At one level this diversity can be viewed as a healthy development and should be encouraged in an attempt to foster innovative and sophisticated responses to often complicated requirements and situations. At another level, the diversity can be seen to reflect the inevitable outcome of uncertainty and the lack of sound models of delivery and a foundation of reliable information, data, and research in the area.

Due to varying stages of development of workplace basic education in different parts of the country, it would be wishful thinking to claim a coherent philosophy of workplace basic education which has been adopted by existing providers. The following selection of definitions of workplace basic education utilized in various programmes provides some insight into the essential ingre-dients of existing definitions.

Perhaps the most generally accepted definition is that which states that work-place literacy 'may be defined as the written and spoken language, math, and thinking skills that workers and trainees use to perform job tasks or training' (Askov, Aderman and Hemmelstein, 1989). Leila Gainer (American Society for Training and Development) adds the following rationale:

> Competitive challenges are driving companies toward employing an array of strategies that require adaptive and innovative workers with a range of skills including interpersonal skills, listening skills, the ability to set goals and implement strategies for achieving goals . . . creativity, and problem solving skills. (Askov, Aderman and Hemmelstein, 1989)

The Training Agency (Britain) states that

> Literacy and numeracy are both broad terms, which describe a wide variety of behaviour. They are not precise definitions capable of exact and objective measurement, they are best seen as a continuum of skills . . . They are better called by their everyday names — reading, writing, practical maths, problem solving, measuring, using a calculator, using numbers, mental arithmetic, spelling and so on . . . Literacy and numeracy are occupational skills; they are not separate and mysterious . . . (Training Agency, 1989)

These definitions of workplace basic education fall well short of those which we attempt to apply to general adult literacy activities. While they contain many of the functional elements of this type of literacy provision, they abandon any notion of 'developmental', transformative or 'active' literacy beyond the specific vocational needs of workers. As such, they are inadequate in defining workplace basic education as an area which can address a range of learning requirements. The limitation of much workplace activity is the view of occupational setting and its requirements as the only or most relevant context for worker's literacy programs. Thus, most workplace basic education activity and programme delivery fail to acknowledge workers as anything more than workers. It is essential, how-ever, to realize that those same workers are also parents, sportspeople, church goers, members of political parties, they are lovers, spouses, neighbours, tenants or mortgaged homeowners, and are involved in social and community organ-izations. That is, first and foremost they are community members or citizens, for whom a specific aspect of their lives consists of their occupation and its particular benefits and burdens.

From this perspective then, *any* working definition of workplace basic education would need to include: a range of written and spoken language skills, maths, reading and comprehension, interpersonal skills, communication and problem solving, required in the effective performance of occupational tasks and functions and enabling participation in workplace and social processes. That is, workplace basic education would provide specific task-related learning with broader social and educational objectives as its context and basis. It would also include effective learning techniques and strategies to enable workers to study efficiently and independently. The structures of workplace basic education would need to incorporate workers in critical evaluation and decision-making. Structures would reflect input and control over course design, content and curricula by workers in consultation with educationists. Further, it would involve utilizing the workplace venue, occupational settings, needs and materials as the context and means for delivery of that education. The content and outcome of learning in the workplace must extend well beyond the restrictions of the workplace and into the world of workers' daily lives.

Accepting this type of definition involves an acknowledgment that there is no overall standard, and no cut off point for workplace basic education. The level of basic skills and methods of programme delivery will be decided by the needs and demands of individual participants and the work they are engaged to do, as well as their other daily life requirements. This definition explicitly identifies a dynamic which must be met by flexible responses and may be as applicable to manual workers as it is to technicians, trades people, supervisors or managers. It assumes a role for educators, not as imparters of knowledge or 'teachers' in the traditional sense, but rather as agents to assist workers organize, manage and better utilize the knowledge which they already possess, and to acquire the knowledge they need or wish to have.

Literacy as Empowerment

As a number of writers have stressed, the definitions we develop of il/literacy also impact unevenly, are invariably arbitrary and ideologically loaded, and particularly disadvantage women, migrant, Aboriginal and other disadvantaged workers. Most definitions in this context are inadequate and in desperate need of revision (Barrett, 1980; Freire, 1985; Freire and Macedo, 1987; Gaskell, 1986, 1987; Giroux, 1987; Horsman, 1989; Junor, 1988; Lankshear and Lawler, 1987; O'Donnell and Hall, 1988; Ramdas, 1990; Rockhill, 1988; Street, 1984; Windsor, 1990).

Ramdas (1990) uses UNESCO statistics to point out that while men dominate in literacy policy-making, some

> 70 per cent of the target group of literacy programs are girls and women. In other words, 70 per cent of the 1,000 million illiterate people in the world today are women and girls, some 700 million . . . Predictably, the illiteracy rates are highest in the least developed countries and amongst the most underprivileged people within them . . . Literacy must be seen as part of the process of empowering underprivileged people. Literacy, I contend, is thus indelibly linked with people's quest for, and attainment, of justice. (Ramdas, 1990)

Thus, to attempt to define literacy as an abstract entity or individual quality, or as politically or socially neutral and devoid of gender, race, class or other social content is at best naive, and does not address worker's literacy requirements, and particularly their workforce requirements.

Ramdas (1990) explains some of the present orientation to literacy in these terms:

> Resources made available for literacy missions are, in most cases, grossly inadequate for making people literate in even the restricted sense of being able to read and write. Given this orientation of development priorities away from the need for literacy, it is economically, organizationally, and administratively inconvenient to most nation states today to define literacy in any but the most narrow sense of the word. (1990, p. 31)

For progressive and critical theorists and practitioners, such as Paulo Freire, the method and practice of education is inseparable from the social, political and economic content, and the interests they represent. As Giroux observes in his introduction to Freire and Macedo's *Literacy: Reading the Word and the World*, Freire's insights go to the political basis of the creation of the illiterate:

> The concept illiterate in this sense often provides an ideological cover for powerful groups simply to silence the poor, minority groups, women or people of colour. (Giroux, 1987, p. 12)

Lankshear argues that there is a common belief among educationists and lay people that literacy is a quality or attribute that people either have or lack. 'Those who lack it are assumed to need it, and ought to acquire it'. Within this general assertion he identifies three closely related misconceptions, namely that 'literacy is unitary; that it is a neutral process or tool; and that it is an independent variable' (Lankshear and Lawler, 1987, p. 39). These misconceptions lead to the view that literacy is essentially the same thing for everyone, and is simply a technical skill, and as such is intrinsically neutral and separate from its social context and the uses to which it is placed.

In contrast to this independent or autonomous view of literacy is Street's (1984) 'ideological' model of literacy, which rejects the professed intrinsic qualities of literacy in favour of understanding the forms literacy practice take and their outcomes within given social contexts. Thus, those who espouse the

> 'ideological' view concentrate on the specific social practices of reading and writing; that is, on the forms reading and writing practice actually take, and the ways reading and writing skills are used, rather than as some abstracted technology. (Lankshear and Lawler, 1987)

These views build on the work of Freire who argues that since language is 'packed with ideology' and reproduces the oppressor's world, reading and writing involve learning to 'read the world, as well as the word'. A quote from a peasant farm worker in Nicaragua, speaking to the mother of his literacy teacher, captures this relationship clearly:

> Do you know that I am not ignorant any more? I know how to read now. Not perfectly, you understand, but I know how. And do you know, your son isn't ignorant any more either. Now he knows how we live, what we eat, how we work, and he knows the life of the mountains. Your son has learned to read from our book. (Lankshear and Lawler, 1987, p. 209)

Implications of this view for Workplace Basic Education (WBE) programmes are that while literacy in itself does not provide emancipation or freedom from poverty or unequal social and political structures, it potentially provides a means to engage in understanding and transforming those structures and power relations. Thus, workplace literacy is a double-edged sword which can serve to empower individuals to transform social relations, or to perpetuate repression and domination.

As Lankshear and Lawler (1987) have described, many standard accounts of literacy fail to see how literacy is integral to gender, cultural and language politics, and consequently view learners and literacy uniformly as an isolatable, measurable, 'uniform' thing, a skill or commodity that can be acquired by participating in literacy programs. Horsman (1990) argues that this process silences and delegitimizes alternative forms of literacy, based on alternative life experiences. 'Consequently, many feminist critiques argue the need, not simply to "add on" a female perspective, but for a re-vision of the world.'

While many adult educationists claim to have some commitment to these philosophies in rhetoric, and attempt to incorporate them through some aspects of their practice, as was stated previously, many of these and other underlying 'principles' of adult education seem to be getting lost, ignored or compromised in a range of workplace basic education activities, and and are instead being driven by the narrowly conceived economic and industrial agenda and directives. Further, approaches aimed at meeting the needs of a range of workers based either on the broader developmental or individual 'empowerment' concepts or even the more restrictive vocationalism are receiving very little attention in theory or practice; they are simply not being considered.

Two seemingly innocuous examples of the types of compromises which educationists are willing to make in workplace basic education occur at the fundamental levels of access to and control of the education process. Programmes are being approached on a so-called 'partnership' basis between adult education institutions and companies, often to the exclusion of worker's interests. In practice, this approach is reflected in the agreement and adoption of the position of the Ford Motor Company (USA) which requires courses to be conducted one-hour in/one hour out of work time, on the basis that both workers and the employer should contribute to the cost of courses. Quite apart from the disproportionately unequal contributions being made by the company and the individual relative to the resources and bargaining position of each in the process (and the world), it effectively denies education to any worker unable to attend out of worktime.

This disadvantages women workers particularly, as the people most likely to have the greatest family and other social commitments outside of paid work, and has proved to be one of the major obstacles to women attempting to access other forms of education. Courses conducted within paid worktime provide a much more real option for all workers to gain education free of domestic responsibilities, isolation, hostility from spouses or other family members, and financial burden. Further, this approach confuses the basis for providing workplace education from the perspectives of different participants. That is, for many companies it is an economic imperative whereas for individual workers the acquisition of basic skills must be viewed as a universal entitlement or right. Very few senior management attend 'training' outside of paid worktime, without substantial compensation in cash or in kind.

Similarly, much of the design of programmes and course content is developed in the absence of the workers themselves, with the control and decision-making remaining squarely with the 'experts' and the boss. Assumptions are made on the basis that these dominant groups know what is needed (although this is often based on superficial needs assessments and speculation) and how best to satisfy these needs, with the result that it is primarily the company's economic requirements which are being serviced.

The present focus of delivery of workplace basic education activity is also problematic for women. The lure of work with large companies in industries and occupations which are predominantly male is already emerging as a discernable trend in the delivery of WBE programmes. The relative ease of developing such programmes in workforces with concentrations of workers in one location, and in numbers to sustain on-going involvement, and the financial temptation and security associated with this leads to a situation where work is not being done in other areas. Because of this trend towards delivery of WBE programmes to large concentrations of male workers, there is no incentive for education organizations to conduct research or develop alternative strategies, curricula or delivery models in areas of specific need. Thus, many of the more difficult and educationally complex 'women's industries' are being overlooked in favour of the larger safer areas which can more readily fill the classes and meet the costs of programmes.

If positive possibilities exist for women, migrant, Aboriginal, geographically and politically isolated workers through workplace basic education, then educationists need to reclaim, defend and extend their principles to be directly relevant to those workers. In many instances education providers will need to take a more active role in determining some of the directions and parameters for workplace basic education, rather than simply uncritically following the agenda and priorities of industry restructuring. It must be acknowledged that many of the restructuring processes and models fit the needs of some workers only poorly, exclude others from substantive gains, and are not the appropriate environment for a range of workplace basic education activity.

The veneer of tripartism needs to be extended to more democratic structures reflecting individual needs, criticisms and learning objectives. Content and format of programs must be more clearly located in the reality of individual worker's lives as they experience them, not as so-called experts or employers perceive and interpret them.

Costs

Here again, one can discern competing agenda which threaten the effectiveness of Workplace Basic Education. WBE is often viewed as a potential revenue raiser, and therefore a lifeline for some education services. The expectation in NSW (New South Wales) is that over the next decade most public providers will generate substantially more of their income than at present (some estimate that as much as 50 per cent of operating costs will need to be generated by the organization). This has already created a scramble in some places in Australia, by some providers to seek those sources of revenue now, so as to avoid 'the rush'.

This situation is exacerbated by the expectations and demands of government, organizational managers, and some sections of the market to provide a range of services which have not been properly developed. This is further compounded by the fact that these expectations and demands are usually only vaguely formulated and conveyed. Much of the responsibility for research and development, priority of provision, and decision-making regarding provision has been decentralized to the local college level, without clear policy direction and resource support.

The expectation of some cost recovery from some services in itself is not impossible or necessarily undesirable. The extent to which this affects current adult education activities and strategies for workplace basic education is an area of concern. The trend of existing attempts at workplace basic education is not surprisingly in those areas with the greatest capacity to pay for provision. It is questionable whether the larger, wealthier companies are in fact the areas in greatest need of workplace basic education provision, and whether concentration on these areas will result in a neglect of more isolated (geographically and industrially) workers, workplaces and industries, small enterprises unable to pay on a fee for service basis, and particularly disadvantaged individuals and companies. These are the areas which pose the greatest challenges for workplace education and will require the largest efforts and a range of creative solutions.

In any discussion of costs we must canvass opinions on general access to workplace basic education, what forms of provision accurately reflects needs, and which approaches will target the areas of most benefit. A simplistic user-pays strategy is destined to result in even greater inequalities in the delivery of adult basic education, a narrow and short-sighted focus by many providers, and the direct exclusion of strategically important sectors of the workforce from this type of education.

Similarly, if we all share the belief that literacy, numeracy and other basic skills are the foundation upon which other training and learning paths must be securely built, then it is a nonsense to develop approaches and pricing structures which effectively preclude access to that very foundation. If workers are fortunate enough to be employed by a company which can afford and has the commitment to pay for basic skills training on the job, they will be a part of an elite few. If they happen to work in small industries and companies, in areas of traditional 'women's' occupations, or in geographically isolated areas, then quite clearly they will probably be among the many who will miss out. Strategies and practices do not include those workers or their industries, even though these areas represent the bulk of the workforce.

It is worth considering this reality in slightly more detail. Statistics available from the Australian Bureau of Statistics provide the following information on small business in Australia. During 1986–87 there were approximately 732,400 businesses operating in Australia, employing 6,835,900 workers. Of these, the Agricultural Sector represented 118,900 enterprises and employed 395,600 people, the Public Sector was 4,600 enterprises employing 1,741,900 people. However, the most significant is the Non-Agriculture Private Sector which consisted of 608,900 enterprises and employed 4,716,400 people (Australian Bureau of Statistics, 1988).

The vast bulk of this sector consists of small business employing less than twenty people (580,900 enterprises employing a total of 2,062,300 people).

Therefore 44 per cent of all persons employed in all industries are in enterprises of less than twenty workers. Of all enterprises across all industry the national cumulative figures are; 90 per cent of all industry enterprises were made up of very small businesses (less than ten employees); 95 per cent with less than twenty employees; 98 per cent with less than fifty employees; and 99 per cent of all enterprises in all industries employ less than 100 employees (Australian Bureau of Statistics, 1990).

The totals for numbers and sizes of all industry emphasize the desperate need to develop training strategies which will service the overwhelming majority of business and the workers. It should be self-evident that most of these small enterprises are not capable of meeting the types of training costs which are currently being proposed. They are unlikely to even consider workplace basic education in this climate. Unless structures and mechanisms are put in place to address this range of needs, the notion of providing workplace basic education (or any other training) on any scale or with anything remotely resembling comprehensive coverage is a nonsense.

Even the recent findings of the Training Costs Review Committee, while accepting that TAFE's industry training will need to occur mainly on a cost recovery basis, distinguished special programmes (including literacy and numeracy) from this approach (Report of the Training Costs Review Committee, 1990). The Committee recommended that additional funding be made available to cater for the needs of disadvantaged groups and the promotion of equal employment opportunity objectives. If, after International Literacy Year we do not view those workers with inadequate literacy skills as a disadvantaged group within the labour force and the community, then the message and the opportunity to respond to it has been lost.

The summary findings of the committee specifically singled out literacy and numeracy as deserving of special attention by governments:

> The community-based providers of adult education should play an enhanced role in these areas and funding arrangements for these courses should be reviewed. The provision of programs directed to literacy and numeracy is primarily a matter for governments. (Report of the Training Costs Review Committee, 1990)

If it is accepted that a range of benefits from workplace basic education flow to employers, industry, local and national economies, the community and society generally, and to individual workers (both as workers and as citizens), then the most sensible and equitable way to proceed is to share the burden of those costs between the main stakeholders. Yet, in the present economic climate this question of who should bear the associated costs is possibly the most keenly contested.

Conclusion

It would be misleading to suggest that shortfalls in basic skills are responsible for lower productivity levels, the majority of industrial accidents, poor product quality or wastage, or missed employment opportunities. Obviously, these processes are determined by a combination of factors. Nonetheless, basic skills upgrading does have a modest but significant role to play in alleviating many of these problems.

The cautionary warning regarding viewing or promoting workplace basic education as the saviour of economic, industrial and personal problems has been stated clearly by James L. Turk (1989), the Director of Education with the Ontario Federation of Labour. He reminds us that

> Limited literacy is not a major cause of unemployment — lack of jobs is. Limited literacy is not a major cause of accidents and disease at work — inadequate capital investment, outdated technology, poor work organization are. Limited literacy does not account for Canadian industry's difficulties in international competition — foreign ownership, small research and development budgets, high interest rates and a high-priced dollar do. Better literacy skills would help deal with all these problems, but in a more modest way than many literacy campaigners now promise. We feel it is important to be more realistic about the gains from increased literacy because overstated expectations will lead, over time, to a withering of broad commitment to resolving literacy problems. (Turk, 1989)

Available research indicates that correlations do exist between low basic skills levels and overall job-performance, but it also implies a certain level of caution regarding the extent of that relationship. Mikulecky and Drew (1990) observe that

> An underlying assumption behind concern about literacy-skill levels in the workplace is that job performance is related to workers' literacy-skill levels. The research suggests that there is a relationship but that it is by no means overwhelming or direct ... Literacy and cognitive performance do not totally explain job performance. Even the highest correlations only explain about 50 per cent of the variance for job performance. Research does suggest, however, that literacy ability is a better predictor of job performance than many other variables ... It has been clear for quite some time that increased literacy-skills training is a requirement of good job training. What has not been as clear is how to most cost-effectively provide such training. (Mikulecky and Drew, 1990)

What we do know is that there is sufficient evidence to demonstrate that workplace basic skills programmes are essential in meeting some of the needs of industry and the labour force, are an integral cornerstone in award restructuring and industry restructuring processes and other vocational training strategies, and that the provision of this type of skills development is clearly economically viable. The information we have about cost estimates also provides telling insights into the current losses or under-utilization of resources being incurred by industry, and signals a clear warning as to the future economic and social costs if the issue of inadequate basic skills in the workplace is not systematically addressed. Employers will ultimately be required to make a judgment regarding the value that basic skills training has in their organizational strategies. Many may come to realize that they cannot afford to ignore the provision of basic skills upgrading.

Likewise, much more work needs to be done by education systems, and by governments who have executive and financial control of those systems, to develop clear and just policies in relation as to the extent of provision of workplace basic education, and the conditions, standards and resource levels under which it will be provided. This will involve substantially greater commitments of funds, research, policy and resource development, and support and co-ordination structures than exist at present. Guidance will need to be given to the main education providers in policy areas, and support and encouragement for massive revision of some practices, delivery models and endeavours aimed at innovative breakthroughs to ensure that this area is being serviced by the most contemporary and sophisticated education methods and technology.

Likewise, education activists will need to clarify their perspectives of workplace basic education, and will need to take a much larger role in the education and training debates in order to meet worker's needs and requirements adequately, to include equality of opportunity and social justice considerations, and to be conscious of these in their own practice. Only then can workplace basic education be conducted at a standard and in an environment which will ensure that workers receive a qualitively 'higher' education which comes close to satisfying some of their essential needs.

Notes

1 These views have been variously stated by government Ministers and Departments:

> Lasting improvements in the quality of Australia's workforce skills will require major changes in the quality and flexibility of our national training arrangements. More training without better will be wasteful and ultimately futile. (Dawkins, 1989)

2 For example; Bureau of Industry Economics (1986) *Manufacturing Industry Productivity Growth: Causes, Effects and Implications*, Research Report 21, Canberra, AGPS; Economic Planning Advisory Council (1988) *An Overview of Microeconomic Restraints on Economic Growth*, Council Paper 32, Canberra, AGPS; John Dawkins and Clive Holding (1987) *Skills for Australia*, Canberra, AGPS; Employment and Skills Formation Council (1989) *Industry Training in Australia: The Need for Change*, Canberra, AGPS; Business Council of Australia (1989) *Enterprise-Based Bargaining Units: A Better Way of Working*, Melbourne, BCA; ACTU/TDC Mission to Western Europe (1987) *Australia Reconstructed*, Canberra, AGPS; Australian Science and Technology Council (1989) *Wealth for Skills: Measures to Raise the Skills of the Workforce*, Canberra, AGPS.
3 For example, Scott (1989) and Parry (1989), Coopers and Lybrand (1990) and Deveson (1990).
4 For example, Mathews (1989) and Campbell (1990).
5 The survey did not tell us what these results might mean in any particular context, or what solutions or strategies might be pursued to address the problems identified in the findings. While there are general implications for workplace literacy from this type of research, there are other sources of information available which indicate that the needs of particular industries deviate wildly from the general trends,

and require significantly more sophisticated analysis and focused research to arrive at meaningful information and solutions. We need to be careful not to limit literacy to a bean counting exercise, but to broaden understanding by providing detailed quantitative and qualitative research supported by sound and thorough analysis. This involves an intimate acknowledgment of particular industries, localities, workplace cultures and the different needs these generate.

6   The following sample of recent newspaper headlines give an indication of media responses: 'One Million Hurt in War of Words' (*Sydney Morning Herald*, 27 January 1990); 'Literacy Alert: Reading, Writing Have Never Been More Important' (*Sydney Morning Herald*, 28 April 1990); 'Work Illiteracy Costs More than 3bn a Year' (*The Australian*, 23–24 June 1990); 'Illiteracy is Handicapping Our Industry' (*The Age*, 15 July 1990); 'Industry Urged to Join Drive on Literacy' (*Sydney Morning Herald*, 29 November 1990); 'Illiterate Might Face Sack: Chamber' (*The West Australian*, 20 September 1990); 'Literacy Classes for Employees Too Costly' (*The Australian*, 22–23 September 1990); 'National Literacy Strategy Called For' (*Canberra Times*, 5 October, 1990).

7   'The greatest danger facing adult education today is, we would assert, an unthinking scramble to teach new skills, to "retrain", to push the priority of economic, vocational training too much at the expense of a broader educative goal' (Ministry of Education, 1987, p. 8).

8   See also Welch (1990) regarding an earlier era in the United States when Taylorism was influential in education.

References

ARONOWITZ, S. and GIROUX, H. (1986) *Education Under Siege. The Conservative, Liberal and Radical Debate over Schooling*, London, Routledge.

ASKOV, E., ADERMAN, B. and HEMMELSTEIN, N. (1989) *Upgrading Basic Skills for the Workplace*, Pennsylvania, Institute for the Study of Adult Literacy.

AUSTRALIAN BUREAU OF STATISTICS (1988) *Small Business in Australia*, Cat.No. 1321.0, Canberra, ABS.

AUSTRALIAN BUREAU OF STATISTICS (1989) *How Workers Get Their Training Australia*, Cat.No. 6278.0, Canberra, ABS.

AUSTRALIAN BUREAU OF STATISTICS (1990) *Labour Force Status and Educational Attainment Australia*, Cat.No. 6235.0 (Feb), Canberra, ABS.

AUSTRALIAN BUREAU OF STATISTICS (1990) *NSW 1990 Year Book*, Cat.No. 1301.1, Sydney, ABS.

AUSTRALIAN BUREAU OF STATISTICS (1990) *The Labour Force Australia*, Cat.No. 6203.0 (Sept), Canberra, ABS.

AUSTRALIAN BUREAU OF STATISTICS (1990) *The Labour Force New South Wales*, Cat.No. 6201.1 (Feb), Canberra, ABS.

AUSTRALIAN MANUFACTURING COUNCIL (1988) *Skills in Australian Manufacturing Industry: Future Directions*, Canberra, AGPS.

BALL, S.J. (1990) *Politics and Policy Making in Education: Explorations in Policy Sociology*, London, Routledge.

BARRETT, M. (1980) *Women's Oppression Today*, London, Verso.

BONNERJEA, L. (1987) *Workbase; Trade Union Education and Skills Project, A Research Report*, London, National Union of Public Employees.

BURGESS, J. (1989) 'Productivity: A Worker Problem?', *Journal of Australian Political Economy*, **24**, pp. 23–29.

BUSINESS COUNCIL OF AUSTRALIA (1987) *Education and Training Policy*, Melbourne, BCA.

BUTLER, A. (1989) *Lifelong Education Revisited: Australia as a Learning Society*, Melbourne, Commission for the Future.

CAMPBELL, I. (1990) 'The Australian Trade Union Movement and Post Fordism', *Journal of Australian Political Economy*, **26**, pp. 1–27.

CANADIAN CONGRESS FOR LEARNING OPPORTUNITIES FOR WOMEN (1988) 'Let's talk about women and literacy', *Canadian Woman Studies*, **9**, pp. 3–4.

CARNEY, S. (1988) *Australia in Accord: Politics and Industrial Relations under the Hawke Government*, Melbourne, Macmillan.

COLLINO, G.E., ADERMAN, E.M. and ASKOV, E.N. (1988) *Literacy and Job Performance: A Perspective*, Pennsylvania, Institute for the Study of Adult Literacy.

COLLINS, S. (1989) 'Workplace literacy: Corporate tool or worker empowerment?', *Social Policy*, **20**, 1.

COOPERS AND LYBRAND CONSULTANTS (1990) *A Strategic Review of Commonwealth/ State Adult Literacy Expenditure*, Canberra, DEET.

DAWKINS, JOHN (1987) *Industry Training in Australia: The Need for Change*, Canberra, AGPS.

DAWKINS, JOHN (1988) *A Changing Workforce*, Canberra, AGPS.

DEPARTMENT OF EMPLOYMENT, EDUCATION AND TRAINING (1989) *Training Needs Analysis, Training Services Australia*, Canberra, AGPS.

DEPARTMENT OF INDUSTRIAL RELATIONS (Metal Trades Federation of Unions and Metal Trades Industry Association) (1988) *Towards a New Metal and Engineering Award*, Sydney, Metal Trades Industry Association and Metal Trades Federation of Unions.

DEPARTMENTS OF LABOR AND EDUCATION (1988) 'The Bottom Line: Basic Skills in the Workplace', Washington, DC, US Department of Labour and Education.

DEVESON, I. (1990) *Deveson Committee Report*, Canberra, Training Costs Review Committee.

DREW, R.A. and MIKULECKY, L. (1988) *How to Gather and Develop Job Specific Literacy Materials for Basic Skills Instruction*, Indiana, The Office of Education and Training Resources.

ECONOMIC PLANNING ADVISORY COUNCIL (1989) *Productivity In Australia: Results of Recent Studies*, Council Paper No. 39, Canberra, AGPS.

FALLICK, L. (1990): 'The Accord: An assessment', *The Economic and Labour Relations Review*, **1**, 1, pp.

FREIRE, P. (1985) *The Politics of Education*, London, Macmillan.

FREIRE, P. and MACEDO, D. (1987) *Literacy: Reading the Word and the World*, London, Routledge and Kegan Paul.

FRENKEL, S.J. (Ed.) (1987) *Union Strategy and Industrial Chance*, Kensington, Aust., NSW University Press.

GASKELL, J. (1986) 'Conceptions of Skill and the Work of Women: Some Historical and Political Issues', in HAMILTON and BARRETT (Ed.) *The Politics of Diversity*, London, Verso.

GASKELL, J. (1987) 'Gender and Skill', in LIVINGSTON *et al.* (Eds) *Critical Pedagogy and Cultural Power*, South Hadley, MA, Bergin and Garvey.

GIROUX, H. (1987) 'Literacy and the pedagogy of political empowerment', Introduction to FREIRE, P. and MACEDO, D. *Reading the Word and the World*, South Hadley, MA, Bergin and Garvey.

GLEESON, D. (1989) *The Paradox of Training: Making Progress Out of Crisis*, Milton Keynes, Open University Press.

GRAFF, H. (1987) *The Labyrinths of Literacy: Reflections on Literacy Past and Present*, London, Falmer Press.

GRIBBLE, H. and BOTTOMLEY, J. (1989) *Some Implications of Award Restructure Proposals for Adult Literacy and Basic Education Provision*, ILY Secretariat, Department of Employment, Education and Training.

HALL, D. (1990) 'Labor's education' in EASSON, M. (Ed.) *The Foundation of Labor*, Sydney, Pluto Press.

HARTLEY, R. (1990) *Literacy and Social Justice: Defining the Problem and its Costs*, Australian Institute of Family Studies.

HORSMAN, J. (1989) 'Something on my mind besides the everyday', PhD Thesis, University of Toronto.

JUNOR, A. (1988) *Women's Place in the New Skills Formation Structures*, Sydney, NSW Teachers Federation.

LANKSHEAR, C. and LAWLER, M. (1987) *Literacy, Schooling and Revolution*, London, Falmer Press.

LONG, P. (1989) *Literacy For Productivity: A Study of Adult Literacy in the Workplace*, Brisbane, Australian Council of Adult Literacy.

LUNSFORD, A.A., MOGLEN, H. and SLEVIN, J. (Eds) (1990) *The Right to Literacy*, New York, Modern Language Association of America.

MATHESON, A. (1989) *English Language Training in the Context of the Current Industrial Agenda*, Melbourne, ACTU.

MATHEWS, J. (1989) *Age of Democracy: The Politics of Post-Fordism*, Melbourne, Oxford University Press.

MATHEWS, J. (1990) *OECD Further Education and Training of the Labour Force Project, Case Studies*, Victorian Ministry of Education.

MIKULECKY, L. (1989a) 'Real world literacy demands: How they've changed and what teachers can do', in LAPP, D., FLOOD, J. and FARNHAM, N. (Eds) *Content Area Reading and Learning: Instructional Strategies*, New Jersey, Prentice Hall.

MIKULECKY, L. (1989b) *Second Chance Basic Skills Education*, Indiana University.

MIKULECKY, L. and DREW, R. (1991) *Basic Skills in the Workplace, in Constructs of Reader Process*, unpublished manuscript.

MILTENYI, G. (1989) *English in the Workplace: A Shrewd Economic Investment?* Sydney, Office of Multicultural Affairs, Department of Prime Minister and Cabinet.

MINISTRY OF SKILLS DEVELOPMENT (1988) *Literacy: The Basics of Growth*, Ontario, Ministry of Skills Development.

MINISTRY OF SKILLS DEVELOPMENT (1990) *How to Set Up Literacy and Basic Skills Training in the Workplace*, Ontario, Ministry of Skills Development.

MTFU/MTIA (1989) *Proposals For Standards Under the Metal and Engineering Industry Award*, Sydney, Metal Trades Federation of Unions.

NURSS, J. and CHASE, N. (1989) 'Workplace Literacy: A tool for recruitment', *Adult Literacy and Basic Education*, **13**, 1.

O'CONNOR, P. (1990a) *Skills at Work: A Guide to the Provision of Workplace Basic Education*, Sydney, NSW Adult Literacy Council.

O'CONNOR, P. (1990b) *Cost Benefits of Basic Skills in the Workplace*, Sydney, NSW Adult Literacy Council.

O'DONNELL, C. and HALL, P. (1988) *Getting Equal*, Sydney, Allen and Unwin.

PARRY, R. (1989) *A Review of Adult Literacy Services in New South Wales*, Sydney, Report for the Minister for Education and Youth Affairs.

PEARPOINT, J. (1989) 'Issues, Trends and Implications in Adult Basic Education. New Frontiers in Literacy Education', in TAYLOR, M. and DRAPER, J. (Eds) *Adult Literacy Perspectives*, Ontario, Culture Concepts.

PLOWMAN, D. (1990) 'Award restructuring: Possibilities and portents', *The Economic and Labour Relations Review*, **1**, 1, pp.

RAMDAS, L. (1990) 'Women and Literacy: A Quest for Justice', *Convergence*, XXIII, 1, pp. 27–40.

ROCKHILL, K. (1988) 'e-Man-ci-patory Literacy', *Canadian Woman Studies*, **9**, pp. 3–4.

SARMIENTO, A.R. and KAY, A. (1990) *Worker-Centered Learning: A Union Guide to Workplace Literacy*, Washington, DC, AFL-CIO Human Resource Development Institute.

SCOTT, B. (1989) *TAFE Restructuring: Building a Dynamic Vocational Education and Training Enterprise for the 1990s*, Sydney, Management Review, NSW Education Portfolio.

STREET, B. (1984) *Literacy in Theory and Practice*, Cambridge, Cambridge University Press.

TAYLOR, M.C. and DRAPER, J.A. (Eds) (1989) *Adult Literacy Perspectives*, Toronto, Culture Concepts.

TRAINING AGENCY (1989) *Literacy and Numeracy: A Guide to Good Practice*, Sheffield, The Training Agency.

TURK, L. (1989) 'Literacy: A Labour Perspective', Address to *L'Institut De Recherches En Dons Et En Affaires Publiques* Annual Symposium, Ontario.

THE UNION INSTITUTE (1991) 'Building Movements, Educating Citizens, Myles Norton and the Highlander Folk School: Commemorative Issue', *Social Policy*, **21**, 3.

WELCH, A.R. (1990) 'Education and the cult of efficiency: Comparative reflections on the reality and the rhetoric', Paper delivered to Australian and New Zealand Comparative and International Education Association (ANZCIES), University of Auckland, New Zealand.

WICKERT, R. (1989) *No Single Measure: A Survey of Australian Adult Literacy*, Sydney, University of Technology.

WINDSOR, K. (1990) 'Making Industry Work for Women', in WATSON, S. (Ed.) *Playing the State: Australian Feminist Interventions*, Sydney, Allen and Unwin.

WOOD, S. (Ed.) (1989) *The Transformation of Work*, London, Unwin Hyman.

Chapter 11

Individualization and Domestication in Current Literacy Debates in Australia

Peter Freebody and Anthony R. Welch

Introduction

Recurring in Australian educational discourse over the last ten to twenty years have been expressions of anxiety over falling literacy standards. It is notable that the nature of these expressions and the contexts in which they appear closely parallel concerns about 'literacy crises' in other advanced industrial nations in North America and Europe — concerns that have formed one of the motifs running through the current volume. We demonstrate later in this chapter that such anxieties over literacy standards are not new in the Australian context; nonetheless, the notion of a 'literacy crisis' has achieved a degree of legitimacy, perhaps through persistence alone, resulting in a popular view that all may not be well.

This chapter sets out to consider and evaluate some of the sources for the perception in some quarters of falling literacy standards, and to place it and its attendant anxieties and calls for 'back to basics' education in the context of features of and changes in the Australian socio-economic framework. Initially, we consider evidence of earlier Australian 'literacy crises', then review pertinent Australian evidence from the last decade or so. We briefly outline parallels, where appropriate, to contemporary 'literacy crises' in other advanced industrial states such as Canada, Britain, and the United States. The bulk of this chapter comprises examinations of policy documents, curriculum statements, and school texts. We sample here from a range of significant educational documents that both theorize and put to work an ideology of literacy education. In doing this, we have also selected documents that have as their audiences the broader community, researchers, teachers, and students. (These discussions are adapted in part from Freebody, 1990, 1991, in press, Freebody, Barnes, and Muspratt, 1991; and Welch and Freebody, 1989, 1991). Similarities in emphasis and omission lead us to describe the ideologies on which these textual materials draw: the main discourse these textual materials embody and inflect is 'the celebrated, causal individual' — the psychologizing of individual literate and economic competence. It is our contention that it is the very modes of presentation of important accounts and data concerning literacy performance, as well as the ways in which literacy is constructed in key texts that constitute a crisis.

Finally we give some consideration to the nature of the Australian inflection of the literacy crisis and its relation to international discourses about literacy of the variety found in this volume. To preview, one of the major lines of argument we develop is that, while pertinent Australian research studies of literacy are often comprehensive with respect to population and task/domain sampling, the analyses are incomplete in that they typically omit consideration of social class as an explanatory variable. For example, while some studies discriminate in terms of age, gender, geographical location, and type of school, they are typically mute on the issue of class differences, thus making it impossible to document and discuss the ideologically crucial aspects of the 'literacy crisis' (other than to remark on the marginalizing of class in debates about literacy education).

Background

Prior to examining aspects of the structuring of the literacy debate in Australia, however, two points need to be made. First, the debate over literacy standards is by no means new: it has a long if not venerable history (Skilbeck, 1977). As Skilbeck has noted, it is safe to assume that one generation's decrying of the declining literacy standards evident in the next has probably been going on since there have been different generations. In particular, and as is illustrated below, since the growth and expansion of mass education in the middle of the nineteenth century, there have been recurring outcries in Australia concerning the desperate and sudden dropping of standards among the population of school children and school leavers.

A second point to note is that the remarks that follow are meant to endorse neither a condemnatory nor a complacent orientation toward current educational practice; they are intended rather to highlight the ways in which the rhetoric surrounding the crisis-versus-defence cycle can cloud genuine and useful educational debate and deflect attention away from productive directions for re-evaluation and reform. The issue of persistently lower achievement among working-class students is a striking example of this deflection. Many of the investigations outlined below have marginalized or ignored this issue in their analyses and reporting of data, and perhaps in their sample selection. The differential access of working-class, Aboriginal, and other groups of students to effective literacy programmes in school has, we will argue, reached crisis point in the context of changing economic and employment conditions. The available data and their attendant accounts of literacy performance typically fail to address these issues, and thus can present, at best, only a partial explanation of overall levels of competence.

Of the major elements that form the web of prevailing beliefs about society, mobility, and education in Australia, one has been that anyone can 'rise' socioeconomically by dint of personal effort, without regard to social-class or ethnic origins. To some extent this has licensed a celebration of the individual as an explanation of differences, in Australia as in other First-World nations, and a corresponding marginalizing of the perception that there are structural barriers to mobility that personal endeavour cannot easily overcome. This is despite the fact that, as Welch (1985), Walton (this volume), and others have indicated, impediments to advancement by, for example, Aboriginals have been a feature of educational provision since white settlement, while all other working-class cultural forms have consistently been marginalized in Australian schools (Connell, *et al.*, 1982). We will demonstrate in the sections below that competence and motivation still tend to be posited as individual psychological attributes rather than explained in their social and historical contexts, as concrete and contingent. Thus literacy debates have often posited and naturalized an individual and a family that are to be blamed for a lack of conformity to middle-class codes, instead of functioning to open out those cultural codes to critical scrutiny and change.

It is in this sense that literacy has tended, particularly in the high school years and beyond, to be confused with more literary modes of expression. The more richly encoded are these modes with the semiotics of ruling class culture, the more they are paraded as class free and culturally neutral. One indication of this belief is that literacy is compartmentalized, including in schools, and still seen by many as a problem of the English teacher — that specialist with acknowledged mastery over the traditions of the literary canon, rather than over the wider problems of literate competences. These assumptions and strategies of theory allow, almost by a professionally sanctioned sleight of hand, the connection between social class and literacy education to be dismissed as itself classist (Atkinson, 1985, pp. 75–7).

Early Expressions of Literacy Crises in Australia

Evidence for crises of confidence in literacy standards in Australia in earlier times is not hard to locate. Both in the popular press and in specialist forums, concerns about falling standards, or failure to teach the basics have been prevalent throughout much of this century at least. The newspaper *Truth*, in September 1915 lamented the proportion of students who had not secured a pass at a school examination, arguing that

> this is truly a deplorable reflection of the education system, which after all these years, and at the expenditure of an enormous amount of public money, has thus shown itself totally incapable of teaching the simple requirements of reading, writing and arithmetic. (*Melbourne Truth*, 9 September, 1915)

Two years later the *Brisbane Daily Standard* argued that reading, spelling, grammar, and writing were all of an unsatisfactory standard, and that '"Back to the 3R's" will be the necessary slogan if improvement does not soon show up' (*Daily Standard*, 4 October 1917). In 1930, the *Sydney Telegraph* railed against the supposed lack of spelling ability it claimed to be associated with state primary and secondary schools, and asked rhetorically whether either sufficient time or effective methods attended the teaching of spelling:

> Many people interested in the intellectual development of the rising generation maintain that, judging by the examples of spelling coming under their notice, the answers must be given in the negative. (*Telegraph*, 27 August 1930)

Later, professional magazines such as *Research and Curriculum Branch Bulletin* spoke of contemporary concerns with respect to the levels of spelling skills among pupils, concerns which prompted the Director General of the time to institute an inquiry. Summarizing the general views of the time, the publication asserted that

> there was a general, but not a unanimous, feeling that a drop in standards had occurred which was especially evident as mis-spellings in written expression. (*Research and Curriculum Branch Bulletin*, 1952)

Examining past concerns with the apparent lack of literacy skills in Australia is only one means of putting the contemporary 'literacy crisis' in perspective. A notable aspect of the 'literacy crisis' in contemporary Australia is that it is not unique; the coincidence of similar 'literacy crises' in other industrialized states at much the same time is striking. Canada, the United States of America, and Britain (Cox and Boyson, 1975; Froome, 1975)[1] also provide contemporary examples of crisis rhetoric that parallel the Australian examples in important contextual respects: the constriction of labour markets, credit squeezes related to actual or potential flights of investment, the rhetoric of nation-states on cold or hot war footings, and an upsurge in the belief of material and cultural advancement through the intensification of technical-education efforts.

Evidence of a 'Slide' in Literacy Standards

What empirical support is there for the hypothesis that there has been a recent and general decline in the literacy competencies of Australian students in recent years? Initially we need to note the difficulty of establishing this hypothesis in the light of the changing composition of students in Australia over the last forty years or so. Australia's large and successful immigration programmes in the post-1945 years have greatly added to the size and diversity of linguistic communities, mainly from Europe, Asia, Latin America, and the Middle East. Thus substantial demographic changes in the student clientele have occurred in recent decades, and these have been reflected in changed contexts in Australian classrooms, particularly for our purposes, with respect to the language background of school children. Policy changes were slow to acknowledge this more diverse cultural context and to implement programmes of change in response.

Of equal relevance to our study, however, is the serious methodological problem presented to researchers aiming to document some generalizable picture of literacy competence. What continuity could be said to inform any attempt to plot performance rates for the average Australian student over a period of time in the face of an average that shifts in terms of certain critical predictor variables? Researchers are faced with making a selection on some basis as to the nature of the average Australian student: a white, English-speaking, middle-class, urban child? Whatever the stereotyped 'norm' is taken to be, the link between observed literacy performance and curriculum or teaching practice changes over the years becomes tenuous, if not impossible, in the light of a clientele that shifts on such a central variable.

The second difficulty is presented by changing statistical/analytic capabilities and fashions among the research community. These changes impose constraints upon our ability to assess studies in standards of literacy over time, and need to be kept in mind when considering the available research. Where is the onus of proof in questions such as this? In a statistical sense, the null hypothesis is that standards of literacy performance among comparable Australian groups of students have not changed. The difficult task, in the light of changing school clientele and changing methods of performance assessment, of proving that standards have either increased or decreased lies squarely with those who wish to argue for an observable change in performance levels. That is, until proven wrong, we need to assume that general standards of literacy have remained roughly stable over time. Some studies that have addressed this issue will now be described and summarized.

Examining the available research prior to 1980, Little (1985) considered three major studies: the Macquarie Survey (Goyen, 1976), a collation of thirty-seven attainment surveys (Skilbeck, 1977), and the Australian Studies in School Performance (ASSP, 1980). The first of these entailed a criterion of 80 per cent correct on an item of everyday verbal and literacy tasks that the researchers expected to be manageable by a ten-year-old, English-speaking child. The survey consisted of approximately 2,000 Sydney people stratified for age, gender, and socio-economic status, over sixteen years of age. The conclusion was that for those individuals under the age of 30, there was a 98 per cent accuracy on the so-called basic functional literacy test; and that for those over the age of 60, the percentage had dropped to 88 per cent correct, with a steady decrease over the age groups towards that figure.

Thirty-seven attainment surveys were summarized by Skilbeck (1977). Examining the literacy-related performance over the period of the mid-1940s to the early 1970s, a period of extraordinary immigration from non-English-speaking countries to Australia, Skilbeck reported no significant changes in mean and modal performance on literacy-related measures, with some tendencies towards more extreme scores at both ends of the performance distribution. Drawing on these and other less comprehensive surveys, and upon his own research, Little (1985) has come to the following conclusion:

> Whatever level is being tested and whatever definition is given to literacy, the surveys show either improvement or no significant change. (p. 5)

State Departments of Education (the States have jurisdiction over pre-tertiary education provision in Australia) have often been the instrument for collecting literacy education data: the Research Services Branch of the Queensland Department of Education (1988), for example, has conducted a number of recent comparisons of reading achievement in Queensland between the years 1980–86. The most relevant of these tested Year 5 (approximately eleven-year-olds) students' performance on a number of literacy-related measures including vocabulary, literal comprehension, and implied comprehension. Consonant with a number of other similar surveys, this project revealed some minor fluctuations in specific sub-skills for this age group in recent times within the context of 'a general trend of a maintenance of performance' (p. 18). The concluding remark in their report is 'the level of reading achievement of Year 5 pupils has remained stable over the last ten years' (p. 19).

One of the most comprehensive and recent studies of literacy performance in Australia was conducted by McGaw, Long, Morgan and Rosier (1989). This study details performance levels of students in Years 5 and 9 (approximate ages eleven and fifteen years respectively) in the state of Victoria on scales of development in mathematics, reading, and writing, identifying the proportions of students in these years achieving at or above certain pre-defined levels of competence. One of its principal aims was to provide comparisons with levels of achievement of similar students in 1975, 1980 and 1988. At each of these three points in time, approximately 1,000 students from each of Years 5 and 9 were tested on an extensive range of literacy-related measures, for example knowledge of alphabet, knowledge of words, spelling, knowledge of language convention, comprehension, drawing simple inferences, knowledge of uncommon expressions, writing captions, writing telephone messages, writing reports, directions, and letters with specific purposes. Furthermore, the statistical analyses performed on the items and on the students' performance levels was of a sufficiently comprehensive and detailed nature to allow considerable confidence in the findings reported. These findings themselves are compatible with the general conclusions drawn from earlier studies as reported above. For example, in summarizing the reading performance measures, McGaw, Long, Morgan and Rosier concluded:

> Compared with 1975, there are indications of improvement in the reading abilities of fourteen-year-old female students. The males at the level, and for ten-year-old males and females, levels of achievement in reading remain at the same levels as they were in 1975 and 1980. This is despite an increase in the number of students from non-English speaking backgrounds. (p. 60)

In summarizing the data on students' writing performance, statistically significant differences on a number of the sub-scales were found, but McGaw *et al.* noted the difficulty of comparing performance across time with particular reference to the assessment of writing skills and reached their final conclusions concerning changes in literacy performance:

> It is not possible to compare directly assessments of expressive writing on the rating scales used by markers. There is no way of knowing if markers are using the same standards as they were on the earlier occasions. They can be given the same marking criteria but the demand levels for the award of each level of marks cannot readily be controlled over the years ... Comparisons of expressive writing over time have been made only in terms of limited and technical aspects of the writing ... Comparisons with the past provide mixed messages of some improvements, some cases of standards being maintained at former levels, and some cases of decline. These comparisons, however, are limited because the past data are limited in that they indicate only whether more or fewer students achieve some levels of minimum achievement. (pp. 102–103)

The comprehensiveness and detail of the study allow us to conclude that, in the light of the increased number of students in Australian schools from non-English speaking backgrounds, the overall maintenance of standards on most measures is impressive. McGaw *et al.* noted that another crucial factor related to changes in performance over time is the differing emphases given by teachers in different periods to various aspects of reading writing. If it is conceded, for example, that teachers in recent times have emphasized expressiveness and quality of ideas in students' writing more than they have certain technical aspects of writing, then the data reported by McGaw *et a.* become increasingly problematic in that, as they noted, it is only the technical aspects of writing that can be reliably assessed and compared over time. Note, however, that precisely the same point can be made about reading.

These studies, then, lead to a clear and unequivocal conclusion: that there is no evidence for substantial decline in standards of literacy performance in the recent past, at least on those measures that can be treated with confidence. But doubts concerning literacy performance may remain, particularly if literacy is taken to entail less quantifiable, less mechanical, and more expressive competencies. Another site of evidence for levels of performance across time on some of the less immediately quantifiable features of literacy performance is in the reports of the examiners of formal external high school examinations. These reports are public documents written partly to inform the State Departments of Education of the appropriateness of certain questions and partly to make comment upon the strengths and weaknesses of each year's candidature. One place, then, in which comments may be found concerning high school leavers' performance in a broad and subtle range of literacy competencies would be in the examiners' reports for the Higher School Certificate in the subject of English, in which diverse reading and writing competencies are called upon, as are students' knowledge and comments upon a range of literature. We have examined these reports of the NSW Examiners for English papers at the Higher School Certificate level from the years 1980–87, looking in particular for their remarks concerning general standards of literacy and appropriate and accurate use of language (see Welch and Freebody, 1990). It turns out that in many of these reports examiners draw explicit attention to comparisons of literacy performance with previous years' candidatures. The following quotes are a representative selection of general comments, and comments specifically relating to certain aspects of the HSC English papers over the years 1980–87:

> Most candidates . . . wrote answers which were literate, well-organized and relevant to the question . . . It was pleasing to note that the level of literacy was, on the whole, high . . . In general, responses demonstrated competence in handling sentence structure, paragraphing, and logical development of ideas (1980). Examiners thought that 1981 answers were appreciably better than the corresponding answers in 1980, and some of the poor sentence structure mentioned in the 1979 report appears to have been remedied (1981). Examiners were impressed by the general standard of the essays and their high level of literacy, fluency, and relevance (1982). Most answers were written in accurate English, and with rather fewer flaws in expression than in some other years . . . Even the weaker candidates were usually able to write coherently, legibly, and reasonably fluently . . . paragraphing, spelling, and appropriateness of language were very good, and scripts overall seemed to be of a higher standard

than in previous years (1983). The Examiners were on the whole favourably impressed by the general standard of competency and literacy demonstrated by the great majority of the candidates . . . It was generally felt that good though 1983 was, 1984 marked a perceptible improvement (1984). The planning of answers seemed better than in recent years: most essays were well structured, with good introductions and thoughtful conclusions, and were relevant, detailed and comprehensive (1985). On the whole the level of literacy achieved in previous years was sustained (1986). The general standard of literacy was pleasing: sentences were properly constructed and spelling was adequate (reading task) . . . literate and creative. Examiners commented favourably on spelling and literacy (1987).

The examiners report at length on the various strengths and in particular the weaknesses of the candidature in each year. A number of textual and planning complaints are consistently raised, and it is not the intent of our presenting the above remarks to suggest that examiners perceived no room for improvement. Further, we certainly do not intend to convey the impression here that the questions set by the examining bodies were capable of affording responses that, in turn, warrant such critiques on the part of the examiners. Nor would we want our remarks to imply that examiners deployed defensible or even explicit criteria in their judgments (Freebody, in press). Nonetheless, on the question of documentable evidence we located no general comments pertaining to standards of literacy competence that were negative or that indicated any decline whatever from one year to the next. It is clear that from 1980–86 an improvement is noted each year, and that in 1987 the standards were deemed to have been at least sustained. If we keep in mind the increased proportion of students staying on to Year 12 examination, the increased proportion from non-English speaking backgrounds, and the stressful circumstances under which HSC scripts are produced, the above impressionistic remarks in the Examiners' Reports indicate an impressive increase in literacy standards as they relate to performance on reading and writing tasks and in responses to literature.

This conclusion, taken together with the statistical evidence relating more reliably to mechanical skills summarized earlier, offers increased and continuing support for Little's (1985) conclusion concerning stability or improvement over time rather than decline. We must look elsewhere for the source of the 'literacy crisis' because it is clear that it has no empirical basis in the available research.

Social Class and Literacy: Domesticating the Research Arena

Our reconsideration of the study by McGaw *et al.* — an essentially 'non-crisis' report — indicates the ways in which genuine bases for reform can be deflected through the suppression of access-related variables such as social class and ethnicity. We can examine the processes of 'domestication' at work as they become inflected in research projects such as this one. The treatment of *social class* differences in literacy performance given in this report is notably different to the treatment of other variables. It deserves special scrutiny, in the light of the otherwise thorough analysis of the data, especially the associations between gender and literacy.[2] On the other hand, the results of the regression analysis which appears a few pages from the end of the data reporting section show clearly that the two consistent and substantial predictors of literacy performance (and mathematics as well) are the two 'surrogate' measures of the socio-economic background of the student: 'father's occupational level' and 'number of books in the home'.

What might explain the fact that the previous eighty pages or so of the report have been spent diligently examining the differences relating to boys' and girls' performance levels (differences that the report reveals are not statistically significant),[3] and almost no statistical attention or discussion is devoted to the significant differences that pertain to socio-economic differences? More standard methodological procedure would involve the initial report of regression results, followed by the presentation of the data broken down by the variables that the regressions had indicated were significant predictors. The matter assumes more intriguing proportions when it is noted that in Appendix B a number of questions relating to socio-economic status (questions 13–17) were asked in the survey, but that only two were included in the regression analysis.

There may be many explanations for why the report marginalizes the one statistically predictive demographic variable it included. Some hint is given in the discussion of the SES (Socio-Economic Status) effect: the authors remarked upon the fact that the 'cultural-intellectual environment of the home' in some families is not as conducive to literacy development as in others (p. 91). It is clear that the authors are either not able or not willing to deploy a sociological perspective on the SES effect, or even to speculate naively on regionally-based or system-based ('private' versus Catholic versus Government) inequalities in the nature of educational provision. Instead they 'domesticate' the SES effect, placing the explanatory arena inside the family home, and hailing an abstraction such as the 'cultural-intellectual environment of the home' allowing the inference of cognitive and motivational deficits.

The strategy used in this report also serves to focus attention on distinctions that are internal to the students themselves and to their membership of a gender community — distinctions that deflect or disallow interpretations based on the differential quality of educational experience offered to various groups in the community. For example, if overall gender differences are found on a particular task, then the explanation that may be most readily afforded, given the assumption that overall boys and girls are exposed to comparable education experiences in a largely co-educational system, is that there are some socio-psychological correlates associated with gender that need to be called into play (such as attentiveness at school, motivation, verbal ability, maturity, diligence). Here is an example of the report's findings:

> Compared with 1975, there are indications of improvement in the reading abilities of 14-year-old female students. (p. 60)

No such improvement is noted in 14-year-old males. What can we actually make of this distinction, if across the board the males and females are assumed to have been exposed to comparable literacy instruction and thus had comparable opportunities to improve in their reading? Simply, how can this gender distinction be explained? No explanation is offered in the report nor do the authors attempt to draw out possible implications for the teaching profession.

If on the other hand, class background variables were to be admitted into the discourse, and those explored as bases for explicating significant differences in performance, the way is opened for an explanation that may be based on the unequal provision of educational experiences in literacy, or in their schooling more generally. This unequal experience may have to do with material and human resources in schools in various areas (with all the class and ethnicity related associations entailed) as well as concern about the class-based nature of educational materials and pedagogical strategies themselves. Clearly, however, such analytic and explanatory strategies would embody a more fundamental challenge to existing literacy-education provision, including teacher-education provision in literacy, than does the imputation that individual difference, gender, or 'family background' is at the root of difference in literacy achievement.

The Federal Government's Literacy Discussion Paper: Domesticating Policy

Documenting expressions of anxiety about falling literacy standards and national and state achievement surveys are not the only pertinent means of contextualizing the contemporary literacy crisis. Comparable emphases and omissions are discernible in other sites, and we now move to consider, successively, government discussion papers, curriculum documents, and selected school texts.

We have termed the construction of literacy as an individual- or family-level problem *domestication*, one of the panoply of 'blame-the-victim' strategies that is neither new nor particularly interesting — nor, of course, is it conspiratorial. Rather, it arises out of a constellation of administrative, academic, and folk discourses that bolster certain lines of formal and informal theorizing. For instance, it rests on the notion that any test that is administered in an educational context is a direct reflection only of the competencies of the testee — the student. This in turn rests on the notion, usually unstated, that the relationship between the form and content of the test, and both the curriculum experienced by the students and the quality of the educational provision is comparable across all the potentially statistically significant sub-groups within the sample. With these two assumptions in place the explanation can go nowhere other than to the individual student's psychologically defined capabilities and 'outward' only as far as the home front.

Domestication is an explanatory strategy resorted to in public documents concerning literacy such as the so-called national 'Green Paper' (July, 1991; at the time of writing about to be redrafted into final policy-recommendation form). This 'Green Paper' is a discussion document circulated by the Federal Department of Employment, Education, and Training, on 'an Australian Literacy and Language Policy for the 1990s'. On page 4 the following definition of literacy appears:

> Literacy involves the integration of reading, writing, listening, speaking, and critical thinking. It includes the knowledge which enables a speaker, writer, or reader to recognize and use language appropriate to different social situations.

The focus here is drawn away from the distinctiveness of literate practices and the special powers afforded those sectors of a community who deploy those practices, and on to an almost impossibly broad notion of 'appropriate' language use — a set of sophisticated competences enjoyed by young children and primary oral cultures in their non-literate mode, but certainly in no sense defining a distinctive 'literacy'. In apparently straining to be inoffensive by simply not identifying what is *not* literacy and the consequences of *not* being able to deploy it effectively for, for instance, working-class, migrant, and the handicapped, the lot of such people can remain unaffected by the policy that dove-tails with the 'definition'. The definition is thus insidious in its appearance of tolerance and neighbourliness, and intellectually perverse in its masquerading of a set of contexts for the individual and community competences needed to effect and operate in those contexts.

Also in this report there are five brief paragraphs on the 'causes of literacy difficulties'. The section is worth extensive examination because it embodies a folk-theorization of literacy difficulties that is sufficiently individualized and mystified that it can be used to strike apparently benign postures toward a number of stakeholder groups in literacy education. The task of the account is at the one time to lift the blame for underachievement from those groups and to keep the explanatory focus squarely on the educational consumer and off the institutionalized provider (Federally-funded State Department of Education). The strategy that simply effects this task is domestication — individualizing the 'problem' and neighbourhooding the 'solutions', constructed in the sections of the text that we have italicized:

Causes of literacy difficulties

Compulsory attendance at school does not mean that all children will learn. Effective learning takes place generally when there is a combination of *appropriate education, stability in the learner's life and motivation to learn.*

The national survey of adult literacy revealed that 23 per cent of adults believed that their schooling and literacy performance had been adversely affected by, in order, *health problems* (with associated lengthy *absences* from school), *socio-economic problems* and absence from or negative *attitude* towards school.

Language or dialect differences may lead to literacy difficulties for some children of non-English-speaking background and Aboriginal children. In both groups, some children will need assistance in learning English as a second or other language.

Schools accept their role in transmitting literacy and in making special arrangements for children with difficulties. However, they will not be successful unless there is a *willingness to learn on the part of children* and unless *families accept their responsibility* to provide an environment conducive to learning. This is not to say that, even under ideal learning conditions, the performance of children will be at the same rate or to the same degree of proficiency.

> *Students* most likely to have literacy difficulties are those *who do not grasp necessary literacy concepts in the first three years of schooling*. These first three years are crucial in terms of literacy development. It is important to design and implement procedures for the early identification of these children so that they can be helped. In most States and Territories, programs are already under way to identify and help such children. While the necessary diagnostic tools are available, there does not appear to be any comprehensive or systematic effort made to identify and report on the extent of the literacy problem at this crucial stage. In many education systems, the identification of the problem relies mainly on the skills of *the classroom teacher* and, in many cases, so does the necessary remedial action. Strategies in education systems must address the processes and resources necessary to support *the classroom teacher* in this vital task. (Dawkins, 1991, p. 15, emphases added)

This text forcefully naturalizes an individuated, domesticated version of literacy education, clearly intertextual with the accounts accorded scientific legitimacy in research reports of the sort quoted above (by McGaw *et al.*). It is instructive to detail how this text works to present an ideologically coherent and apparently seamless fabric: in the first paragraph three variables are given as associated with effective learning, 'appropriate education, stability in the learner's life and motivation to learn'. The first of these is unproblematically causal at a systemic level, precisely because it is virtually tautological; the second implicitly relegates the problem to the family hearth; the third, while having some folk resonance, confounds explicandum and explanation. That is, the socio-economically uneven distribution of motivation is what calls for an account; it does not in any systemic sense stand as an account itself.

The second paragraph inserts 'socio-economic problems' between health and negative motivation, as if class were one of a list 'personal setbacks'. The third paragraph admits the significance of a systemic variable — first language status — as an educational problem, but this is acknowledged to be special difficulty, and this apparent concession sets the stage for the final individuation and domestication of the problematic of literacy. The correlate given causal status by association in the first paragraph and by attribution in the third is now able to be instated explicitly as a cause, and further, designated the principal obstacle to an assumedly standard and effective programme of 'transmission' offered by schools.

In these discursive ways social science and related policy statements construct the phenomenon it purports to describe, in our case, literacy education: (1) by delimiting a human field of participants (in our case, a nation, families, and individual boys and girls); (2) by recruiting this field apparently to allow the data to establish the patterns of causes and effects (in our case the causes of instability, family irresponsibility, and personal lack of motivation); and (3) thus by naturalizing a redefinition of all correlate-cause-effect associations in the terms 'dictated' by the data (in our case, recreating uneven literacy accomplishment across social class as a personal problem of motivation and parental encouragement). As summarized by Henriques and others (Henriques, Urwin, Venn and Walkerdine, 1984):

... all knowledges are productive in the specific sense that they have definite effects on the objects one seeks to know. For the social sciences these effects are not separable from the practices of administration to which these sciences are tied. (p. 92)

That is, policy does not simply respond to needs created in some socio-political context; it uses versions of folk- and specialist-wisdom to recast the field of intended activity such that the phenomena themselves are constructed in ideologically and administratively convenient ways. Defining literacy and the causes of literacy 'difficulties' in the above ways, celebrating the individual and family bases of literacy achievement, and ignoring the powerful associations among ethnicity, class, and literacy not only constructs literacy only as a personal achievement, but also calls into play certain policy responses while marginalizing others.

Framework Guidelines: Domesticating the Curriculum

If the processes of domesticating literacy competence is as prevalent as we have suggested, then the texts of curriculum — for teachers and students alike — should also provide documentation of similar processes. Here and in the section following we take a close look at a set of curriculum framework documents for the first ten years of schooling, and the actual student materials for a high-school subject: Economic/Cultural Studies.

How might curriculum guidelines and source materials reflect the process of domestication? We hypothesize that a crucial social learning for students is the individuated society — a construction of social experience that places at the centre the individual, who is endowed unproblematically with explanatory power for emergent social, cultural, and economic phenomena. In considering Social Studies curriculum documents, therefore, we first examine the particular ways in which, of the many options available for describing human reference groups and social networks, curriculum documents, written by State-Departmental offices for teachers' and school administrators' use, present the individual in relation to the social world. The focus here is on how ways of presenting the social world constrain significantly the type of explanation that may be offered as to how the world got to be the way it is, and the kinds of responses that are explicitly or implicitly afforded the reader as a way of acting in his or her world.

As an example, we examine the Social Studies Curriculum and its attendant guidelines and background papers developed by the Queensland Department of Education (referring to framework and materials documents published between 1986–90; see Freebody, Barnes, and Muspratt, 1991). The first general observation we can make concerning these curriculum documents is that they place at the centre of their construction of the social world a notion of the 'individual' both in theorizing the student-learner as a participant in this curriculum itself, and in presenting the topic of study that is central to this curriculum, human society. There is, for example, one entire element devoted to 'understanding individuals'.

The over-arching P-10 Curriculum, of which the Social Education curriculum forms a part, is explicitly stated to cater

- for the commonalities and variabilities within and among children during the P-10 years. (*P-10 Curriculum Framework*, p. 1)

It does this by making the following assumptions about children and students:

- each child has a unique background and unique capabilities and interests . . . children have individual styles and rates of learning . . . children construct personal knowledge bases which allow them to make sense of their own experience . . . schools provide children with a place for self-expression, for self-development, and for enhancing self-concept within structured and appropriately challenging contexts . . . schools offer essential learnings for all children and cater for the particular strengths and interests of individual children . . . which represent an appropriate balance between the needs of individual children and groups of children (*P-10 Curriculum Framework*, pp. 4–6);

- attitudes, feelings and sensitivities and a complex mixture of cognitive and affective elements. They vary from individual to individual, and within the same individual at different times (*Primary Social Studies Syllabus*, p. 6);

- social control involves processes which regulate the actions of individuals or groups to ensure they behave in expected and approved ways. Group norms, mores, rules and laws are made and enforced by groups to ensure individuals within that group conform (*Primary Social Studies Syllabus*, p. 12);

- to understand the uniqueness of each child's development in these areas, the results of such research should be balanced against observations of individual children and groups of children (*Social Education Framework*, p. 14);

- to develop their intellectual, social and emotional capacities so that they: appreciate themselves as unique (*Social Education Years 8–10 Draft Syllabus*, p. 5).

Generally, we see throughout documents such as these an insistence upon the centrality of the individual as 'unique' in his or her pattern of differences. This uniqueness, however, is rarely explicated in any specific way other than through the use of such generalization as developmental rate or style or background. Even then, background issues were linked to cultural or sub-cultural variables. The unexplicated individual is, then, placed at the centre of this social world, thus reinforcing statements concerning the function of the curriculum as a device whereby personalized knowledge, self-expression, and self-concept maybe enhanced or at least facilitated. The sanitized and sanctioned nature of 'the individual', is protected by a close patrolling of the boundaries between individual and society. The individual is, in effect, put, in oppositional terms to society:

The balance between programs based on individual needs and the needs of society, ensuring that both are given proper emphasis in the curriculum for the P-10 years. (*Social Education Framework*, p. 37)

The ways in which individuals are socially constituted are not explored, and are in fact effectively marginalized relative to the transcendent importance of the individual throughout these curriculum documents.

As a corollary of the centrality of the individual in the particular taxonomy that is constructed in these documents, we find that socio-cultural distinctions are generally characterized in terms of individual differences, again at the level of the person as a subject of study in this curriculum and as a student in this curriculum. With respect to the student, for example, the major differentiation that is at work in this document is dependent upon the notion of age level, a point that will be developed more fully in the following section. There are occasional but undeveloped mentions of other potentially significant parameters in the social world (for example, gender, class, race), but these seem to act generally as somewhat legalistic reminders of equality as a matter of policy, rather than an issue that is built into the fabric of this curriculum. For instance, on p. 7 of a document titled *P-10 Curriculum Framework* there is the statement concerning equal educational opportunities for all — boys and girls, multiculturalism and so on. In the *Social Education Framework*, p. 9, the Department of Education acknowledges the importance of providing young people with equal life chances through effective participation in, and contribution to Australian society but takes account of their location, gender, cultural heritage, race or socio-economic status.

A thorough examination of these documents indicates that the legalistic sensitivities of this curriculum are not, in fact, representative: the curriculum acknowledges the jeopardy to equality that arises out of, for example, location, gender, cultural heritage, race or socio-economic status but does not problematize it. It does not make that jeopardy a topic of historical and cultural interest in the study of human society itself as it proceeds through its topics. The sociality of humans is constructed in a manner that precludes the cross-referencing of human sociality to the concrete business of hierarachy and privilege.

The portrayal of the individual 'in' society offered in documents such as these, while emphasizing individual freedoms and respect for others, has serious implications for the mechanisms of critique and change that might be afforded to explain disadvantage or patterned injustices. The liberal-democratic fallacy, which justifies the conditions of patterned and systematic inequality, is disguised.

The emphases upon individual freedoms and respect in the curriculum documents, then, need to be supplemented with explicit theorization of the ways in which patterned inequalities are developed. As it stands, this omission tacitly licenses voluntaristic social models — 'individuals choose to reject, modify or adapt to new circumstances resulting from change' (*Primary Social Studies Syllabus*, p. 12). With the individual-agent thus celebrated it is difficult for a curriculum such as this to deal systematically with the material inequalities that characterize history in anything other than a trivial way (Welch, 1985) or through devices that blame the victim.

Classroom Texts: Domesticating the Disciplines of Instruction

The texts used in school, in that they portray the socio-cultural world, are also necessarily structured in ways that document particular versions of the relationship between individuality and sociality. One way of looking at the ideological work done by texts is to consider how the features of a text, the patterns of choices exercised by the author, serve simultaneously to reflect and build particular discourses, themselves the articulations of ideology. These choices in part affect this work through a logic comparable to the above documents: how the phenomenon is characterized — what is taken to be a legitimate, scientific, educationally appropriate description — affords certain explanations of how it and its context came to be as they are, often tacitly excluding other possible forms of explanation. In turn, this constrained explanation licenses certain responses with respect to what a person might/should (and, again, by exclusion, might/should not) do in the light of this phenomenon.

We can exemplify this process through the examination of texts written for high school students on inequality in the distribution of economic resources (in High School Economic or Development Studies). Such texts can be interrogated for their representations of the themes of individuation and domestication that have guided the discussions above. To preview the analyses, the texts describe Less Developed Countries (LDCs)[4] in synoptic, 'correlational' terms; that is, lists of social, cultural, political, and economic characteristics are presented as characterizing or typifying 'poor' countries. The student-readers' (and for that matter the teachers') intellectual resources are drawn to the task of assimilating this multiplicity of features, importantly, in isolation, and without any cohering historical, interconnecting argument. The account is clearly synchronic — the LDC is problematized as a complex 'thing' in space, without history.

It is worth considering in some linguistic detail one comparatively comprehensive attempt at characterizing the phenomenon of the LDC in order to attain an impression of how 'inequality' is articulated and conveyed as an 'academic body of knowledge'. Consider the following key sections from a prominent text on economics for upper secondary school:

> Less-developed countries (LDCs) tend to be characterized by the following features:
>
> 1) Subsistence living and limited use of markets: most individuals in less-developed countries use their output for their own family [. . .] and exchange little of their production. [. . .]
>
> 2) A high proportion of the workforce in less-developed countries is engaged in agriculture and in other primary industries. [. . .] The manufacturing sector and the tertiary sector in underdeveloped countries are also comparatively small.
>
> 3) Technical change in less-developed countries is normally slow and producers often cling to traditional methods. In some circumstances, however, traditional methods may be more appropriate than Western capital-intensive methods. [. . .]
>
> 4) Savings are small and the rate of capital accumulation is low. [. . .] those on high incomes in the LDCs are reputed to spend most of their income on ostentatious consumption rather than to invest in productive works. [. . .]

5) Business motivation or entrepreneurship of a productive nature may be lacking. [. . .] Capitalistic entrepreneurship may be lacking.

6) Unemployment, labour-intensive methods, underemployment. [. . .]

7) Life expectancy is low, nutrition and health poor. [. . .]

8) High growth rates of the population and a distorted age distribution of the population add to poverty. The higher rate of (population) increase in the LDCs may reflect the less frequent use of birth control techniques [. . .]

9) Urbanization problems but a proportionately low urban population. [. . .]

10) Lack of social overhead capital. The supply of roads, ports, hospitals, schools, telephone services, water and sewerage facilities is limited. This is a reflection of overall poverty. The ability of the government to raise revenue for public works through taxation is limited [. . .]

11) Illiteracy is widespread and the technical skills required in modern industry are in short supply.

12) The distribution of income in LDCs is very uneven [. . .]

13) Dualism. [. . .] an urban monetary economy consisting of individuals engaged in Western style industry and a rural traditional barter economy. [. . .]

14) Export dependency on one or two primary products. [. . .] The prices of primary products tend to be very unstable and specialization in such a limited range of primary products (lack of diversification) adds to risk as a rule. (Tisdell, 1979, pp. 173–9)

We can document the way in which the field is constructed in accounts such as this. In this particular text the nature of human participation and the abstract agencies of 'poverty' are central features. Yet, of the eighty-seven participant-items in this account of the characteristics of LDCs, only eighteen entail human participants. The remaining sixty-nine themes include mainly abstractions and nominalizations, for example:

- growth rates of populations
- high proportion of the population
- LDC(s)
- the rate of capital accumulation
- entrepreneurship
- technical change
- the ability of governments to raise revenue
- specialization in a limited range of primary products

- most incomes
- life expectancy.

Here, the author's chosen themes display the agenda of abstraction of the causes of Third World status. The human participants are not just important only in the terms of their relative infrequency, but also in terms of how they serve to construct the socio-political 'world' of the LDC, and how other accounts and responses are thus constrained. It is notable that the human participants in this text present the following hierarchical societal composition: individuals may be producers, combine into families, into workforce, into a population, into a country. That is the human taxonomic tree that this text presents. No descriptive terms for people are given that rely on sub-groups within a nation state and that would thus afford an explanation or response based on contestation or the struggle for resources or decision-making power.

We can also consider the activities performed by the most common human term, 'individuals': what are the verbs with which this term is associated? The following is the exhaustive list of the verbs accompanied by their attendant predications in our textual example:

'individuals . . .'
use (their output for their own families)
exchange (little of their production)
need to consume (most of their products to survive)
can expect to live (for shorter periods)
die (before they reach an economically productive age)
are (dependent)
(are) engaged in (western-style . . .)
(on high incomes) *are reputed to spend* (their income on ostentatious consumption)
(with funds to invest) *have* (a preference for money-lending)

Some individuals, in the world presented in the text, will die at an economically inconvenient age and are dependent. By the same token, some are clearly part if not the whole of the problem — consuming, spending, and lending. Both perpetrator and victim are there in the text, both relentlessly individualized.

In this section we have briefly documented and exemplified the important link between the ways in which the topic is described, the explanations, implicit or otherwise, that can be adduced, and response-positions thus afforded the reader. The topic we have chosen to exemplify this point — school text accounts of material inequality — may be thought to be something of an easy target, because the writers of these texts are faced with the task of presenting phenomena to school students that are complex and inextricably embedded in historical, cultural, and economic considerations. Our defence here is threefold: first, it is almost certainly the case that the textbook accounts of economic forces at work in the world presented in the upper secondary are easily the most complete, scholarly, and complex accounts most students will ordinarily encounter in their lives.

Second, the point has not been to quibble about the need for simplification *per se*, but rather to explore the particular form of that simplification, and the positioning work effected by the resultant texts. Those forms function to reify the phenomenon of inequality, through the mutually complementing content and logic of the field, and the theoretically unmotivated and non-programmatic nature of the individual and communal response options thereby afforded. It is in this crucial respect that the synoptic work of the text remains difficult to contest, and thus remains capable of pulling off an impressive and creative ideological feat — a subject who can stay mute and ineffectual in the face of gross, dangerous, and patterned inequalities.

Third, we have found in these texts for use by students the same patterned ideologies that underpin the discourses that shape research, policy and departmental/ministry guidelines. Thus, in a substantial and profound sense, the 'stories' that are told to or assumed to be held by the distinct readership that these texts address are similar in their centralizing of the individual and their apparently warranted domestication of the problems and solutions available in 'the literacy debate'.

Conclusions: Literacy as the Object of Standards and Policy

Part of the contestation that arises about literacy has to do with whether this term covers a set of private abilities and moral dispositions or public practices in any given text: on the one hand, literacy been construed as the arch-private act, drawing upon and drawing out personal knowledge, idiosyncratic dispositions and feelings, and moreover having as its ultimate purpose the development, and even the moral fulfilment of the individual. In other sites, literacy is characterized largely or solely as a public informational resource playing an equally transcendent role in the building of a community's economic well-being. Expressions, sometimes critical, of this 'human-capital' recruitment of literacy are not difficult to locate (Fuller, Edwards and Gorman, 1987; Lankshear, 1989). Some expressions are blunter than others, the bluntest often coming from eminent psychologists of language (Miller, 1972):

> The fact is that our technological progress is creating a socioeconomic system in which the ignorant, illiterate individual is useless. (p. 375)

Interestingly, both of these orientations de-historicize and thus de-politicize the cultural resource of literacy by assigning it the status of a commodity (Apple, 1985; Welch, 1988) in two contrasting markets — markets whose legal capital is on the one hand cultural and on the other material/economic. Thus, these versions of the private or public status of literacy in fact enjoy a fundamental compatibility: from the discourses of literacy as the high road either to individuation or to communal economic fulfilment comes a research interest in documenting the prevalence of reading success among the individuals in an economic community — usually construed as a nation-state. The consequent legitimacy (Welch, 1991), from both orientations, of such documentations allows their incorporation into significant policy positions and research agenda.

The accomplishment of the dominant account of the 'why' and 'how' of the unequally distributed resource of literacy competence, and the forms of consciousness that accompany differing relations to literacy achievement, themselves become crucial determinants in the achievement of authority in the area of literacy-education policy — an object in the circuits of literacy-power: 'the knowledge that is used to structure and fix representations in historical forms is the accomplishment of power' (Clegg, 1990, p. 152).

Our argument thus far has tended to support the view that the Australian 'literacy crisis' may be something of a confection, but that the silence about class segmentation of literacy is systematic. It could be argued that there are no major problems with respect to overall level of literacy in Australia: the existence of 'underachieving' groups of predictable composition — Aboriginals, long-term white poor, and students of non-English speaking background — does not constitute a literacy 'crisis' in the usual sense of that word, since the provision in Australia of literacy education to such groups, while undertaken by committed individuals, has been systemically under-resourced.

Given that the discourse of literacy crisis is something of a confection, we need to seek an explanation of its origins and timing. Why has talk of a crisis surfaced at this time, and what does it signify? Are these correlative arguments about the nature of schooling and society that are associated with particular interest groups? Is the crisis one of literacy, or a crisis of a wider form?

We have pointed in the Introduction to some parallels in 'literacy crises' in several advanced industrial states. At this point, it may be seen that part of the explanation for the occurrence of a 'literacy crisis' at this time, both in Australia and other advanced industrial states, is the changed international economic and political context. Here again international and historical comparisons are pertinent. We argued in the Introduction that there are political interests involved in presenting literacy crises in particular ways at particular times. For example, in the late 1970s and during the decade of the 1980s, increasing critical attention has been given to literacy. The most stringent critics of allegedly poor standards of literacy in Australia have found voice in conservative journals and magazines, representing political ideologies of the right, both in and beyond the field of education. For example, as one of the *ACES* reviewers argued in the late 1970s, in the course of a critique of using schools for 'social engineering', 'We want to reinvigorate the world we live in, to renew society', by which was meant 'renewal and reinvigoration of the existing social order' (Paterson, 1977, p. 11). One of the earlier examples of such views in *ACES* railed against the 'distressingly low' standards of literacy and numeracy, and imputed this state both to the lack of attention to the 'basic skills' and the prevailing, and naive, current of 'freedom' in schools and teachers' colleges, which it argued should be supplanted by 'planned conditioning', such as operated in the animal kingdom. (Williams, 1977, pp. 9–10). Progressives were the enemy within:

> Progressives who dismiss literacy and numeracy as 'irrelevant' or as something their socially adjusted charges will just 'pick up' (like measles or venereal disease) are free to indulge their fantasies. (Williams, 1977, p. 9)

In reviewing articles in such journals over a number of years, a clear, if not always explicit, sketch of an ideal society is revealed. The image that emerges is one of a world where the 'great traditions' in literature and philosophy are destined to go on unchanged, and where discipline connotes more than an ordered corpus of knowledge. The effects of the 'egalitarian myth' feature largely in such articles, as do assertions as to the apparent abandonment of what are loosely termed *standards*. In some articles can be discerned an assertion that state-administered schools are failing to teach literacy and numeracy skills, which are still being successfully taught in the private sector.[5] This concern with literacy standards can now be seen to signify much more in the ways in which it is deployed in the discourse of the political right: 'Literacy' carries with it the semiosis of a desire to return to a traditional disciplined society, with traditional moral codes,[6] and less moral and racial diversity than are present in contemporary Australia.

Thus one of the highly visible critiques of literacy standards is part of a reiteration of a conservative socio-political agenda, and a desire to return to a traditional, heavily romanticized idyll. The crisis may well be of a much wider form; what is being rejected may be the notion of socio-economic modernity itself, an egalitarian emphasis, as much as literacy standards. But, as the chapters in this volume demonstrate, there is a crisis of another form which again puts literacy in a different light. Over recent years, substantial changes have occurred in Australian society. These changes are paralleled by circumstances overseas, particularly in other industrialized states, as argued most particularly in the chapters by Limage and Collins.

The optimism that was a feature of the first three post-war decades has largely been replaced by a more opportunistic and pragmatic set of values and practices. Part of this change has involved a diminished faith in education. The decades after the war saw an expansion in the Australian education system in both sheer size and demographic coverage. For the first time, secondary education became a prospect for large sectors of the population. There developed a considerable faith in the individual value of education, in terms of personal development and social mobility.

The faith has largely been withdrawn. Over the last decade and a half, accompanied by substantial increases in unemployment, particularly among Australian youth,[7] Australian schooling has become subject to increasingly strident attacks. The school is the scapegoat for a variety of social and economic ills that are not of its making. Why is this occurring in a nation otherwise sympathetic to education?

To answer this question we turn to the main objective of our argument so far, that the modern state itself is the locus of crisis, and that literacy education — as evidenced in the texts of research, policy, curriculum, and instruction — is implicated and blamed through a system of interconnected ideologies much wider and more labyrinthine than literacy educators have to date imagined (as forcefully demonstrated in the chapters by Hasanpour, Ahai and Faraclas, and Walton). The eroded legitimation of the modern capitalist state is attested to by the report of the Trilateral Commission (Crozier, Huntingdon and Watanuki, 1975) by the resonance of Habermas' characterization of modernity (Habermas, 1976). Both concur on the issue of the increasing lack of governability of the modern state. One of the avenues the state employs to shore up its failing legitimacy is the education system. Here too, however, the gap between the rhetoric of equal opportunity and the increasing reality of active socio-economic reproduction is apparent in most nations, and, as the preceding chapters (especially Kwan-Terry and Kwan-Terry, and Kumar) describe with various inflections, it is literacy education that is traversed most dramatically in the state's efforts to resolve this fundamental tension.

So attacks upon the alleged failure of literacy education in Australia can be seen as part of a wider concern to deflect attention away from social class issues and the operation of a fundamentally inequitable social system, in which literacy problems are meted out unequally, especially to traditionally marginal groups such as Aboriginals, the traditionally indigent, and those of non-English speaking background.

> Whenever dominant groups declare there is a crisis, we must always ask 'whose crisis is this?' and 'who benefits from the proposed "solutions"?' The recent declarations of a crisis in literacy in a number of nations are not immune to these questions. It is possible to claim that by shifting the public's attention to the problems of education, the real sources of the current crisis are left unanalyzed. That is, the crisis of the political economy of capitalism is exported from the economy onto the state. The state then in turn exports the crisis downward onto the school. Thus, when there is severe unemployment, a disintegration of traditional patterns of authority, and so on, the blame is placed upon students' lack of skill, on their attitudes, on their 'functional illiteracy'. (Apple, in Lankshear and Lawler, 1987, p. viii)

Culture clothes power. Cultural practices are about unequal distributions of power and privilege and about the need to occlude these processes of distribution. The cultural capital upon which that power is based is differentially available to different groups in society, and differentially distributed through schooling (Bourdieu, 1974, 1984). As they are currently realized, attacks upon general standards of literacy in society generally seek to obscure this process rather than to illuminate it. Moreover, their function is precisely to naturalize this connection between certain privileged forms of literacy and the perpetuation of cultural and economic power in society. It is the belief that making visible the variety of ways in which these processes are acted out around the world can initiate and reinforce programmes of genuine reform that have motivated this anthology.

Notes

1 See, for example, Froome, S., 'Reading and the School Handicap Score', Cox and Boyson (1975, pp. 9–12).
2 Considerable attention is given to gender in the report by McGaw *et al.* In each of the chapters dealing with reading and writing the mean performance scores are broken down by gender, resulting in twenty-one tables relating to gender differences. It is therefore somewhat surprising to find, close to the end of the data report, that gender is in fact not a statistically significant predictor of literacy performance among these students.
3 We have no wish to argue that gender is not important as a basis for literacy differences, but rather to highlight the fact that on methodological grounds there is no basis for the silence on class issues in this report.
4 We need merely note already the pre-formed narrative built into that label.
5 See, for examples of the implication that private schools often represent the solution to reading problems fostered in the state schools (Thomas, 1987, pp. 1–4).

6 See the allusion to the Protestant ethic as a basic element of the 'old' education, which is celebrated as against the 'new' education, which contains permissiveness, and etc. (Webster, 1987, p. 15).
7 In the second half of 1991, youth unemployment, in the midst of a major recession, was running at around 25–30 per cent, about three times the general figure.

References

APPLE, M. (1982) *Education and Power*, London, Ark.

APPLE, M. (1987) 'Foreword' in LANKSHEAR, C. and LAWLER, M. *Literacy, Schooling and Revolution*, London, Falmer Press, pp. vii–xii.

ASSP (1980) *Australian Studies in School Performance*, Canberra, AGPS.

ATKINSON, P. (1985) *Language, Structure and Reproduction. An Introduction to the Sociology of Basil Bernstein*, London, Methuen.

BOURDIEU, P. (1974) 'The school as a conservative force' in EGGLESTON, J. (Ed.) *Contemporary Research in the Sociology of Education*, London, Methuen, pp. 32–41.

BOURDIEU, P. (1984) *Distinction: A Social Critique of the Judgement of Taste*, Cambridge, MA, Harvard University Press.

BRISBANE DAILY STANDARD, 4 October 1917.

CLEGG, S. (1989) *Frameworks of Power*, London, Sage.

CONNELL, R.W., ASHENDEN, D.J., KESSLER, S. and DOWSETT, G.W. (1982) *Making the Difference*, Sydney, Allen and Unwin.

COX, C. and BOYSON, R. (Eds) (1975) *Black Paper. The Fight for Education*, London, J.M. Dent and Sons.

COX, C. and DYSON, R. (Eds) (1977) *The Black Paper Two*, London, Temple Smith.

CROZIER, M., HUNTINGDON, S. and WATANUKI, J. (1975) *The Crisis Of Democracy Report on the Governability of Democracies to the Trilateral Commission*, New York, New York University Press.

DAWKINS, J. (1990) *The Language of Australia: Discussion Paper: An Australian Literacy and Language Policy for the 1990s*, Canberra, AGPS.

EXAMINERS' REPORTS (1981–87) English, Sydney, NSW Department of Education.

FREEBODY, P. (1991) 'The ideology of language', Paper presented to the Second Annual Systemics Linguistics Conference, Brisbane, January.

FREEBODY, P. (in press) 'Inventing cultural-capitalist distinctions in the assessment of Higher School Certificate English examination papers: Coping with inflation in an era of "literacy crisis"', in CHRISTIE, F. (Ed.) *Literacy in Social Context*, Darwin, Northern Territory University Press.

FREEBODY, P. and BAKER, C.D. (1987) 'The construction and operation of gender in children's first school books', in PAUWELS, A. (Ed.) *Women and Language in Australia and New Zealand*, Sydney, Professional Publications, pp. 80–107.

FREEBODY, P., BARNES, C. and MUSPRATT, A. (1991) 'A critical perspective on the Queensland P-10 Social Education Curriculum', Report to the Queensland Education Department.

FROOME, S. (1975) 'Reading and the School Handicap Scores', in COX, C. and BOYSON, R. (Eds) *The Black Paper*, London, Temple Smith, pp. 9–12.

FULLER, B., EDWARDS, J. and GORMAN, K. (1987) 'Does Rising Literacy Spark Economic Growth? Commercial Expansion in Mexico', WAGNER, D. (Ed.) *The Future of Literacy in a Changing World*, New York, Pergamon.

GOYEN, J. (1976) *NCTE Newsletter*.

HABERMAS, J. (1976) *Legitimation Crisis*, London, Heinemann.

HENRIQUES, J., HOLLOWAY, W., URWIN, C. VENN, C. and WALKERDINE, V. (1984) *Changing the Subject*, London, Methuen.

HIGHER SCHOOL CERTIFICATE 2 UNIT GENERAL ENGLISH PAPER, NSW Government Printing Office.

LANKSHEAR, C. and LAWLER, M. (1987) *Literacy, Schooling and Revolution*, London, Falmer Press.

LITTLE, G. (1985) 'There is no decline', *Curriculum Development in Australian Schools*, 1, pp. 4–7.

LUKE, A. (1988) *Literacy, Textbooks and Ideology*, London, Falmer Press.

MCGAW, B., LONG, M.G. MORGAN, G. and ROSIER, M.J. (1989) *Literacy and Numeracy in Victorian schools: 1988*, Hawthorn, ACER Research.

MELBOURNE TRUTH, 9 October, 1915.

PATERSON, I. (1977) 'Book Review, New Schools in a New Society', *ACES Review*, 4, 1.

QUEENSLAND DEPARTMENT OF EDUCATION (1987–1991) 'Social Education Materials (Guidelines, Framework Documents)', Queensland Department of Education, Brisbane.

RESEARCH AND CURRICULUM BRANCH BULLETIN (1952), 6.

SKILBECK, M. (1977) 'Beyond the Standards Debate', *Education News*, 16, 3, pp. 8–11.

SYDNEY TELEGRAPH, 27 August 1930.

THOMAS, C. (1987) 'Illiteracy as a Barrier to a Skilled Workforce', *ACES Review*, 14, pp. 1–4.

TISDELL, C.A. (1979) *Economics in Our Society: Principles and Applications*, Milton, Qld, Jacaranda.

WEBSTER, D. (1987) 'The Garden State's Educational Crisis', *ACES Review*, 14, 2.

WELCH, A.R. (1985) 'The Functionalist Tradition in Comparative Education', *Comparative Education*, 21, 1.

WELCH, A.R. (1988) 'For Sale by Degrees. International Students and the Commodification of Higher Education in Australia and the UK', *International Review of Education*, 34, 3.

WELCH, A.R. (1988) 'Aboriginal Education as Internal Colonialism. The Schooling of an Indigenous Minority in Australia', *Comparative Education*, 22, 2.

WELCH, A.R. (1991) 'Education and Legitimation in Comparative Education', *Comparative Education Review*, 35, 3.

WELCH, A.R. and FREEBODY, P. (1990) 'Crisis de alfabetizacion o crisis de estado? Explicaciones de la actual "Crisis de alfabetizacion"', *Revista de Educacion*, 293, pp. 255–279.

WILLIAMS, J. (1977) 'Imparting Basic Skills', *ACES Review*, 4, p. 1.

List of Contributors

Naihuwo Ahai, Language and Literacy Secretariat, Department of Education, Port Moresby, Papua New Guinea.

James Collins, Anthropology Department, State University of New York at Albany, New York, USA.

Nicholas Faraclas, Department of Language and Literature, University of Papua New Guinea, Port Moresby, Papua New Guinea.

Peter Freebody, Division of Education, Griffith University, Mount Gravatt, Brisbane, Queensland, Australia.

Amir Hassanpour, Department of Communication Studies, University of Windsor, Ontario, Canada.

Krishna Kumar, Central Institute of Education, University of Delhi, India.

Anna Kwan-Terry, School of Mechanical and Production Engineering, Nanyang Technological University, Singapore.

John Kwan-Terry, Division of Language, Literature and Arts, Nanyang Technological University, Singapore.

Colin Lankshear, Education Department, University of Auckland, New Zealand.

Leslie Limage, International Year Secretariat, Division of Basic Education, UNESCO, Paris, France.

Peter O'Connor, Co-ordinator, Workplace Basic Education Unit, Sydney, New South Wales, Australia.

Christine Walton, Faculty of Education, Northern Territory University, Casaurina, Australia.

Anthony R. Welch, School of Social and Policy Studies in Education, University of Sydney, New South Wales, Australia.

Index